MW00755233

EVERYDAY READING

Everyday Reading

*Poetry and Popular Culture
in Modern America*

Mike Chasar

COLUMBIA UNIVERSITY PRESS   NEW YORK

COLUMBIA UNIVERSITY PRESS

Publishers Since 1893

NEW YORK   CHICHESTER, WEST SUSSEX

cup.columbia.edu

Copyright © 2012 Columbia University Press

Cover design: Noah Arlow

All rights reserved

Library of Congress Cataloging-in-Publication Data

Chasar, Mike, 1970–

Everyday reading : poetry and popular culture in modern America / Mike Chasar

p. cm.

Includes bibliographical references and index.

ISBN 978-0-231-15864-0 (cloth : alk. paper) — ISBN 978-0-231-15865-7 (pbk. : alk. paper) — ISBN 978-0-231-53077-4 (e-book)

1. American poetry—20th century—History and criticism. 2. Poetry—Social aspects—United States—History—20th century. 3. Literature and society—United States—History—20th century. 4. Public opinion—United States—History—20th century. 5. Poetry—Public opinion—History—20th century. 6. Poetics—History—20th century. I. Title.

PS325C49   2012

811'.5209—dc23

Columbia University Press books are printed on permanent and durable acid-free paper.

This book is printed on paper with recycled content.

Printed in the United States of America

c 10 9 8 7 6 5 4 3 2 1

p 10 9 8 7 6 5 4 3 2 1

References to Internet Web sites (URLs) were accurate at the time of writing. Neither the author nor Columbia University Press is responsible for URLs that may have expired or changed since the manuscript was prepared.

CONTENTS

ACKNOWLEDGMENTS

In opening the study that follows, which traces the forgotten and often anonymous readers and writers who sustained and fueled the culture of popular poetry in twentieth-century America, it is a particular pleasure for me to identify and remember the people and institutions that helped to make this book possible.

I am especially grateful to Willamette University, which in a time of economic uncertainty, unyieldingly provided me with a wide range of support mechanisms, including an early junior-faculty research leave as well as monetary grants for research, publication, and travel; without these resources and gifts, and without the support of Gretchen Flesher Moon in the English Department and Marlene Moore in the College of Liberal Arts, the book as it has been produced would not have been possible. Much of the research and early writing for this project began at the University of Iowa, with the assistance and support of the English Department, the Graduate College, the University of Iowa Center for the Book, and the Obermann Center for Advanced Studies. The final stages of this book were completed with the financial help of a National Endowment for the Humanities summer stipend.

Dee Morris, Loren Glass, Cary Nelson, Ed Folsom, and Garrett Stewart were early and influential readers, respondents, and inspirations; this book would have been worthwhile if only for the chance it afforded me to experience and learn from their generosity and guidance. Rachel Blau DuPlessis, Edward J. Brunner, Stephen Burt, and Virginia Jackson offered especially close and valuable feedback, assistance, and encouragement during the later stages of this project, and I am also grateful to Heidi R. Bean, Jeff Charis-Carlson, Melissa Girard, and Catherine Keyser for the intellectual insight, wit, and friendship they extended to me as this book took shape. Many other individuals deserve my gratitude as well, including Bartholomew Brinkman, Matthew P. Brown, Holly Carver, Kathleen Diffley, William Fogarty, Jeffrey Gore, Jenna Hammerich, Everett Hamner, Jessica Helfand, Kembrew McLeod, Frank Miller, and Sean Scanlan; Faith Barrett, Gunnar Benedicktsson, Lauren Berlant, Marsha Bryant, J. P. Craig, Maria Damon, Karen Ford, Steve Healey, Meredith Martin, Phil Metres, Scott Nowka, Jed Rasula, Matthias Regan, Bradley Ricca, Susan B. A. Somers-Willett, Angela Sorby, Jeff Swenson, Michael Thurston, and Mark W. Van Wienen; Roberto Ampuero, Adam Diesberg, Drew Duncan, Patrick Oray, and Cheeni Rao; friends, students, and colleagues at Willamette University and the University of Iowa; and many and various interlocutors at Dave's Foxhead, George's Buffet, Venti's Café and Basement Bar, and the F/Stop Fitzgerald's Public House.

I would like to thank the Special Collections departments at the Iowa State University, University of Iowa, and University of Missouri at Kansas City libraries, which extended me their assistance and patience on many occasions; the Indiana and Minnesota state historical societies; Kristi Ernsting at Hallmark Cards for her assistance with Hallmark company archives; Clinton Odell, who allowed me access to his family-owned archive of Burma-Vita Company records for the writing of chapter 3; Arthur B. Church Jr., Hualing Nieh Engle, and family members of Doris Ashley and Myrtle Eckert; and William Bartlett at NBC, Amanda Chapman at Energizer Personal Care, Ray Daniels at Nissan, and Emily Moran at Crate & Barrel, among others, for helping to guide me through corporate infrastructures in search of permissions.

A version of chapter 3 appeared as "The Business of Rhyming: Burma-Shave Poetry and Popular Culture" in *PMLA* 125, no. 1 (January 2010): 29–47; a much shorter version of chapter 5 appeared as "Remembering Paul Engle," in the *Writer's Chronicle* 41, no. 2 (October/November 2008); and I had the opportunity to discuss material in this book at several conferences, including those of the College Book Art Association, Midwest Modern Language

Association, Modernist Studies Association, and the Western States Folklore Society, as well as at Fiske Matters: A Conference on John Fiske's Legacy (University of Wisconsin), Lifting Belly High: A Conference on Women's Poetry since 1900 (Duquesne University), and Studies in Sound: Listening in the Age of Visual Culture (University of Iowa).

I am grateful for the support of my parents, Ann and Dwight Chasar.

Lastly, and most importantly, how do I thank you, Meridith Brand—old soul, spouse, finder of flattened frogs, slayer of slugs, and yin to my yang? You are the book to my scrap, the Ted to my Malone, and the Burma to my Shave.

EVERYDAY READING

Introduction

Poetry and Popular Culture

The 1918 mayoral race in St. Paul, Minnesota, was in part a referendum on popular poetry. That year Democratic candidate Laurence C. Hodgson (1874–1937)—a Twin Cities newspaper personality better known as the poet "Larry Ho"—defeated his Republican and Labor party challengers to become the city's twenty-eighth mayor. Reflecting on the election a year later the *Modern Highway* newsletter reminded readers of an ironic disconnect between the world of poetry and the world of politics that had come to the fore of the campaign, explaining that even though Hodgson's "plurality was a big one," only by "some queer caper of fate" could a "poet-giver"—a man "whose greatest pastime is sunshine making" and "who could see a shining soul right through the dirtiest skin of the least inviting newsboy"—have been elected to public office.[1] A Minnesota native, Hodgson had been a political reporter for the *St. Paul Dispatch*, the *Minneapolis Times*, and the *Minneapolis Tribune* and had worked in government before, most notably as secretary to the speaker of the house as well as secretary to two St. Paul mayors, including his immediate predecessor, Vivian R. Irwin. But as the *Modern Highway* suggests, it was the poetry Hodgson published as Larry Ho that the opposition identified as a potential weakness and election-year issue. Hodgson's competition, the *Modern*

Highway recalled, "sneered at the idea of a poet making a good mayor—sneered publicly" (10).

That negative campaign strategy appears to have backfired, however, for instead of casting doubt on Hodgson's political acumen—one can certainly imagine a poet "who is always finding something to sing about in the doings of the dullest day" being characterized as soft on crime—Hodgson's "poet-giver" alter ego ultimately served, like Bill Clinton's saxophone, to highlight his human side and inspired people to consider his candidacy more seriously (ibid.). Indeed, the *Modern Highway* recalled, "that reminded a great many people of the identity of this Laurence C. Hodgson. They began getting down scrapbooks filled with his poems, for his verse and scraps of philosophy are the kind that find their way pretty regularly into scrapbooks" (ibid.). As an election-year poster from 1918 suggests, Democrats in fact turned the issue of Hodgson's extracurricular activities into a strength, advertising his double identity for maximum public appeal (see figure 0.1). Larry Ho not only won the election in 1918, but he also went on to win three more terms as mayor of St. Paul before returning to the newspaper business in 1931.

In many ways the story of Hodgson and his readers is not unique. Like Berton Braley, Anne Campbell, Edgar A. Guest, Don Marquis, Walt Mason, James Metcalfe, Jay Sigmund, Frank L. Stanton, Helen Welshimer, and Ella Wheeler Wilcox, Hodgson was part of a modern America that was crazy for poetry—that wrote and published it, read it as part of everyday life, bought it, collected and shared it, and afforded it a great deal of prestige for its many aesthetic, emotional, social, political, and even commercial ways of communicating. Known as the "people's poet," Guest, for example, authored more than twenty books, regularly wrote advertising verse, and for thirty years published a poem each day in a *Detroit Free Press* feature that was syndicated to more than 300 newspapers nationwide and carefully saved by people like Hodgson's St. Paul scrapbookers (see figure 0.2). In 1955 the University of Michigan awarded Guest an honorary degree—seven years before it would bestow the same recognition on its official poet-in-residence, Robert Frost. Called "Eddie Guest's Rival" by *Time* magazine, Campbell began publishing in the *Detroit News* in 1922 and wrote a poem six days a week for twenty-five years, producing more than seven thousand five hundred poems, whose syndication reportedly earned her up to $10,000 per year. A 1947 event marking her silver anniversary at the paper drew fifteen hundred fans, including Detroit's mayor and the president of Wayne State University, who claimed

FOR MAYOR
L. C. HODGSON
"LARRY HO"

FIGURE 0.1. Election poster for Laurence C. Hodgson's 1918 campaign for mayor of St. Paul, Minnesota. Reprinted with permission of the Minnesota Historical Society.

that Campbell "has helped to make our town great."[2] While working as an insurance executive in Cedar Rapids, Iowa, Sigmund wrote over twelve hundred poems during a sixteen-year span, during which time he also mentored fellow Cedar Rapids native Paul Engle, who would go on to shepherd the University of Iowa Writers' Workshop to national prominence after World War II. Sherwood Anderson, then a newspaper editor in Kentucky, liked Sigmund's verse so much that he not only solicited Sigmund's contributions but then proceeded, as an act of homage at the time of printing, to remove Sigmund's name from the byline and substitute his own. Metcalfe was an FBI agent who participated in the ambush of John Dillinger outside of Chicago's Biograph Theater in 1934 and later wrote rhyming prose poems—a form that Sinclair Lewis's fictional newspaper poet, T. Cholmondeley Frink, called "poemulations" in *Babbit*—for the *Chicago Sun-Times*, 750 of which made up the first of his over fifteen books.[3] And Marquis's poems in the *New York Evening Sun* and *New York Tribune* were so well known and liked—especially the verses about the adventures of Archy, the prohibition-era, vers-libre-writing cockroach, and Mehitabel, an alley cat, which were illustrated by *Krazy Kat* comic strip creator George Herriman and formed the basis for a 1957 Broadway musical—that in 1943 the U.S. Navy christened a ship, the *U.S.S. Don Marquis*, in his memory.[4]

As much as these and other writers had national followings—and, in some cases, very respectable incomes—theirs was hardly the only poetry that Americans were reading or hearing in the late nineteenth and the first half of the twentieth centuries. Mark W. Van Wienen has described the World War I era as a period in which "just about anyone might consider himself or herself fit to write poetry and even called upon to write it."[5] Reporting for the *American Mercury* in 1926, the successful Iowa novelist Ruth Suckow explained that her state's literary culture "is snatched at by everybody—farmer boys, dentists, telegraph editors in small towns, students, undertakers, insurance agents and nobodies. All have a try at it."[6] Historian Joan Shelley Rubin writes that Americans "encountered poetic texts at a number of public, or at any rate, observable venues: in school, at civic gatherings, in women's clubs, as parlor entertainment and bedtime routine, within religious ceremonies, at celebrity performances, and around Girl Scout campfires,"[7] and Kansas newspaper poet Walt Mason suggested in 1914 how such verse enjoyed popularity beyond the simple fact of its publication. "A man," he explained in the *Literary Digest*, "sees in the newspaper a clever rhyme full of hope and encouragement, and he cuts it out and shows it to his friends, and carries it in his pocket-book, and takes it home and reads it to his family, and his wife pastes it in the scrap-book for future reference."[8]

In short, Americans living in the first half of the century—the period during which the U.S. culture industries were rapidly expanding and the national economy was settling into what we have come to call consumer capitalism—lived in a world saturated by poetry of all types and sizes, ranging from clever,

FIGURE 0.2. Notebook of Edgar A. Guest's poetry, assembled by one of Guest's fans in the mid-1930s. Author's collection.

two-line advertising jingles to full-length collections such as Khalil Gibran's *The Prophet*, which appeared in 1923 and went on to become the best-selling single-author volume of poems in U.S. history. Poetry appeared in books, daily newspapers, and magazines. It was preserved in scrapbooks and photograph and autograph albums, and it was included in classroom readers, comic books, song books, farmers' almanacs, church services, civic events, citizenship handbooks, nature field guides, propaganda, and in a wide variety of advertising media. It was on the radio, billboards, broadsides, drug store window and trolley card placards, Chautauqua circuits, picket lines, wax cylinder and other recording formats, magic lantern slides, and stereoview cards. And it decorated many ephemeral, commemorative, value-added, and/or commercial goods, ranging from postcards to greeting cards, calling cards, playing cards, business cards, bookmarks, matchbooks, posters and wall hangings, stickers, calendars, event tickets, notepads, menus, fans, trivets, thermometers, milk bottles, pinup girly posters, bird-food and breath-mint tins, packages for drafting tools, candy boxes, souvenir plates, handkerchiefs, pillows, and table runners.

The sheer amount of poetry embedded in so many aspects of modern American life—commercial, political, educational, occupational, domestic, and otherwise—can come as a surprise to poets and literary critics today who have long imagined poetry to have occupied at best a marginal place in the twentieth-century United States, even though the energy of the period I study in this book helped to underwrite a current American publishing climate in which, according to David Alpaugh, literary journals alone print more than one hundred thousand poems each year and in which enormous amounts of poetry are woven, whole or piecemeal and often so seamlessly that they escape notice, into the fabric of television programs, talk shows, movies, novels, advertisements, Web sites, blogs, new video formats, and interactive social media, including chat rooms, Facebook, and Twitter. In arguing about whether poetry "matters" (Dana Gioia) or whether it "makes nothing happen" (W. H. Auden), poets and critics convinced of poetry's cultural marginalization in modern America have a tendency to wrongly mythologize previous eras as the genre's "golden age"—times when, as Stephen Burt has claimed, "more people read more poems, at home and at school."[9] In *Would Poetry Disappear? American Verse and the Crisis of Modernity*, John Timberman Newcomb has shown that pronouncements about poetry's purported decline or death in the twentieth century were even being made during the period that this book examines, a time when poetry was rapidly proliferating. Reports of poetry's death are greatly exaggerated. The fact is that more people in the modern United States were producing and consuming more verse than at any other time in history—poems, to borrow Stuart Hall's phrasing, that we understand "to be 'popular' because masses of people listen to them, buy them, read them, consume them, and seem to enjoy them to the full."[10] In a modern America fueled by consumer capitalism and new media and communication formats, poetry had tens of millions of readers.

Most of this poetry, however, has never been studied, even though poets and poetry critics have been extending their attention to increasingly diverse types of verse for decades. Academic components of modern social movements such as Marxism, feminism, and the civil rights movement expanded the literary canon to include poetry written by women, writers of color, and working class writers, in the process developing new ways of understanding that work in relation to the broader artistic, cultural, and political histories it helped to shape. Writers and critics affiliated with the avant-garde Language poetry movement in the 1970s and 1980s helped to dislodge the lyric poem as the privileged genre of poetic study and admiration; practitioners of the new lyric studies have subsequently shown the very category of the lyric to have been an "idealization of poetry" obscuring the diversity of other verse forms in the historical record as well as the social and material circumstances of its composition, distribution, and consumption.[11] Claiming "we no longer know the history of the poetry of the first half of this century; most of us, moreover, do not know that the knowledge is gone," Cary Nelson's *Repression and Recovery: Modern American Poetry and the Politics of Cultural Memory* reintroduced a large, complicated body of work by leftist American poets and compelled the development of yet another set of frameworks for understanding how poetry operated in American culture as well as the various aesthetic systems informing it.[12] And more recently, Rubin's historical study, *Songs of Ourselves: The Uses of Poetry in America*, revealed how, for many amateur or nonspecialist readers, poetry was not necessarily or primarily a private endeavor pursued by trained or elite audiences but was regularly experienced as part of, or made to be a highlight or centerpiece for, institutionalized social situations and occasions like school classrooms, civic events, religious meetings, bedtime rituals, and girl scout troop meetings.[13]

This history has produced a disciplinary field that is now predicated on the study and evaluation of multiple, diverse sets of poetic phenomena—a field best described in the plural as the study of American poetries. *Everyday Reading* starts with that momentum, which has challenged if not dismantled the idealization of "poetry" expressed in the singular and with a capital letter P, in order to argue that a critical study and evaluation of popular and commercial verse is not only warranted but necessary to understanding the impact that poetry as a whole had on modern American life. At the same time this book grows out of cultural studies as a now well-established critical methodology in American English and humanities departments—a methodology some poets and poetry critics have been reluctant to embrace but that has nonetheless deeply affected the practice of today's poetry criticism.[14] Insofar as it has driven and legitimized scholarly work on popular subjects as diverse as romance and dime novels, *Star Trek*, fanzines, soap operas, popular movies, toys, comic books, and *Buffy the Vampire Slayer*, and insofar as it has expanded the definition of the word "text" to encompass virtually any cultural production as a formally and ideologically complicated event to be taken seriously, cultural studies offers a rubric or set of rubrics for the assessment and evaluation of popular poetic texts and especially their intersection with

American mass media and popular practices. By virtue of its shared emphasis on producers and consumers, on media and distribution formats as well as textual composition, and on the importance of studying texts for the formal and cultural ways that hegemony is reinforced and challenged, cultural studies provides this book with another framework and impetus for assessing popular verse and its impact on everyday life in twentieth-century America.

In focusing on popular poetry this book does not offer an argument about whether T. S. Eliot's "The Waste Land" is a better poem than a Burma-Shave advertising jingle, or whether either or both should be included in the next big poetry anthology. If that is the argument you are looking for, then I reluctantly have to send you elsewhere. Rather, this is a book about how and why millions of people read the poetry they did; how and why that poetry influenced the reading, mass media, and communication practices we experience today; and how, at times, that poetry intersected with literary culture in the United States. That is not to say that *Everyday Reading* is unconcerned with the subject of aesthetic value and evaluation. For one of the byproducts of studying this material seriously is the recognition that it, too, has clear aesthetic components—that it was written, published, and consumed in relation to a range of different aesthetic systems and expectations, and that uncredentialed or ordinary readers were concerned with the subjects of poetic genre, form, tradition, and taste. People edited large poetry scrapbooks that not only helped them to think through their personal lives but also shaped and worked to define their aesthetic ones as well. Radio shows, newspapers, and magazines broadcast and printed poems that would have been rejected for publication in other formats and frequently made the subject of taste a talking point. Businesses conducted poetry-writing contests with stated judging criteria, and sometimes that criteria overlapped with, or was articulated in relation to, the aesthetic goals of modernism or belles lettres. It is tempting to reduce the history of American poetry in the twentieth century to a set of binaries like "high" and "low," "modern" and "genteel," and "avant-garde" and "quietist." But just as poetry criticism of the past thirty years has revealed how other types of poetry were written, published, and consumed in relation to multiple aesthetic systems and traditions, so a study of popular poetries reveals that the aesthetic values of modern America's popular literary landscape were many and various. The culture of popular poetry was not unlike a music store with recordings filed according to genres like classic rock, Christian contemporary, rap, hip-hop, classical, and country western, each tag suggesting and defining different sets of tastes, aesthetic traditions, types of social capital, listening communities, and even circulation networks. What those various aesthetic filing systems were; how they operated; how they were produced, met, and challenged by readers and writers whom we wouldn't normally consider to be experts on poetry; and how they might be better understood by today's scholars and critics figure into *Everyday Reading*, even though the particular categorical claim that Eliot's poem or Burma-Shave's poem must have a spot in the next poetry anthology is not. If you are Garrison Keillor, then the Burma-Shave poem gets the nod and is set alongside verses by John Donne, Walt Whitman, Emily Dickinson, Don Marquis, and others.[15] If you are Norton, it does not. The reasons why are part of the story I want to tell here.

In bringing the histories and methods of poetry criticism and cultural studies to a consideration of popular poetry and its connections to American communication practices more broadly, I have four overarching theses for this book. First, I argue that ordinary readers of popular poetry were more self-aware, discerning, creative, and socially engaged than literary critics and historians have typically assumed, even though those audiences' reading methods, habits, and characteristics don't necessarily or even frequently map neatly onto those recommended by poets, educators, experts, or other cultural curators seeking what Eliot called a "correction of taste" in American life.[16] During the first half of the twentieth century ordinary readers like those in Larry Ho's St. Paul came to be cartooned as an unreflective, easily manipulated, affect-driven, sentimental, and often female demographic that was sincere but ultimately misguided when it came to issues of taste and poetry's purpose in the world; frequently, this caricature pitted the knowing, cynical, modern worlds of the mass media and East Coast literary cultures against the local color of a simpler, more earnest Midwest, where many modern poets had in fact been born or raised.[17] (It is no accident that my study begins in the Twin Cities and spends considerable time in Missouri, Minnesota, Iowa and, to a lesser extent, Michigan, Illinois, and my home state of Ohio.) This depiction was partly a function of a broader and by now much-studied discourse of modernism in which, as Andreas Huyssen has explained, "woman . . . is positioned as reader of inferior literature—subjective, emotional and passive—while man . . . emerges as writer of genuine, authentic literature—objective, ironic, and in control of his aesthetic means,"[18] and it was propagated by influential voices like Ezra Pound, who championed a "harder and saner" modernist poetry as an antidote to the genteel, "nice" poetry or "emotional slither" that "Aunt Hepsy liked,"[19] and Eliot, who claimed that, compared to "the mind of the poet" in which "experiences are always forming new wholes, the ordinary man's experience is chaotic, irregular, fragmentary."[20]

The distinctions Pound, Eliot, and others made between elite and popular tastes and texts were themselves a function of a discourse that predated modernism—a cultural logic, traced by Lawrence Levine in *Highbrow/Lowbrow: The Emergence of Cultural Hierarchy in America*, that had been redrawing and demarcating cultural boundary lines between refined and mass/popular cultures since the middle of the nineteenth century. While those distinctions were established firmly in relation to a range of art forms (including drama, opera, classical music, and fine art) by the 1910s and 1920s, that was not the case with poetry, in part because poetry had so many different popular forms and uses that it took much longer to tease them out from the fabric of people's everyday lives and recast them as highbrow or lowbrow in character. In fact, it wasn't until what Joseph Harrington has called the "poetry wars" of the 1930s that the discourse of high and low caught up with, and began to reform, perceptions of American poetry on broad cultural and institutional scales; ironically, the aesthetic distinctions that have been attributed to modernism and New Criticism, and which modernism used to distinguish itself from nineteenth-century genteel literary culture, are really a twentieth-century extension—even a culmination—of a nineteenth-century cultural project.[21] Prior to the 1930s, as some of the poetry scrapbooks I examine in chapter 1 vividly illustrate, readers may have recognized differences between genres of poetry, but they felt licensed to range widely across them, using them for their own purposes and thus becoming, as Rubin observes, "repositories of both the high and the popular—aware of, but not constrained by, a shifting boundary between them."[22] What poetry signified in a culture that read in such a way, and what it contributed to and fulfilled for that culture, is the first part of the narrative I want to trace here.

The lines of demarcation between high and low poetries—signaled, in some conversations, as a difference between "poetry" and "verse" (a distinction I do not want to make in this book except to ventriloquize other viewpoints)—are thus a relatively recent rhetorical feature in the history of American cultural hierarchies, which perhaps helps to explain why the cartoon of the deficient or even nonexistent popular poetry reader has maintained a strong purchase on poets and critics in an otherwise postmodern and contemporary America that has had plenty of poetry in circulation and plenty of high-low intersection in other art forms: a reason why Randall Jarrell, speaking at Harvard University's 1950 Defense of Poetry conference, would strongly, if incorrectly, assert that most American readers were "unused to any poetry" at all, "even of the simplest kind."[23] A quick look at the *New York Times*, which was printing poetry on its Op-Ed pages in a press run of about 500,000 during the very week Jarrell spoke at Harvard, would have shown his statement to be factually problematic. Nevertheless Mark Harris echoed Jarrell when he told audiences at the University of Iowa in 1959 to "no longer quibble over the question of whether our country men can receive or appreciate literature of the first rank. The fact is that they cannot."[24] Over the years these views—that few ordinary people read Poetry (in the singular, spelled with a capital P) and that they wouldn't be able to deal with it even if they did—would become a truism if not a certain sort of religion, moving Dana Gioia, the future head of the National Endowment for the Arts and a former vice president of marketing at General Foods Corporation, to describe the bulk of potential American poetry readers in 2002 as "the incurious mass audience of the popular media,"[25] and underwriting Adam Kirsch's judgment in his 2007 review of *Songs of Ourselves* that "the common sense of [ordinary] readers is a bit like the proverbial sausage factory. You don't want to look at it too closely, for fear of what you might find."[26]

If my first goal is to resist this mythology and its narratives—and to follow, instead, Stuart Hall's more sympathetic picture of uncredentialed readers who are not "cultural dopes" but, rather, creative and critical audiences who "are perfectly capable of recognizing the way" their life experiences "are reorganized, reconstructed and reshaped"[27]—then this book's second point is that the actual poetry such audiences consumed was not only more various but more aesthetically and culturally complex (and perhaps even more pleasurable) than mainstream literary histories would suggest. Pound disparaged popular poetry as "poppycock."[28] The press regularly called it "piffle." Jarrell described the verse read aloud on nationally broadcast radio poetry shows as "one-syllable poems."[29] And a wide array of terms with mostly pejorative connotations—verse, jingles, rhymes, poesy, ditties, poemulations, newspaper poetry, advertising poetry, children's rhymes, genteel verse, doggerel, Hallmark poetry, tripe, light verse, inspirational verse, sentimental verse, schoolroom poetry—were (and still are) used to obscure the different and wide-ranging aesthetic, social, political, and emotional aspects of poetries that were purportedly too full of what Pound called "painted adjectives" and "rhetorical din, and luxurious riot" to merit serious consideration.[30] In addition to homogenizing and dismissing this verse along stylistic or aesthetic lines, critics also came to disparage it because of its frequent connections to commercial, for-profit endeavors and not just its popular audiences—because of its marketability, and because it at first blush does not appear to have resisted being instrumentalized or pressed into what Theodor Adorno called "enforced service . . . of economically organized purposes and goals."[31] In the midcentury United States, Edgar Guest—whose verse "A Friend's Greeting" first appeared in a Hallmark card in 1916 and went on to become the company's best-selling poem—was a lightning rod for critics opposed to popular poetry and poetry's use for commercial gain. Mark Harris opened a 1959 symposium, The Writer in a Mass Culture, at the University of Iowa by saying, for example, "Let us declare once and forever . . . Edgar Guest was never a poet."[32] In the paragraph concluding his *New York Times* review of Rubin's *Songs of Ourselves*, Tom Sleigh suggests that even though Guest no longer serves as a primary straw man in such arguments, the mixture of poetry and marketing savoir faire he cultivated nonetheless remains offensive. "As I read about Guest's savvy self-marketing and the weepy faux sincerity of his public performances," Sleigh writes without referencing a single line of Guest's verse, "I was completely repulsed."[33]

It is partly because I, too, believe that poetry can be—and, as I show in parts of all five chapters, regularly represented or harbored—an alternative discourse to the economic values of the commercial marketplace that I find wholesale dismissals of popular and commercial verse forms based primarily on their marketing appeals and relative proximity to certain aspects of the marketplace to be inadequate and intellectually unsatisfying. For starters, marketing strategies, elaborate self-branding efforts, showmanship, and performances of sincerity were regular aspects of highly monetized but otherwise "literary" cultures in the first half of the twentieth century, just as they are today. Taking a whip to Edgar Guest or any other aspect of commercialized or mass-cultural poetry not only works to obscure the economic underpinnings of highbrow literary culture and perpetuate a fantasy of "authentic" poetry and poetry writing as what Fredric Jameson calls "the locus of some genuinely critical and subversive, 'autonomous' aesthetic production";[34] it also hides the ideological complexities of commercial verse culture itself, letting its texts go about their oftentimes sophisticated cultural work unexamined and unchallenged, while incorrectly and chauvinistically assuming that popular readers did not recognize, question, or even attempt to reverse or counter those hegemonic interests while encountering or consuming it. Thus, despite the different types of verse I study in this book, every chapter attempts to understand poetry's intersections with commercial America in ways that are more nuanced than prevailing binaries suggest are possible. Chapter 1, for example, examines how readers excerpted texts from their commercial surroundings and repurposed them for noncommercial and even subversive ends in personally assembled poetry scrapbooks; chapter 2 tracks in part how radio listeners resisted the application of capitalist economic logic to poetry, a genre that, for them, frequently represented and sustained a noncapitalist gift-giving impulse in American life; chapter 3 finds advertising poetry to be a site for some of the same innovative poetic strategies that would later come to be associated with anticapitalist, avant-garde writing; chapter 4 explores how commercial billboard advertising provided a linguistic resource for William Carlos Williams; and chapter 5 argues that University of Iowa Writers' Workshop director Paul Engle envisioned (but failed to create) an MFA program that might encourage university-trained writers to engage, not separate from, a variety of poetic discourses, including the verse of mass-market periodicals and Hallmark greeting cards.

Although I examine poetry belonging to sentimental, genteel, advertising, greeting card, schoolroom, political, newspaper, religious, and other popular traditions in addition to more conventionally literary ones, it is not possible for a single book to study each of those traditions in full, let alone parse the range of skills, talents, cultural associations, and aesthetic pleasures that they entailed or inspired. In using them to represent a complex and diverse archive—as well as networks of writers, texts, media formats, and readers—I also want to argue, as the third and fourth major points of this study, that the culture of popular verse was not self-contained but influenced the work of now-canonical modernist writers and the development of popular culture more broadly. While scholars have examined how popular- and mass-culture phenomena (such as audio recording and broadcast technologies, marketing techniques, book-club selections, Hollywood film, comics, celebrity culture, and so on) affected modernist literary production, the field has been slow to conceptualize the relationship between popular poetry and modernist poetry as anything other than strictly adversarial in nature, presuming that so-called highbrow, or elite, writers identified and categorically abandoned the forms, media, and other characteristics of popular verse.[35] This critical predisposition toward an adversarial narrative of American poetry has not been reserved solely for characterizing the relationship between the popular and the elite. Cary Nelson has argued, for example, that a parallel dichotomy frequently made between (twentieth-century) modern and (nineteenth-century) genteel verse forms in histories of American poetry is more "melodramatic" than accurate and obscures the exchanges that actually occurred between the two traditions. "Indeed," he writes in *Repression and Recovery*, "one of the striking things about the gradual emergence of modernist forms in American protest poetry . . . is the lack of a sense of a radical break with the past. The thematic continuities in this hundred-year-old American tradition are so strong that a sense of opening out and diversification, of thematic conservation and formal variation, overrides the adversarial model of modernism wholly rejecting the more formal traditions in American poetry. . . . And the rhetoric of the genteel tradition and the rhetoric of modernism were oftentimes counterpointed in the work of individual poets."[36]

Just as Nelson suggests the adversarial model of genteel and modern poetries is limited or incomplete, so I propose that a similar model of how elite and popular poetries related (or didn't relate) also obscures continuities and exchanges between literary poets and popular verse. Gertrude Stein collected Burma-Shave advertising jingle booklets. Pound used his grandfather's scrapbook as source material for the *Cantos*. Well-known writers published in magazines like *Ladies' Home Journal* only partly because those publications paid well. As I explain in chapter 4, Williams made central to his writing a popular mode of reading that developed in America's speed-reading road-and-billboard culture of the 1920s and 1930s. And, as I show in chapter 5, Engle did not see an inherent contradiction between writing in high and low poetic forms when, even as he was hiring Pulitzer Prize–winning poets and mentoring future ones at Iowa, he also spent time composing greeting card verse for Hallmark.

In addition to proposing that the culture of popular poetry offered sets of resources, materials, and models that helped broker exchanges between popular and elite traditions, I also want to claim that the culture of popular verse from the first half of the twentieth century affected the development of popular culture more broadly. In a period when consumer products and participatory media formats that we more commonly associate with popular culture (radio, television, comics, popular music, blockbuster films, popular novel genres, and the Internet) were in nascent form or nonexistent, poetry served as a common and primary ground on which the dynamics of our current-day popular culture were initially worked out and established. Embedded in the first forms of mass media, including newspapers, periodicals, and advertisements, poetry dignified, familiarized, and helped people experiment and become comfortable with the dynamic interface between the culture industries and everyday life that Stuart Hall argues is the site of popular culture proper—the "constantly changing field" or "arena of consent and resistance" in which people acquiesce to, or resist, hegemonic power structures.[37] Before call-in talk shows, long distance song dedications, and *American Idol*, for example, poetry radio programs not only solicited listener feedback and contributions but also based much of their success on consumer-generated content. The cutting-and-pasting practices that yield mix tapes, fanzines, digital mash ups, and much online media find a direct historical precedent in the cutting and pasting of American scrapbookers, who often imagined the sampling and splicing of poetry to be the highest form of album-making more generally. The contest structure of the Burma-Vita Company's annual Burma-Shave jingle-writing contest, itself based on nationally conducted poetry-writing contests that soap advertisers like Ivory sponsored in the 1890s, helped routinize a practice in which people are invited to participate in shaping the very marketing campaigns they are later subjected to as consumers. If we want to know about the workings of mass and popular culture in the early twenty-first century, we can look back to the early twentieth century when poetry—a literary form we do not readily associate with the workings of the mass media and its audiences—served as a laboratory for, if not one of the very foundations of, how popular culture would come to operate in the United States.

It is thus the relationship between the industrially produced text and the reader, consumer, or user that drives my investigation in this book, as that relationship constitutes popular culture more generally. There are many other ways a study of popular verse might take shape. I could have written five chapters about five different popular poets, such as Guest, Campbell, Metcalfe, Welshimer, and Mason, for example. I could have focused more specifically on the workings, forms, discourses, and characteristics of individual genres of popular verse—newspaper, magazine, greeting card, souvenir pillow, business card, advertising, and radio poetry, as well as others—or on how modern popular poetry developed from its nineteenth-century precedents. Given the heavily gendered aspects of popular verse culture, each chapter might have focused more specifically on that topic, or I could have oriented each chapter in relation to literary regionalism, which has so far been studied primarily as a prose phenomenon. These and other possibilities are visible in the material that follows and would be compelling frameworks for other studies. But because most of the material I present in this book has never in fact been read or considered at any length in an academic context, I have chosen for the moment to prioritize not select individual talents, individual genres, historical precedents, or other more narrowly focused critical rubrics but, rather, the relationship between the culture industries and the consumer that is the constitutive dynamic of popular culture, the culture of popular poetry included.

In establishing this agenda I follow two other approaches that today's poetry critics typically do not take. First, I take seriously what Lauren Berlant might call the "silly object" of American poetry—the often ephemeral, and what many critics would take to be the banal, product of "mainstream documents and discourses" that nevertheless functions "not as white noise but as powerful language" in relation to people's lives, the larger culture, and even canonical literary production.[38] As critics ranging from Roland Barthes to Stuart Hall, Michael Denning, Fredric Jameson, and Sianne Ngai have revealed, the silly, easily overlooked objects of everyday life can be sites of intense ideological coding and negotiation as well as aesthetic activity or innovation.[39] Following Berlant, I want to reveal, beyond the established critical motif of elitism, the complexities of popular and commercial poetries as a form of powerful language that demands critical scrutiny. Second, I do not privilege the little magazine and what Bob Brown in 1931 called "the antiquated, word-dribbling book" as the primary or even most important sites of twentieth-century poetic production, distribution, and study.[40] Most popular poetry did not and does not circulate in little magazines and traditional codices, and limiting a study of popular verse—even poetry in general—to those media incompletely assesses it by a measure best suited for the study of other items, like dime or romance novels. In "Verse and Popular Poetry," their 1988 contribution to M. Thomas Inge's *Handbook of American Popular Culture*, Janice Radway and Perry Frank limit their discussion of best-selling poetry to "single volumes," for example, and thus determine that the most popular verse of the twentieth century was Khalil Gibran's *The Prophet*, which sold over three million copies—a number that not only pales in comparison to best-selling prose volumes of the time but that gives the mistaken impression that poetry was not as popular, prevalent, or profitable as other literary genres in American life. In applying a unit of prose measurement to the genre of poetry, Radway and Frank disregard phenomena like Guest's *Free Press* newspaper feature that was syndicated to 300 papers across the United States and thus possibly reached Gibran-like distribution figures every single day; they similarly overlook the poetry radio shows of the 1920s and 1930s that, in their national broadcasts, likely exceeded Gibran's audience as well—or else expanded it by having sections of *The Prophet* read on air.[41] My approach in this book has been to track poetry in multiple media—clippings, scrapbooks, radio, billboards, promotional booklets, mass-market periodicals, newspapers, and greeting cards, as well as the book and the little magazine—in order to understand and thus better gauge the nature and extent of poetry's embeddedness in American life.

While the following chapters all engage my four major themes, they do so in different ways so as to assess the culture of popular poetry—its producers, consumers, texts, media networks, and influences—from multiple vantage points and thus provide a more complete picture of its landscape. I begin with a study of poetry scrapbooks—personally assembled verse anthologies that extended Renaissance and Enlightenment practices of commonplace book keeping into the modern era of mass communication—not just because they offer a glimpse into the lived literary landscape of modern America (what poetry people read, where they got it, how they read it, and so on), but also because they materially manifest how, as Michel de Certeau has put it, "the activity of reading has . . . all the characteristics of a silent production."[42] As some of the first documents of popular culture in the historical record, they offer a portrait of ordinary readers as a creative, engaged, discerning, and even subversive "species-in-formation" that, in "migrating and devouring its way through the pastures of the media,"[43] repurposes and thus transforms the materials of mass culture into individualized and often (so I find) moving and sophisticated compositions and artifacts.

Between the Civil War and World War II Americans regularly made and maintained poetry scrapbooks, as rising literacy rates, increasing tides of print, the expansion of the public education system, and the development of middlebrow America fueled a cut-and-paste culture that helped lay the foundation for many of the communication practices we've come to associate with popular culture and modern media more generally. By focusing on poetry readers whose collections have not been preserved by libraries or archives—I have purchased more than 150 orphaned collections on eBay over the past half decade that, in aggregate, form an archive of the practice at the height of its popularity—I want to depict the cutting and pasting of these albums not only as a vernacular companion to literary or modernist acts of bricolage and collage but also as a method of thinking that people used to process, articulate, and remake their life experiences. While there is not enough space in this book for me to spotlight each of the albums I've collected, I offer as many specific examples as possible while still speculating on some of the key issues they bring to light as a diverse but nonetheless relatively coherent genre. In their methods of cutting and pasting, for example, they reveal as a group a widespread cultural sense that literary property ownership did not function in relation to poetry in the same way that it did to prose—readers cut off copyright notices, author bylines, and publication information and formed alternate bibliographic systems based on how poems were used rather than who wrote or published them—and thus poetry became, over time, a repository or magnet for other values (such as love, patriotism, religion, friendship, and so on) that were incompletely capitalized as well. At the same time that they harbored and sustained what were sometimes fugitive discourses, though, poetry scrapbooks also schooled readers in the acquisition and maintenance of private property, so that if the album's compositional freedoms and various discursive registers offered opportunities to keep alive alternative value systems, then the practice itself often served as a training ground for the construction and preservation of American bourgeois identities.

Produced by the drama of "consent and resistance" that, in Hall's formulation, constitutes popular culture, poetry scrapbooks took many shapes and forms, were compiled by individuals and groups, by men and women, by adults and children, and by people of different races and immigrant backgrounds. As de Certeau suggests, we can read these compositions as a type of literary production, or writing, and I begin chapter 1 by examining two albums assembled in the 1920s—one by Doris Ashley of New Bedford, Massachusetts, and the other by Myrtle Eckert of Skykomish, Washington. I find both collections to be rich, deeply expressive texts, and I juxtapose them here not to endorse one over the other but to show how differently rich and expressive individual albums could become and to give some sort of range for the political, social, and aesthetic forces that such objects allowed readers to put into play. I conclude this chapter with a discussion of two scrapbooks as well: one by Odell Shepard, a Pulitzer Prize–winning author and onetime English professor at Trinity College in Connecticut, and the other by Joyce Fitzgerald, an aspiring and probably teenage writer about whom I know nothing except her name and what I can extrapolate from her collection. Working in an era before creative writing programs made institutionalized workshops available to writers, both Shepard and Fitzgerald turned their albums into virtual writing communities and workshops where they could situate their work in relation to that of their peers and forge relationships to literary tradition. Both are noteworthy collections, but I conclude with Fitzgerald's because it not only finds and establishes a workshop space and writing community as Shepard's presumably more professionalized scrapbook does, but then turns that very act into an extended expressive and feminist literary project that I propose we can read from traditional literary-critical perspectives as a piece of literature as well.

If chapter 1 focuses on the consumer as maker or producer, chapter 2 uses the phenomenon of old-time radio poetry shows to shift attention to the dynamic interface between the consumer and the culture industries. The activity of poetry scrapbooking was so familiar to Americans that, seeking a metaphor by which to instruct first-generation radio audiences in the participatory feedback-loop dynamics of the new medium in the 1920s and 1930s, early poetry radio shows adopted the model of the poetry scrapbook to cast themselves as an on-air version of the print practice. Immensely popular and often profitable—*Between the Bookends* with host Ted Malone received upwards of twenty thousand fan letters per month at the height of its popularity, and Tony Wons earned a reported $2,000 each month including royalties from the sales of *Tony's Scrap Book*, his annually updated print extension of CBS's *R Yuh Listenin'?*[44]—such shows not only depended on listeners to mail in original and favorite poems that comprised their broadcast content but also, in doing so, served as an interface through which the relationship between corporate and popular interests was worked out. By soliciting listener contributions, for example, Malone and Wons helped to incorporate a diffuse set of independent or otherwise uncoordinated scrapbook practices into the structure of the culture industries with the host and national network, not the individual consumer, positioned as final editor and voice of popular America. At the same time, however, such shows also connected and gave voice to audience members who were old, sick, poor, living in rural areas, or otherwise isolated or disenfranchised during the Great Depression. As an archive of fan letters sent to Malone in 1935 suggests, programs like

Between the Bookends and *R Yuh Listenin'?* served as a resource for poems that listeners would use to help survive the economic, social, and emotional pressures of the 1930s.

As with chapter 1, chapter 2 introduces part of an enormous but now largely unfamiliar archive; radio poetry programs produced a huge amount of material in terms of broadcast hours, fan letters that circulated millions of poems and editorial commentary on those poems, news reports and features, and print spin-off or tie-in products that took highly visible magazine and book formats. (In 1932 alone, for example, *Tony's Scrap Book* sold over two hundred twenty-five thousand copies.)[45] In chapter 1 I approach my archive by extending attention to individual albums themselves—by bracketing the chapter with extended discussions about two pairs of scrapbooks. I could certainly privilege close reading of this type in chapter 2, but I purposely do not, as I am interested in what the culture of popular poetry reveals when pressured by other methods of reading. Thus, I also look for patterns between different texts that become visible via "distant" reading practices, such as those proposed not only by literary theorist Franco Moretti but also, as I show at the beginning of the chapter in an analysis of a 1940 *Between the Bookends* broadcast, by some of the hosts of old-time radio poetry shows themselves.

In reading more distantly I take as my object of study the set of fan letters, which I mentioned earlier, sent to Malone in 1935. As Huyssen's analysis of modernist discourse would lead us to suspect, Malone's almost unbelievable popularity was regularly explained by the press as the product of a shrewd ability to program for hysterical, love-struck, and easily manipulated female audiences; in an attempt to establish and increase his credibility in media circles, Malone himself encouraged this view by leaking select, outrageous details from fan letters. Reading these letters individually can leave today's scholar with the impression that Malone and his press coverage carefully cultivated, but reading them distantly—as a group, for the language they share and for the topics and concerns they raise that might otherwise be invisible in the context of a single letter—a different picture of Malone's audience begins to emerge. Seeking resources by which to survive the Depression's effects, listeners not only used the show as a way to practice and keep alive an emotional language of hope and empathy that they had little occasion to use in daily life, but they also found in it a way to practice and sustain the dynamics of value economies that weren't primarily mediated or fueled by capital and that took on new urgency after the stock market crash of 1929. Time and again *Bookends* listeners responded to, or even preempted, what they perceived to be a corporate commodification of their poetry by spelling out the terms of their participation and ongoing listenership in relation to the logic of gift exchanges that Malone was expected to understand, honor, and respond to in kind. Rooted in the non- or extracapitalist exchange economy of poetry visible in some of the poetry scrapbooks I examine in chapter 1, these responses were never aired publicly; they helped, instead, to facilitate a private relationship between Malone and his audience that nevertheless affected the public operation of *Bookends*, keeping that product of mass culture, Walter Ong might say, unexpectedly "close to the human lifeworld."[46]

Chapters 3 and 4 work less panoramically than 1 and 2 and with comparatively discrete archives—a single advertising campaign in the case of chapter 3, and a single feature in the poetry of William Carlos Williams in chapter 4. For chapter 3 I focus on the genre of advertising poetry, because it was extremely common in the modern era, because highbrow literary culture of the time frequently constructed its artistic and political agendas vis-à-vis the advertising industry and its jingles, and because advertising copy has long been the target of poets' scorn for being spiritually and, if we are to take Hart Crane at his word, even physically debilitating because of its aesthetic simplicity, commercial orientation, and utilitarian purpose. (Explaining why he resigned his job at Madison Avenue's James Walter Thompson Advertising agency in 1923, Crane wrote to his friend Charles Harris, "I got so I simply gagged everytime I sat before my desk to write an ad.") But in studying the history of advertising verse and especially the billboard poetry of Burma-Shave— rhyming, balladlike jingles that, from the 1920s to the 1960s, were sequenced line by line on billboards along American highways in order to advertise the Burma-Vita Company's signature shaving-cream product, Burma-Shave—I have found the culture of advertising verse to be more aesthetically, socially, and economically complex than traditional accounts or Crane-like gut reactions would lead us to believe.

When we study the Burma-Shave poems—and, by extension, the larger genre of advertising poetry—with an eye turned to the dynamics of popular culture that I highlight in chapters 1 and 2, it is possible to make at least two major claims. First, the billboard poems themselves (often composed by consumers participating in Burma-Vita's annual jingle-writing contests) cultivated and exploited the material nature of language in ways that critics would typically attribute to the work of literary writers or even the oppositional poetics of the avant-garde. This literariness, which depended partly on the thrill of a drive-through poem with hundred-foot-long line breaks and appealed to readers to coproduce the text and complicate the process of signification, made the billboard poems more, not less, popular, and suggests that current literary-critical ways of distinguishing between high and low culture (or between oppositional and commercial uses of language) during the modern era fail to capture the reality of a period in U.S. history when popular culture could drive artistic innovation, and vice versa; indeed, a Burma-Shave jingle booklet left among Gertrude Stein's papers when she died in 1946 suggests the appeal of the campaign's innovative poetics was not limited (in Stein's mind, at least) to popular audiences or to commercial verse forms, nor did modern poets uniformly believe that one or another type of language use was inherently complicit or oppositional.

Second, as a reception history of the campaign shows, consumers were not as easily or completely manipulated by the campaign as some advertising theories would have us think. In fact, the spirit of linguistic play and poetic innovation at the core of Burma-Vita's billboards—a participatory form fueled by the company's ongoing invitation for consumers to contribute to the campaign as writers and producers, not just as passive target demographics—ultimately distracted consumers' attention away from the commercial message and toward the creative forces of reading and writing poetry. Prospective customers wrote alternate rhymes, played with and riffed on the form, found the hundred-foot gaps between the signs to be invitations to make their own meanings, reveled in the pleasure of reading messages backward as well as forward, and read socially, collaboratively, and out loud, vocalizing the "silent production" of de Certeau's reader/ consumer rather than simply capitulating to the commercial messages in solitude and silence. For years Burma-Vita managed to harness or direct this enthusiasm toward product sales. However, the company's increasing double identity as a producer of a straightforward commodity and a publisher of a not-so-straightforward aesthetic experience caused something of a corporate identity crisis, and in the midst of decreasing sales in the 1950s, company personnel began blaming neither the new medium of television nor the advent of electric shavers and aerated shaving cream for its dwindling market share, but instead the poems that had been pitching their product. In calling for more "simple, direct selling copy" to replace the jingles, one member of the company's board of directors in effect acknowledged that poetry might be temporarily yoked to the needs of the market but never completely instrumentalized.[47]

As the Burma-Shave jingle book in Stein's papers suggests in miniature, modernist writers did not always respond with antipathy to popular or commercially cultivated reading practices; sometimes, as I argue in chapter 4 by using the poetry of William Carlos Williams as a case study, they found in it models, strategies, and resources for their own writing. I focus on the relationship between Williams and billboards and other types of commercial signage in part because that relationship links to the culture of highway reading I describe in chapter 3, but also because it is not uncommon for Williams to be described as a sort of poet laureate of early American automobile and road culture—"perhaps," writes Robert Pinsky, "the first poet to describe the landscape as it looks . . . from a car."[48] Indeed, as a country physician Williams spent extensive time driving through a billboard-studded signscape that, while he was writing the poems he would publish in 1923 in *Spring and All*, asked American motorists to develop a new set of speed-reading skills. The textual landscape between 1910 and 1940 was vastly different from the one we experience today, as billboards, fliers, signs, posters, banners, and other pieces of advertising had yet to be fully regulated by state and federal agencies and frequently jockeyed for position by overlapping or blocking each other, producing in the process a chaotic, sometimes difficult to read, text-heavy landscape of incomplete, combined, and juxtaposed messages.

For first-generation automobile users, moving at high speeds produced what Mary Austin called a new "automobile eye view" that "blurred" features of the landscape, commercial messages included, and while that experience frustrated some people, it inspired others.[49] People in marketing and advertising, for example, developed a new idiom of automobile, road, and petroleum-fueled words like "motel" (motor + hotel) or ESSO (a phonetic rendition of Standard Oil's initials, S.O.) that aimed to convey maximum amounts of information as efficiently as possible. And creative readers sought out and reveled in the unintentional messages created by overlapping and juxtaposed signs—messages with incidental but nonetheless legible secondary or tertiary meanings that disrupted the otherwise well-lubricated functioning of marketplace communication. Williams, I argue, not only registered these phenomena as an individual driver and reader but sought to position their juxtapositions, overlaps, and especially their short-circuits at the center of his poetry. The popular readiness to read for the friction or contradiction in commercial communications ultimately offered Williams one way to go about handling what many people have observed to be a dominant feature of his poetry—the citation and incorporation of signs and other instances of the commercial vernacular—without simply replicating the linguistic strategies of what he called "the money boys."[50] Part of what we identify as his innovative poetics, in other words, is founded on, and in part made possible by, his engagement with the popular reading practices of everyday life.

The culture of popular poetry that I track in this book would not last. It emerged and flourished in the late nineteenth and first half of the twentieth century in relation to a particular set of historical conditions, including, most crucially, the emerging and stabilizing consumer economy and the development and maturation of modern mass culture. In the fifteen or twenty years following World War II, the culture of popular poetry would undergo substantial reconfiguration, as the development of the popular music industry, the advent of television, the expansion of the college and university system buoyed by the G.I. Bill, and other forces would change not the structural dynamic but the face of American popular culture. Newspapers and magazines began dropping poems from their pages. Poetry radio shows dropped off the air. Perhaps due to the lack of poetry being printed in newspapers and magazines, poetry scrapbooking declined rapidly. The Burma-Vita Company, whose signs were regular features of the American highway for almost forty years, would go out of business, dismantling its billboards at the same time that American advertising as a whole was using less and less poetry. These changes don't mean, however, that the culture of popular poetry—or poetry in general—disappeared so much as it changed in relation to new sets of influences. It would take another book to fully describe and study these influences and the new formations that came about as a result of them, but in chapter 5 I begin thinking about that historical transition by way of the relationship between two symbolically important literary institutions of the Cold War era that remain in operation today: Hallmark Cards Inc., which became a prominent face of popular and commercially rewarded poetry in the 1960s, and the University of Iowa Writers' Workshop, which in the 1950s and 1960s became the most lauded and influential creative writing program in the country.

Led for nearly twenty-five years by poet Paul Engle, and known for employing and having trained Pulitzer Prize–winning poets, the Writers' Workshop has been celebrated and historicized as a beacon of refined, high-art writing in an era of mass culture and debased popular tastes—as exclusive and elite an institution as Hallmark Cards has been thought to be commercial and artless. In the late 1950s and early 1960s, however, Hallmark and Engle embarked on a partnership that, for a time, brought the forces of popular and elite writing in the United States into unexpected alignment. Engle helped to create a Hallmark Hall of Fame television broadcast. He edited *Poetry for Pleasure: The Hallmark Book of Poetry*. And, at the same time that he was working with or teaching poets such as Robert Lowell, John Berryman, Robert Penn Warren, W. D. Snodgrass, Philip Levine, and Donald Justice, he was writing verse for Hallmark greeting cards. For Engle, I argue, this was not an unexpected partnership between the spheres of high and low writing but in fact a logical and desirable one. Raised in Cedar Rapids, Iowa, where, as fellow Hawkeye Ruth Suckow wrote, literary production was "snatched at by everybody,"[51] Engle's aesthetic vision was rooted in the democratic, midwestern, brow-crossing poetry world of the early twentieth century when, as Van Wienen described it, "just about anyone might consider himself or herself fit to write poetry and even called upon to write it."[52] Early in life Engle was mentored by a Cedar Rapids insurance executive who wrote poetry. He himself wrote poetry for newspapers, special occasions, and mass-market periodicals as well as literary magazines. He envisioned poetry finding readers in a wide variety of ways—Hallmark cards included—and were it not for the forces of the period's cultural hierarchies that stood in opposition to this sort of engagement with everyday readers, he might well have developed an Iowa Writers' Workshop that trained poets to write with popular culture as well as with the Pulitzer Prize in mind.

While we might be inclined to explain Engle's involvement with Hallmark as a strictly promotional or financial arrangement benefitting the Workshop or himself, the greeting card and periodical verse he wrote invites us, I think, to take it more seriously. As with most of the material I discuss in this book, it is more aesthetically complex than it first appears. It is marked by the complexities of its relationship to American capitalism; it works in fascinating ways with the media of its distribution and in relation to a range of readers; and it is produced by a mutually informative relationship between high art and low art that renders that dichotomy unsatisfying. In extending attention to three of Engle's poems—two from greeting cards and one from *Ladies' Home Journal* that I found pasted inside Joyce Fitzgerald's scrapbook, whose album I examine in chapter 1—I argue that in Engle's view, the trained poet's skill and facility with language was measurable not just in terms of how he or she wrote for people involved with creative writing programs and prize committees but also by how he or she reached the "farmer boys, dentists, telegraph editors in small towns, students, undertakers, insurance agents and nobodies" that Suckow discussed.[53] These were, after all, the people who propelled the culture of popular poetry in modern America—a culture of everyday reading and writing that, as I hope this book begins to show, was a dynamic and complex phenomenon with far-reaching effects that we have only begun to understand.

CHAPTER 1

Saving Poetry

In the late 1920s and early 1930s, just as Laurence C. Hodgson was completing his fourth term as mayor of St. Paul, Minnesota, and preparing to return to life as journalist-poet "Larry Ho," Doris Ashley of Freetown and New Bedford, Massachusetts, began putting together a 230-page poetry scrapbook. The collection took shape inside a former day planner or journal for 1928—a "year book" initially distributed for promotional purposes by the United States Fidelity and Guaranty Company of Orlando, Florida. Only the pages for May 1 though the end of the year remain, however, as Doris (or "Dottie" as she was known to her family) removed the pages for January through April, very likely to accommodate the extra thickness she would add when she began pasting poems directly on top of the handwritten record she had sporadically kept in 1928.

The combination of extant handwriting and scrapbooked items is an intimate, even charming, literary self-portrait of Dottie, who was in her early twenties at the time, unmarried, and the youngest of five children. Her father, Frank H. Ashley, surviving relatives have told me, was a sawyer who moved his family from one mill town to the next as his work required, though they never strayed far from the Freetown and New Bedford area in Bristol County, forty miles south of Boston. Dottie was particularly close with her sister,

Naomi (Ashley) Keaton, who was known as a musician; she stayed in touch with Asenath Ashley, a cousin who received an art-school scholarship; and she was perhaps an aspiring author herself—that is, if a typed rejection letter from *Liberty: A Weekly for Everybody* included in the scrapbook is any indication (see figure 1.1). She traveled to Florida with Naomi and wrote about tooling around town in a "machine" with a number of (mainly) male friends and relatives, as well as visiting the Olympia Theater for entertainment, attending a class reunion, and hosting a tea party at her home. She appears to have been somewhat comfortable in society but not quite a part of it. "I've been in society before," she says of the class reunion, for example, "but whoever heard of anyone eating a sandwich with a knife and fork?" Dottie's world was not so small, however, that she did not take a good deal of interest in the sociopolitical landscape around her. She records on Tuesday, November 6, that Herbert Hoover "was elected and by a large majority. Carried 40 states in the Union. Poor Old Al Smith." And on Sunday, November 11, she takes time to ruminate about the history she has been living through: "Just ten years ago today the Armistice was signed," she writes. "I was just a little girl—12 years old. Wonder what we shall consider it in twenty-five years?"

The nearly three hundred poems that Dottie pasted in her journal create a striking cross-section of American poetry from the 1920s and 1930s that demonstrates, in part, the ease and willingness with which many of the age's readers read across what we often imagine to have been fairly rigid aesthetic brow lines separating the popular from the high, the genteel from the new, and the sentimental from the modern. In her collection work by Emily Dickinson and Edgar Allan Poe is mixed with modernist writing by Ezra Pound, Stephen Crane, H. D., Edna St. Vincent Millay, Carl Sandburg, and Vachel Lindsay, which in turn appears alongside popular verse by Edwin Markham, Edgar Guest, and a host of other, either largely forgotten or critically dismissed, authors who wrote poems with titles like "Loneliness," "My Love for You," and "What Are the Waves Saying?" Some of the poems in the scrapbook—and some of the articles about, or pictures of, American arts and letters that Ashley included along the way—are dated before 1928, which suggests that she had been gathering and saving material for several years before the collection took its final form, and while most of the poems and articles appear to have been clipped from newspapers and periodicals, there are also typewritten copies and even carbon copies, indicating the variety of ways in which poetry changed hands outside of more circumscribed or institution-

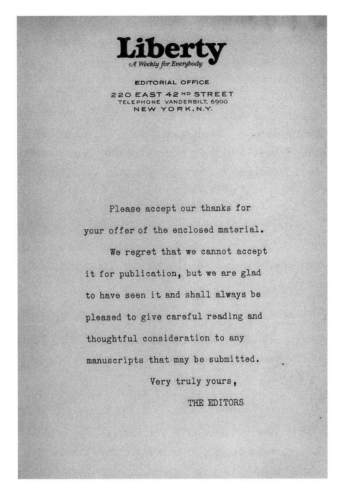

FIGURE 1.1. Rejection letter from *Liberty: A Weekly for Everybody* in Doris Ashley's scrapbook, circa 1930. Author's collection.

ally sanctioned newspaper, periodical, and educational contexts. Most of the poems by modernist writers, for example, have been typed by hand—some in blue ink, some in black, most likely copied (by Dottie? Naomi? Asenath?) from Louis Untermeyer's third revised (1925) edition of *Modern American Poetry: A Critical Anthology*—which offers provocative evidence that not only did popular poetry circulate by scrapbook and among ordinary readers but modernist poetry did so as well, as aspiring middlebrow readers moving comfortably between "high" and "low" materials augmented the literati's network of little magazines and anthologies (and, increasingly, college and university classrooms) in playing a larger role in disbursing—even popularizing—modernist poetry than one might be inclined to think.

In this regard the appearance of H. D.'s "Oread" and Pound's "In a Station of the Metro" on facing pages two-thirds of the way through Ashley's album is a particularly compelling moment (see figure 1.2). Here—even though her source book, Untermeyer's *Modern American Poetry*, does not print them together—Ashley links two poems that are frequently joined in academic or literary accounts of modern poetry as examples of the "harder and saner" imagist verse that Pound hoped would serve as a corrective to the "poppy-cock" and "emotional slither" of what he perceived to be outdated poetic modes.[1] But while Ashley may have recognized the shared method or avant-garde origin of "Oread" and "In a Station of the Metro," she doesn't let her composition be structured entirely by those aspects, as she juxtaposes the poems with a gossipy report on H. L. Mencken's marriage as well as sentimental verses by Frank L. Stanton ("A Rain Song") and Anne Campbell ("And So Are You") that exhibit many of the flaws that Pound hoped the new poetries would offset. Despite the distinctions that Pound and others wanted to make between modernist writing and poetry that "Aunt Hepsy liked," however, Ashley's scrapbook, like other such collections, suggests how modernist, elite, or art writing might have in fact gained a measure of cultural traction by virtue of its proximity to, not distance from, the very tastes it was seeking to correct.[2] The result of this juxtaposition, at least in Ashley's hands, is an object that appears to us as both "cute" and "interesting"—an unexpected overlap of two aesthetic categories that Sianne Ngai has argued are foundational to the consumer marketplace and popular culture.[3]

There are many things worth knowing that we don't know about Ashley and that surviving family members were unable to tell me. She married Raymond Lang, a mechanic, in 1937. They didn't have children. And Dottie never—so far as relatives can recall—evinced any interest in poetry, although the collection was among her belongings when she died in 1975. What motivated her to start keeping a poetry scrapbook in her twenties (a time in her life for which her family can't account)? What did she do with the scrapbook after she compiled it? Where did she get her poems, how closely did she read them, and—a question that particularly intrigues me about this volume—how and why did she go about organizing the poems as she did? In one of the more prominent studies of handwritten commonplace books that people kept

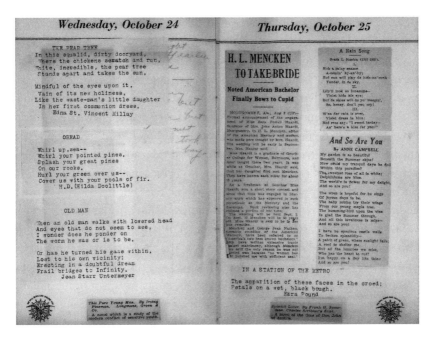

FIGURE 1.2. Page spread from Doris Ashley's scrapbook featuring "The Pear Tree" (Edna St. Vincent Millay), "Oread" (H. D.), "Old Man" (Jean Starr Untermeyer), "A Rain Song" (Frank L. Stanton), "And So Are You" (Anne Campbell), "In a Station of the Metro" (Ezra Pound), and a newspaper article reporting on H. L. Mencken's marriage to Sara Powell Haardt, circa 1930. Author's collection.

during the early modern period, Ann Moss argues that "the commonplace-book is a totally archaic object, surviving in the cultural memory, if it survives at all, in the last of several metamorphoses, as an album of favorite lines of poetry put together haphazardly for purely private perusal and meditation."[4] Is it fair to say that Ashley put together her scrapbook haphazardly? Or is it possible that she joined the poems more deliberately? In the page spread pictured in figure 1.2, for example, is it plausible that she combined verses not on the basis of their stylistic characteristics (as scholars, poets, and little magazines might suggest we combine them) but according to a chain of associations provoked by thematic and discursive relationships between the verses—a chain that at once moves imagistically from poem to poem (from Millay's "Pear Tree" to H. D.'s "great pines," Pound's "wet, black bough," Campbell's "maple tree," and the rain of Stanton's poem that waters them all) and thematically via the related ideas of youth, love, and marriage that the verses evoke individually and in concert with one another?

If such linkages are plausible—and I think the arboreal conceit in figure 1.2 makes it clear that they are—then how possible is it that Ashley built on or deepened those linkages in other ways as well? For instance, is it also possible that she combined "In a Station of the Metro" and the newspaper article "H. L. Mencken to Take Bride" on the same page because of the homonymic rhyme she heard between "bough" in Pound's poem and "bow" in the newspaper article's subtitle ("Noted American Bachelor Finally Bows to Cupid")? Such an association would not only develop a relationship between nature and marriage on a linguistic as well as figurative level—many poetry critics would praise Ashley for reading "at the level of language" if so—but might also encourage us to consider the poetics of scrapbooking and the activities of ordinary readers more carefully than Moss suggests. For Ashley, I would argue, this was not a haphazard project at all; rather, this part of the album, at least, has become a sort of extended composite poem or textual mash up of which she is both critical reader and producer or author. For scholars reading it today, it not only has implications for how we think about issues of intentionality, authorship, and the ways that poems assumed meaning as they were produced, distributed, circulated, and consumed in modern America, but it also raises questions about how we imagine the relationship between popular and modernist poetics. How, for example, might the collage and quoting techniques of modernist poetry be rooted in popular scrapbooking or album-keeping practices? Might we imagine Ashley's juxtapositions as a vernacular form of Pound's imagism, where the white space on the album's page functions in much the way as the semicolon in "In a Station of the Metro"? And if Pound is being indexed among popular poets and poems we might call cute, to what extent does that make Pound's poetry popular or cute as well?

As the albums kept by Larry Ho's fans in Minneapolis and St. Paul suggest, Ashley wasn't the only one keeping a poetry scrapbook. Far from it. Between the U.S. Civil War and World War II, Americans—men and women, children and adults, students and independent learners, African Americans, native-born white Americans, and immigrants who collected and mixed English and non-English materials—were avid scrapbookers, often devoting entire albums to poems and song lyrics culled from newspapers, commercial magazines, advertisements, greeting cards, calling cards, church bulletins, carrier's addresses, and other sources. Over the past decade I have studied an archive of over

150 such collections, which represents a culture of extremely engaged poetry reading and do-it-yourself anthology making that, however much a part of everyday life it once was, is virtually unknown to most poets, literary critics, and historians today.[5] Some of these albums are similar to Ashley's collection, and some are very different, but howsoever they may resemble each other—in form, content, compositional method, and in relation to various sets of historical and cultural impulses that I will elaborate on later in this chapter—they are each unique, even idiosyncratic, compositions in spite of the fact that most of their raw materials were mass produced for national distribution by the emerging U.S. culture industries. As such, even though these anthologies represent, in aggregate, an untold and unexamined history of poetry reading as well as a transformation of commonplace book practices in the era of mass culture, there is no single album that can, at the beginning of this chapter, stand in for the full range of critical and aesthetic faculties that ordinary readers brought to their projects or the various ways in which such collections might contribute to, or help to reboot, conventional literary-critical narratives about who consumed what poetry and how in modern America, to say nothing of the central role that poetry played in the development of popular culture more broadly.

Ashley's album offers provocative evidence of how one person actually read and processed the poetry of her time. At the moment, though, I do not want to privilege her scrapbook, or any other, as either the most sophisticated, valuable, or exemplary document in a vernacular method of poetry reading that helped to make cut-and-paste literacy practices foundational for later media formats and acts of literary appropriation. Because of the variety of collections in this archive, and because I want to suggest over the course of this chapter some of the possible ways that further collection and study of such poetry albums (and, by extension, a study of popular verse phenomena more generally) can reshape how we think about the cultural provenance and impact of poetry in U.S. history, I want to introduce another anthology before moving on to a broader consideration of the practice. It may be tempting for current scholars to presume poetry scrapbooking to have been uniformly one thing or another. (An early reader of this book, for example, judged the poetry in albums like Ashley's to be "mainly an extension of 'schoolroom poetry'" even though, as my discussion indicates, that is not always or even predominantly the case.) Thus, in presenting a comparatively modest, thirty-four-page collection assembled in 1921, I do not intend for it to complete a picture of scrapbooking in American life but, instead, for it to provide another example of the many ways that such homemade anthologies functioned in the lives of ordinary readers.

Ten years before Ashley converted her "year book" in Freetown or New Bedford, Massachusetts, Myrtle Eckert of Skykomish, Washington, collected forty-four clippings, mostly poems, inside of a commercially produced five-by-seven-inch "Snapshots" photo album, which she then gave to her son Fred for Christmas. (A small Christmas gift tag on the inside cover reads "A Merry Christmas / To Fred / From Mother / 1921.") Myrtle's surviving relatives tell me that she was born in Wisconsin in the early 1870s, making her part of a generation that included Edgar Lee Masters, Paul Laurence Dunbar, Gertrude Stein, Robert Frost, Amy Lowell, Carl Sandburg, Wallace Stevens, and Vachel Lindsay. Myrtle moved West, to Idaho, by covered wagon with her first husband, Fred Farnham. When Farnham died—he was accidentally poisoned to death a few years into their marriage when a doctor mistakenly gave him iodine instead of cough syrup—Myrtle married George Eckert and had two sons, including Fred. By 1921 she was working in Skykomish as a maid and housekeeper, and George was a night watchman for the railroad. Fred would soon get married, and he and his brother, Vern, worked in the timber industry, very likely at the local shingle mill where Vern ran the donkey at the millpond. Neither Myrtle nor George had finished high school; George, in fact, could write only his name.

According to Fred's nephew Roy, now in his seventies and a retired journalist living in Oregon, "there was a great emphasis put on published and written things" in the family, and so when Myrtle wanted to give something of importance to Fred—in advance of his marriage, to both tie him to the family and instruct him in the making of one—she made him this album, using a homemade paste of flour and water to glue the clippings in place. Most of the poems are inspirational verses that aim to impart, largely via truism or proverb, life lessons about the value of persistence, work, thrift, honesty, and cultivating and maintaining an appreciation for, and close relationship with, mothers (presumably referring, in this context, to both Fred's mother, Myrtle, and the mother that Fred's fiancée would likely become). It is not difficult, in sum, to see the album as a homemade conduct manual for a young man going out into the world to start a family of his own. Myrtle—or perhaps Fred—had a particular fondness for the poetry of Berton Braley, author of about a third of the album's poems. Like Myrtle, Braley was born in Wisconsin and had also gone west, in 1905, to write for newspapers in

Montana. By 1921, however, he was living in New York City and working as a news correspondent, a freelance writer, and here and there in the publishing industry. As part of his freelance business he sold clever, entertaining, and uplifting verses as copy for postcards, envelopes, calendars, ink blotters, posters, lithographs, advertising campaigns, magazines, and newspapers—poetry like the following excerpt from "Residence Immaterial":

Love in a tenement, love in a hut,
    Love in a palace or cave,
It isn't the kind of a figure you cut,
    And it isn't the money you save;
Love that is real will surely endure
    Wherever, however it dwells;
It isn't the fact that you're wealthy or poor,
    But the fact of your LOVE that tells!

As popular as such poetry was, there is little like it in Doris Ashley's album. It is not schoolroom poetry. Nor is it sentimental poetry. Nor is it modern poetry traditionally conceived, even though the sets of market relations in which it was embedded certainly make it part of a modern literary economy. Whatever we want to characterize it as—and I think inspirational or greeting card poetry is not a bad start (American Greetings was founded in 1906, Hallmark in 1910)—this is the type of verse that comprises the bulk of Myrtle's collection.

What intrigues me most about this scrapbook is a Braley poem that does not appear to fit easily with the others—a topical, political poem titled "Cleared" that responds to the 1914 court decision that absolved factory ownership of responsibility for the famous 1911 Triangle Shirtwaist Factory fire that killed 146 workers, mostly women, in New York City. Myrtle pasted "Cleared" near the middle of her album as part of a page spread that also includes Braley's "The Spendthrift," a list of "Cupid Commandments by Star Readers," and "My Mother," a well-traveled verse by May Riley Smith that dates to at least 1874 (see figure 1.3). Focusing on a single current event, rather than on an abstract or dehistoricized concept like love in "Residence Immaterial," Braley nonetheless motivates a similar set of democratically available proverbs, truisms, or clichés to turn unoriginal (some might say predictable) language into a memorial and condemnation. Indeed, it is precisely this

unoriginal language, part of a shared working-class vernacular, that allows
Braley to articulate outrage not in an original or individual voice and style
but in a collective one:

> Cleared! By the word of judge and jury,
>   Beating in vain at the bolted door,
> And the long-drawn wail of the mothers crying,
>   Shall haunt their memory evermore.
> The prison bonds may never bind them,
>   They walk, free men, in the open air,
> But wherever they go their past shall find them,
>   And haunt them and mock them everywhere.
>
> "Cleared." By the word of judge and jury,
>   Freed as guiltless, without a flaw,
> But they still must face—not hate and fury—
>   But the vengeance calm of a higher law.
> They shall go their ways in fear and trembling.
>   They shall toss by night, they shall start by day.
> For they face a court where there's no dissembling.
>   And for all their deeds they must surely pay.

The inclusion of "Cleared" in Myrtle's scrapbook—probably seven years after
the verse first appeared in print—is not only a good example of how a poem
acquires new significance when cut out, saved, and repurposed by ordinary
readers, but it also makes political and historical an album that does not ini-
tially appear to be political or historical in nature.

No doubt some of the poem's appeal had to do with the moral lesson
that the court's verdict gives Braley an occasion to express: that justice is not
contained and distributed by institutions alone but is a good that ordinary
people have a part in administering as well. In the working-class world of
Skykomish (no stranger, probably, to Wobbly organization), this sense of
justice, as well as the competing interests of ownership and labor at the cen-
ter of the 1914 court case, would have also signified more specifically, as the
Triangle Shirtwaist Fire and subsequent legal fight became a rallying point
for laborers and labor movements nationwide. It is the poem's third line
("the long-drawn wail of the mothers crying") that I think signifies especially

CUPID COMMANDMENTS BY STAR READERS

"Thou shalt not bear false witness against thy rival. He may be a coming 'white hope.'"—G. T.

"Honor thy sweetheart, so that thy days may be long in the home she will make for thee."—M. J.

"Thou shalt not covet the position of her poodle dog—but endeavor to deserve it."—P. C. H.

"Remember the tryst, to keep it holy."—M. J.

"Thou shalt not steal a kiss, when you can have all you want for the asking."—L. R.

"Thou shalt not endanger the life of any girl, or thy own, while she is riding behind thee on a motorcycle. Wait until thou dismount-eth."—W. O. S.

"Thou shalt not tell her of thy undying love and then chase around with some gay affinity."—W. W.

"Thou shalt not talk about the high cost of living to thy beloved, and then tell her the salary thou receivest."—Mrs. G. H. K.

"Thou shalt not throw kisses at a girl, lest thou shouldst not hit the one at whom thou hast aimed."—G. G. G.

"Thou shalt not spend all thy money upon a girl before thou marryest her. She wants something afterward."—L. M. A.

"Thou shalt not say unto thy sweetheart, 'I am not worthy of thee,' lest she believe thee and choose another."—W. G. C.

"Thou shalt not go begging, but thou shalt do like the Romans of old—Come, see and take."—Mrs. M. C. D.

"Thou shalt partake of no high-scented sweetmeats before thou makest thy call, lest she say, 'Lo, I have snared me a wine-bibber.'"—W. D.

"Thou shalt praise no other woman before her. Nay, not even her own side-kick, lest she say in her heart, 'He is a fool, for what can any man see in her?'"—W. D.

The Spendthrift

BY BERTON BRALEY

I'd rather take my pleasure while I'm young and have a chance
Than wait until I'm older, when I cannot lightly dance;
I know that life is smiling in these days of careless youth,
But I don't know what'll happen when I'm bent and gray, in sooth.
I may sorrow for my folly when my folly's fully done,
But at least I shall remember that I had a heap of fun.

I've toiled for all I squander, I have robbed no man on earth,
I have harmed no living creature in my laughter and my mirth.
If I scatter by the wayside all my store of hard-won pelf,
There is no one any poorer save that prodigal, Myself;
Time may come I'll wish for money that so carelessly was spent—
But what profits my repentance till the time comes to repent?

I am fain for love and laughter, I am avid after joy,
There is something pagan in me which no lessons can destroy,
And although the sages warn me of a rainy day afar,
I can only think of sunshine where the pleasant meadows are;
And if skies shall cloud and darken and a rainy day befall,
I will seek a drier climate where it never rains at all!

Cleared
by Berton Braley

(Harris and Blanck, in whose New York shirt waist factory 140 girls were burned to death last spring, have been acquitted of the charge of manslaughter growing out of the fire.—News Item.)

"Cleared!" By the word of judge and jury,
Beating in vain at the bolted door,
And the long-drawn wail of the mothers crying,
Shall haunt their memory evermore.
The prison bonds may never bind them,
They walk, free men, in the open air,
But wherever they go their past shall find them,
And haunt them and mock them everywhere.

"Cleared!" By the word of judge and jury,
Freed as guiltless, without a flaw,
But they still must face—not hate and fury—
But the vengeance calm of a higher law.
They shall go their ways in fear and trembling,
They shall toss by night, they shall start by day,
For they face a court where there's no dissembling,
And for all their deeds they must surely pay.

"Cleared!"—But for all that they made to suffer
They, too, must suffer, and suffer long;
For there's never a path more harsh or rougher
Than that of the mortal who does a wrong.
Though the prison walls do not enfold them
And they joy in their "freedom," duly won,
They shall find that the laws of fate still hold them
And shall serve their time until life is done!

MY MOTHER.

The sweetest face in all the world to me,
Set in a frame of shining silver hair,
With eyes whose language is fidelity:
This is my mother. Is she not most fair?

'Tis counted something great to be a queen,
And bend a kingdom to a woman's will,
To be a mother such as mine, I ween,
Is something better and more noble still.
—Selected.

FIGURE 1.3. Page spread from Myrtle Eckert's scrapbook that includes Berton Braley's poem "Cleared," circa 1921. Author's collection.

strongly in the context of Myrtle's scrapbook, however, as that line privileges motherhood as a primary site of objection to the court decision and thus ties the event directly to the album's pervading concern with the importance of motherhood. Myrtle's interest in the subject is not unusual for the time, as the United States was saturated with poetry about mothers that contributed to a cultural hagiography of motherhood more generally. Pillows featuring poems in praise of mothers were common souvenir and gift items. Framed odes to mothers were sold and hung in houses nationwide. Mother's Day was made official in 1914. And the values and activities that mothers purportedly exemplified—peace, compassion, religious virtue, social work, education, and a moral compass like the one suggested in "Cleared"—were impulses behind many Progressive-era movements, including the fight for women's suffrage, which was achieved with the passage of the nineteenth amendment one year before Myrtle made this album for Fred.

I am confident that Myrtle included "Cleared" because of how the mothers' inarticulate but nonetheless unambiguous wailing in line three—what V. N. Volosinov might have described as "the pure response to pain in the organism" that is made socially relevant by Braley—contributes to the album's composite argument about the importance of motherhood.[6] The contrast between this expression of motherhood and Smith's poem "My Mother" pasted immediately below it in the album cannot be much greater:

> The sweetest face in all the world to me,
>   Set in a frame of shining silver hair,
> With eyes whose language is fidelity:
>   This is my mother. Is she not most fair?

Compared to the portrait of a mother in Smith's lines—where the implied picture frame domesticates her, the silver hair ages her, and the language of fidelity she speaks through her eyes more or less mutes her—the mothers in "Cleared" respond to, interact with, and affect the public sphere by way of an action or sound that cannot, in fact, be framed, aged, or domesticated. The distress of Braley's wailing mothers (who wail for the loss of real children rather than for the "demon-lover" of Samuel Taylor Coleridge's "Kubla Khan") thus becomes an especially charged relay point between Myrtle and Fred where the subject of industrial labor is concerned. Myrtle is not just giving Fred idealized or essentialized motherly advice about morality, religion, and temperance but—tied to the Shirtwaist Fire by virtue of her gender and to Fred by her blood—is finding another language of fidelity in which to warn her son about labor relations between capitalists and workers, the consequences of assembly line production, and what happens, perhaps, when folkways get left behind. What is especially moving to me is not just the sound of Myrtle wailing, via Braley's poem, for a fate her son may meet, but how that audible but inarticulate critique of industrial labor finds material form as well. Myrtle doesn't just give Fred a book instructing him how to be a good man, son, or husband but also gives him a physical *example* of an economy counter to the economic logic of enterprises such as the Shirtwaist Factory's: a handmade, hand-delivered, one-of-a-kind repurposed photo album full of poems hand picked especially for him and then glued down with homemade paste. The scrapbook ties Fred to the family and folkways thematically but also materially; the paste doesn't just cement Myrtle's words into place (they are hers, even though they were written, distributed, and even paid for by someone else) but aims to metonymically secure Fred—as reader, son, worker, husband, potential father—into place as well.

Assembled by white working-class women with familial ties to the timber industry shortly after the passage of the nineteenth amendment, the poetry scrapbooks by Ashley and Eckert resemble each other in understandable ways, as many homemade albums were put together and maintained by women who were charged with managing family reading material, conducting children's education at home and at school, and sustaining book or other cultural awareness groups in their local communities. That said, I start this chapter with these two examples not only because I hope they will introduce and partially represent what was a widespread method of American poetry reading and book making between the late Progressive era and World War II, but also because of their important differences. The content of the respective collections, the private or social uses they appear to have served, and even the nature of their physical construction suggest that despite their initial similarities the scrapbooks are perhaps just as significant for how they differ from each other. To do justice to their makers, and to the various and complicated life experiences and verse cultures informing the albums they created, we should not lose sight of these differences by attempting to cast their work as essentially one type of literary activity or another.

I feel certain, however—based on the materials I have studied, on records and accounts of the historical practice, and on a long tradition of commonplace book and verse miscellany making that helped provide a foundation for American poetry scrapbooking—that we should not assume any of the albums to have been haphazardly assembled by ordinary readers. One only has to look, for example, at a thousand-page poetry scrapbook apparently kept, compiled, and indexed by a turn-of-the-century convent to see just how unhaphazard and systematic the practice could be (see figure 1.4). Organized by use value and intended as a reference book for poems to be recirculated in "Cards and Calendars," the collection, left unfinished, was a collaboration assembled over time from printed clippings, prayer cards, and verses handwritten in numerous scripts. As this album additionally suggests, neither should we presume that such objects were assembled for "purely private perusal and meditation"—a presumption that wrongly applies John Stuart Mill's famous description of poetry writing ("feeling confessing itself to itself, in moments of solitude") to poetry reading.[7] Rather, in many cases these items appear to have served as engines for deliberate, often sustained, and even social or public ways of thinking, reading, and communicating. Seen the way I suggest, a scrapbook served as a sort of print-based "thinkertoy"—the term that early computer theorist Ted Nelson coined to describe the computer-based "system that helps you envision complex alternatives" to linear and institutionally privileged cognitive processes.[8] In the independent and associative ways of reading, thinking, and "teacherless learning"[9] they represent and preserve, poetry scrapbooks are a striking record of popular activity—if not popular intelligence—from an emerging mass-cultural age when "it is said," Ezra Pound wrote in *How to Read*, "nothing is ever consciously related to anything else."[10]

United as a genre by a collagist's or bricoleur's compositional method that regularly repurposed the poetic content of mass culture by cutting and pasting it into new or different configurations, such amateur poetry collections are certainly part of what Chris Baldick has called "a great age of anthologies."[11] They range in size from just a few poems to thousands of poems. Some are devoted exclusively to poetry while others mix poems with newspaper articles, pictures, flowers, comic strips, and other items. They were assembled by individuals working alone and in groups, including school classrooms, and they were sometimes continued from one generation to the next. As the album by Ashley indicates, some readers commandeered previously existing book structures and converted them into scrapbooks (a practice that was especially common before World War I), while others purchased blank books of varying design concepts marketed specifically for scrapbooking. While some albums resemble what we think of when we imagine scrap-

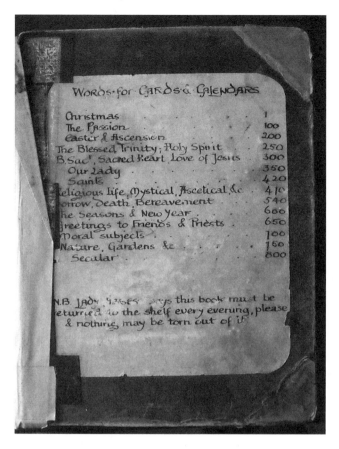

FIGURE 1.4. Cover and table of contents for a thousand-page scrapbook assembled at a turn-of-the-century convent. Author's collection.

booking today—collections of photos, report cards, prizes, vacation and school souvenirs, and/or other items of identifiably biographical significance that comprise a sort of idealized life narrative—they more frequently begin with material of a public nature, collating, organizing, sampling, arranging, juxtaposing, counterpointing, adding to, sorting through, saving, or otherwise making individual sense of an expanding print (and poetry) culture. They are no doubt a function of many cultural variables and impulses, including, but hardly limited to, soaring literacy rates, the wide dissemination of affordable print material and innovative and attractive advertising formats, national values of thrift and resourcefulness, the birth of the middlebrow class and its members' desire for cultural legitimacy, and a growing interest in home libraries fueled in part by the 1,689 new "Carnegie" public libraries constructed in the United States between 1883 and 1929.

Taken individually, and as documents representing a widespread cultural practice, these items promise to illuminate many aspects of America's literary cultures, though it is impossible and impractical for me to describe and pursue, much less try to exhaust, all of those aspects or every type of poetry collection here.[12] For the more narrow purposes of this book, then, I want to use such albums to follow and illustrate two primary arguments that I will trace over the course of this chapter and that will be ongoing concerns in later chapters. First, in their constant incorporation of, and engagement with, products of the U.S. culture industries, poetry scrapbooks offer us some of the first material documents of popular culture in the historical record. Therefore, they not only afford us a window onto the development of consumer culture's participatory, disciplinary, and ideological aspects more generally, but they also suggest that poetry—often imagined to have had only a marginal relationship to mass culture and everyday life—played a foundational role in shaping activities and exchanges that we now associate with mass media phenomena ranging from radio and television to rock and roll and Web technologies. Second, in addition to providing evidence of America's thriving poetry landscape—and entirely befitting these albums' status as popular culture artifacts that predate zines and mix tapes—poetry scrapbooks became not just a documentary form but an *expressive* genre that we can read as a vernacular companion or counterpart to the quoting, cut-up, and collage practices of modernist writing. Indeed, the fact that modernist writers were born in, kept scrapbooks in,[13] and learned to write in an America where poetry scrapbooking (and clipping in general) was common at home and at school should prompt us to reimagine the synchronicities between various types of literary production in an age of mass culture that longstanding binaries like "high" and "low" have so far worked to obscure.

I devote the rest of the chapter to these two ends, hoping along the way that my reader will follow with a certain generosity as I situate poetry scrapbooking in a longer history of such projects, as well as in turn-of-the-century U.S. contexts when scrapbooking became a way that readers could exercise and cultivate independent poetry-reading practices while at the same time being schooled in, and incorporated into, the ideology of the period's developing consumer capitalism. The resulting set of negotiations—of ideological incorporation and counterhegemonic activity—is not unique to scrapbooking, but would have implications, by way of scrapbooking in particular, for how popular audiences imagined the cultural significance of poetry from this period forward. And then, because I start this book by focusing on ordinary or uncredentialed readers whose critical capacities and tastes (for "poppy-cock" and "emotional slither") were regularly deemed in need of correction by literary elites, so I conclude this chapter with an extended reading of a single scrapbook. I do this in part to show how, in some people's lives, the scrapbook served as a sort of workshop space for aspiring writers looking to gain access to authorship in an age before institutionalized creative writing programs and widespread college and university admission, but also—and primarily—to demonstrate how such albums might be read as literary compositions in their own right and how they might teach us to be better readers as well.

How to Read a Poetry Scrapbook

The term "scrapbook" has a nineteenth-century origin, and while the *Oxford English Dictionary* dates it to 1825 in Britain, the practice would reach a crescendo in what Todd Gernes calls the "pervasive culture of scrapping" of late nineteenth- and early twentieth-century America.[14] "This is an age of albums," a writer for the *New York Sun* observed in 1903. "A score or more of different kinds of albums, portfolios, memory books and diaries are in current use."[15] The effects of this enthusiasm were felt in the worlds of literature, book arts, the decorative arts, and graphic design, as prose and poetry writers became increasingly interested in the poetics of the fragment, as everyday pieces of furniture were covered in lacquered scraps, and as scraps were even used to create wallpaper designs. In describing a sharecropper's "fireplace wall . . . crusted deep with attractive pieces of paper" in *Let Us Now Praise Famous Men*, James Agee suggests the combination of utilitarian and aesthetic values in scrap work that many Americans living in a culture that prized resourcefulness would have found appealing; no doubt the practice of turning recycled materials into art is also foundational for the patchwork quilt.[16] There was an active market in collectible die-cuts and lithographed ephemera. Boys and girls were encouraged to become young members of the emerging business and professional class by selling "scraps and gleanings" door to door.[17] And inventors ranging from Samuel Clemens (who developed and patented *Mark Twain's Adhesive Scrap Book*) to Emma Goldman's lover Edward Brady (who was working "on a novelty in albums") sought to profit from this phenomenon as well.[18]

Cultural anthropologists Tamar Katriel and Thomas Farrell have argued that scrapbooking became an American "indigenous practice" that "even in its native habitat . . . tends to remain invisible to cultural outsiders—so much so that many non-Americans who have spent several years living in the United States are completely unfamiliar with this practice, and often with the word *scrapbook*."[19] There are nevertheless distinct, if awkwardly demarcated, historical antecedents to scrapbooking that help us understand some of the dynamics at play in the homemade poetry collections from modern (or modernizing) America. Scholars studying personally assembled collections from the Middle Ages know them as "florilegia," a term that means "flower collections" in Latin and that anticipates our current use of the Greek term for flower collections, ἀνθολογία, or the "anthology."[20] The medieval practice of handwriting and compiling passages copied from other texts—usually religious writings by the church fathers or classical philosophers—developed into many forms (the hold-all book, the verse miscellany, the portfolio, and various types of memory albums) that would persist well into the nineteenth and twentieth centuries. The most famous and frequently studied of these forms—the handwritten Renaissance-era commonplace book, which contained excerpts from one's reading organized by topical or thematic headings—became a formal and informal educational tool with rules, strictures, and sometimes intricate indexical procedures made most well known, perhaps, by John Locke's widely distributed and much-imitated 1706 treatise *A New Method of Making Commonplace Books*. The effects of such a systematized practice of reading on three centuries of educational and intellectual life in Europe and the United States have been difficult to overstate. Ann Moss, for example, argues that insofar as the commonplace book "provided the apparatus for detailed critical comparisons in which we recognize an activity we would call literary criticism," it "may be said to have invented the critical reader, in a modern sense."[21]

Scholars have approached this history in many ways, but a primary line of inquiry in recent years has focused on how these documents served as sites of hegemonic and counterhegemonic activity—that is, how their compilation and use was social in orientation and thus served to affiliate readers with dominant power structures (church fathers, governmental or social orders, etc.), and how the compositional freedom and what Susan Stabile calls the "associative logic" of their construction provided people with opportunities to resist those structures.[22] David Parker, for example, has argued that commonplace books allowed the mostly male members of early-modern England's new and growing middle class to articulate antiestablishment political views "at a time when [they] could have been persecuted" for airing those views in public.[23] Similarly, for Stabile, the hyperlocal, domestic focus of eighteenth-century American women's memory and commonplace books resulted in collections that were fundamentally "at odds with nationalist narratives that emphasize[d] shared origins, unbroken continuity, or universal memory."[24] And Arthur F. Marotti has revealed how aristocratic, often female, writers and readers composed and circulated poetry in manuscript books during the Renaissance not to challenge, but to preserve, their class standing by resisting what they felt was a threat in the form of "the commercializing and democratizing features of the print medium."[25] This social aspect of reading, writing, and collecting is a major reason leading Marotti to argue that, "in many ways, these anthologies of . . . verse are more interesting than anything comparable in print at the time."[26]

As the albums by Doris Ashley and Myrtle Eckert suggest, it is possible to understand poetry scrapbooks as an extension of the intellectual and social practices that Parker, Stabile, Marotti, and others see in commonplacing. Eckert, for example, uses the occasion of her gift album to Fred to raise a female, working-class voice against the encroachment of an industrial order she feels affecting her family and folkways. In her early twenties and unmarried, Ashley (possibly an aspiring writer) juxtaposes marriage-themed poems with a report on Mencken's late-life marriage to a published woman writer (Sara Haardt) in order to think through and even justify her own unmarried status and its relation to her literary pursuits. The fact that some aspects of the commonplace book remained present well into the "pervasive culture of scrapping"[27] further indicates we can read scrapbooking in conversation with its earlier instantiations, not just because scrapbooking needed to reference the familiarity and prestige of earlier notebook forms in order to gain conceptual and cultural purchase, but also because—during a period of transition from one method of anthology making to another—people were likely reading and collecting in multiple ways, even within single albums. Some people purchased scrapbooks with indexes printed in them, for instance, but then never used those indexes or used them incompletely. Other people added their own indexes to blank books where none were supplied. Some readers established commonplace-like thematic or subject headings to structure certain parts of their collections, then used other parts of their books as hold-all or miscellaneous sections with more open, exploratory rubrics. Still other scrap-bookers pasted clipped-out poems alongside, and even over the top of, hand-written poems and quotations, sometimes creating palimpsests that don't just layer different texts but different textual interfaces as well (see figure 1.5).

As we examine how the scrapbook slowly disentangled itself from this history and matured as a modern genre in both formal and ideological aspects, two elements of its identity become increasingly evident and suggest that we should not read such collections entirely within frameworks set up for study-ing florilegia and commonplace books. On one hand, it becomes clear—most prominently in the highly commercialized, mass-produced texts that make up most scrapbooks' content—that the U.S. culture industries, and there-fore the consumer capitalism for which they work, supplanted earlier forms of cultural authority, taking over the position that the church fathers and humanist ideals once held. That is, the culture industries became the main authoritative source of material worth reading, thinking about, saving, and sharing, and therefore every album took place, was made possible, and must be read in relation to this particular power regime. On the other hand, con-sumers exercised an unprecedented amount of liberty and agency when it came to reading and anthologizing—so much so that, from our perspective today, they not only challenged the integrity of the authoritative, mass-pro-duced text by cutting it up and repurposing it but also disfigured the very communicative organs of capitalism in the process. Propelled by what John Fiske has described as a "sense of equality with, if not superiority to, the pro-ducers of the industrial text,"[28] people—like Louisa May Alcott, who claimed that she read "with a pair of scissors in my hand"[29]—not only cut off the bylines, copyright, and bibliographic information that anchored texts within a capitalist system of ownership, but also resituated clippings into compet-ing literary economies (such as gift economies and Eckert's folk economy) in which capital was not paramount.

This relationship between the hegemony of the industrially produced text and the liberty afforded to, or taken by, the individual consumer is a structural aspect of popular culture that, as Ellen Gruber Garvey has shown, was rec-ognized by early advertisers who encouraged consumers to collect, exchange, and creatively scrapbook promotional trade cards as a way of learning and rehearsing the language of national brand names, logos, and the "celebrations of plenty" on which the emerging consumer economy depended.[30] As one of the foundational activities of popular culture, the collecting of advertise-

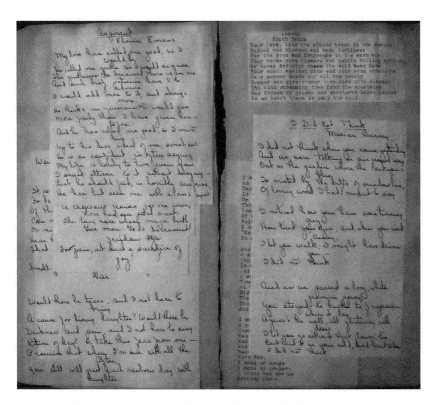

FIGURE 1.5. Depression-era scrapbook with a palimpsest of written and typewritten material. Author's collection.

ments (which were often poetry-heavy) remained part of scrapbooking well into the twentieth century, when, for example, Campbell's Soup ads were providing design elements for both an unidentified scrapbooker making her album inside of a recycled 1908 Bowdoin college yearbook (see figure 1.6) and for nineteen-year-old Anne Sexton, who in 1948–1949 included a soup can among the various objects she set in orbit around the central handwritten poem "Us" (see figure 1.7).[31]

At the same time that the marketplace encouraged such interaction, it also sought additional ways to discipline or supervise the potentially disruptive creativity that scrapbooks' open-page, no-rubric layout made possible. An industry of scrapbooking how-to guides emerged, resulting in the publication of anthologies and source books like *Clippings for Your Scrapbook: 52 Famous Writings Reproduced for Your Convenience* (1937) that

FIGURE 1.6. Scrapbook assembled inside a 1909 Bowdoin College yearbook, with Campbell's soup advertisements as design elements, circa 1930s. Author's collection.

FIGURE 1.7. Page from Anne Sexton's scrapbook featuring the handwritten poem "Us" surrounded by advertisements, including a Campbell's soup can, circa 1948. Reprinted by permission of SLL/Sterling Lord Literistics, Inc. Copyright © Anne Sexton.

identified for consumers the types of texts that were most appropriate for collection. Publishers issued—and therefore authorized—sample albums like *Elbert Hubbard's Scrap Book* (1923), *The American Scrap Book* (1928), *A Farmer's Scrap-Book* (1930), *Old Brother's Scrap Book of Poems* (n.d.), and *Bob White's Scrap Book* (1934) that effectively modeled scrapbooking best practices for readers. Newspapers printed poems boxed in under the headline "Poems for Your Scrapbook" to further differentiate between items that were proper to cut out and save and those that were not. As the innovative and extremely well-selling album invented by Samuel Clemens suggests, even "blank" books were enlisted in this effort. The adhesive industrially applied to the pages of *Mark Twain's Adhesive Scrap Book*, for example, doesn't blanket the whole page—as it does in late twentieth-century versions of this design that have pull-off plastic page covers—but was applied in three distinct newspaper-sized columns providing a template for composition that urges readers to reproduce a newspaper's layout rather than a more individualized, discontinuous, or associative one (see figure 1.8). Arguably, Clemens's celebrity endorsed attempt to standardize Americans' reading practices in relation to the privileged mass media of his day combines with the album's investment in mass production, technological innovation, and nationwide distribution to mark the emergence of a specifically modern disciplinary form.

In the economy of this literary activity, poetry occupied a doubly prominent and even privileged place. Short and thus eminently clippable, and available on all sorts of printed matter, poetry was also culturally prestigious (both in terms of the "gem" status that nineteenth-century anthologies had conferred on it, and in comparison to popular fiction and newspaper articles) and was thus not just a general part of scrapbooking but, in some people's minds, the height of it. *Elbert Hubbard's Scrap Book,* for example, begins with a publisher's foreword referencing both John Keats and the "scented rose gardens of Poetry" that Hubbard was said to frequent for his reading material—language that not only literalizes the notion of the anthology (i.e., a flower collection) by way of the rose garden, but that also situates poetry as a natural thing for people to save. True to form, the publishers printed a poem in the middle of nearly every following page, creating a layout that Sexton may have imitated twenty-five years later and that certainly privileges poetry as both physically and conceptually central to scrapbooking (see figure 1.9).[32] In "The Scrap Book as Educator," a brochure issued by the After School Club of

FIGURE 1.8.
Pages from *Mark Twain's Adhesive Scrap Book* showing columns of adhesive and items pasted onto the columns. Author's collection.

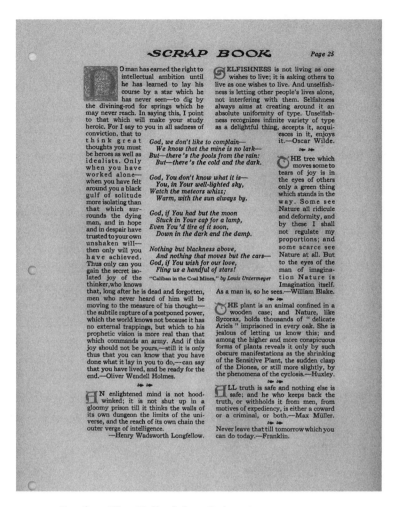

FIGURE 1.9. Page from *Elbert Hubbard's Scrap Book*, 1928.

America in the late 1920s or 1930s, Nathaniel Dawson underscores this poem-scrapbook link with his guiding example of "my little friend, Ned Hoskins," a reluctant learner who discovers the joys of reading only when he's encouraged to start keeping a scrapbook full of things he collects himself. "Gradually," Dawson writes, "there came a change over the once unstudious boy. At length, quite naturally, Ned began asking his mother for different volumes of her own favorite poets . . . The final surprise came one day, she said, when she picked up the Scrap-Book herself to read for awhile, and found her own beloved 'Ode to a Skylark' copied out in childish hand."[33]

In 1914 newspaper poet "Uncle Walt" Mason of Emporia, Kansas, explained to the *Literary Digest* what happened to the poems he and others wrote for newspapers. "A man," he said, "sees in the newspaper a clever rhyme full of hope and encouragement, and he cuts it out and shows it to his friends, and carries it in his pocket-book, and takes it home and reads it to his family, and his wife pastes it in the scrap-book for future reference."[34] In addition to the conceptual synchronicity between poetry and scrapbooking I have already highlighted, there was also, as Mason indicates, a sense that the "poem" and the "scrap"—and definitely the "poem" and the "clipping"—were more closely related, socially and generically speaking, than the scrap and other genres that came ready-made in codex formats. Fulkerson of William Dean Howells's *A Hazard of New Fortunes*, for example, has "some of [Basil] March's verse in his pocket-book, which he had cut out of a stray newspaper and carried about for years."[35] The nameless, suicidal tramp in Willa Cather's *My Antonia* is found to be carrying only a penknife, a wishbone, and "some poetry [Samuel Woodworth's "The Old Oaken Bucket"] . . . cut out of a newspaper and nearly worn out."[36] And in delivering the annual address to the Zenith Real Estate Board, George Babbitt prefaces his reading of a poem by T. Cholmondeley "Chum" Frink (Sinclair Lewis's fictional version of writers like Mason and Edgar Guest) by stating, "I always carry this clipping of it in my note-book."[37] None of these readers and writers would have been surprised—given the time, social relationships, and personal aspirations one could invest and express in both poem clippings and scrapbooks—that people would value them accordingly. On October 14, 1935, for instance, radio listener Miriam Garrison, whom I will return to in the next chapter, wrote a fan letter to the on-air poetry show *Between the Bookends* in which she explained, "My poem notebook is my hobby and my most treasured literary possession."[38]

To be sure, people used scrapbooks for poetry-related purposes other than, or in addition to, the expressive and artistic purposes in which this chapter is most interested. The first poetry scrapbooks in the historical record, for example, were assembled by seventeenth-century British ballad collectors who sought to preserve popular, ephemeral broadsides from London's alehouse and street cultures by pasting them into specially made blank books; some of the ballads they collected, in what was then a leisure-time activity among upper-class men who wouldn't have had the word scrapbooking to describe their activity, are the only copies of those poems known to have survived.[39] In a sense, then, the birth of the scrapbook form and the preservation of popular verse go hand in hand. While scrapbooking in postbellum America was a less elite practice than it was in seventeenth-century England, it was nevertheless fueled by a similar, though much broader, cultural impulse to save and catalog valuable but otherwise ephemeral texts that could quickly disappear in the period's seas of print. Commercial clipping bureaus were formed, new filing rubrics like Dewey's decimal system were invented, and the turn of the century saw the publication of standard library reference books like *Granger's Index to Poetry* (1904) to help readers better navigate a booming print culture.[40] As the thirty thousand entries in *Granger's* first edition suggest, recording and tracking verse was especially motivational since poetry, more than other genres, was ubiquitous and in demand yet always on the verge of disappearing or being lost.[41] Finding the *Index* only partly helpful—*Granger's* catalogued poems printed solely in books and anthologies—the Public Library of Cincinnati and Hamilton County in southwest Ohio started an additional, in-house card catalog dedicated to preserving poems from local newspapers and other similarly ephemeral print media. By World War II what came to be called the library's "Auxiliary Poetry File" would grow to include more than sixty thousand index cards tracking verse that librarians were worried would otherwise disappear; about 40 percent of the time, library workers actually cut out poems from their source publications and pasted them on back of the appropriate index cards for easiest reference, creating in the process a card catalog that is part scrapbook, part filing system, and part poetry preserve.

While scrapbooks were certainly produced at what John Fiske calls "the interface between the products of the culture industries and everyday life,"[42] I would caution against thinking of their makers as "poachers," a now-famous metaphor that Michel de Certeau uses in *The Practice of Everyday Life* to describe consumers who "move across lands belonging to someone else, like nomads poaching their way across fields they did not write, despoiling the wealth of Egypt to enjoy it themselves."[43] Far from feeling like trespassers, many American readers believed that they in fact had a perfect right to the poems they were collecting—that no one owned them (copyright holders included), and that they comprised, instead, a cultural commons that users had a right to access and use however they saw fit. This belief has roots in at least two entangled discourses and practices of nineteenth- and early twentieth-century America, one of which has to do with how Americans imagined and contested the notion of copyright, and the other of which stemmed directly from the public's perception of poetry and the values it represented (at least in the abstract if not in daily practice). As Meredith L. McGill argues, many people in antebellum America felt that the right to reprint and recirculate written material was a central expression of American democracy—one of the "characteristic features of a social structure that many thought could fend off the stultifying effects of British publishing monopolies."[44] No one group of people—or so opponents of developing U.S. copyright laws would argue—could manage or own the social life of a text while staying true to America's republican ideals.

While this sensibility would be disciplined out of the mainstream during the rest of the century, it persisted as a sometimes ambivalent or contested but nevertheless guiding spirit in relation to poetry. A variety of factors contributed to this, not the least of which was the fact that most poetry circulated *outside* of books, and intellectual ownership stakeholders were unwilling or (more likely) unable to police a vast print world in which, for example, a majority of the nation's newspapers published and republished poems, often on a daily basis. Over time the lack of copyright enforcement in relation to poetry became convention if not permission for reuse. Reinforced by popular poetry's regular—even stereotypical—appeals to, and associations with, values and goods (such as religion, patriotism, motherhood, and nature) that the public did not want to see measured completely in terms of capital, such de facto permission helped to create a poetry-reading culture in which readers felt, as Joseph Harrington has argued, that "the poem's presentation context becomes just as important as its textual contents in determining its 'value.'"[45] To return to de Certeau, then, one might say that scrapbookers were not poaching poems, because poems were to some extent unpoachable; not only were they not owned by anyone, but in many cases they represented a separate or parallel value system in which ownership was defined differently, and thus poaching wasn't even possible.[46]

However—and here the ideological work of the poetry scrapbook becomes most evident—this doesn't mean that de Certeau's metaphor of nomadic, poaching readers "despoiling the wealth of Egypt to enjoy it themselves" is wholly irrelevant to the culture of scrapbooking. For, as the postscript at the bottom of the convent scrapbook I referred to earlier indicates—"N.B. Lady Abbess says this book must be returned to the shelf every evening, please & nothing may be torn out of it" (see figure 1.4)—it became possible to poach or steal poems and scraps once those items had been removed from the public commons, resituated into personal presentation contexts, and thus effectively privatized. Indeed, the very fact that a group of nuns needed to be warned not to tear up their communal scrapbook suggests the extent to which such poaching—a certain "cliptomania" if you will—did exist. As the examples of Fulkerson, Cather's tramp, Babbitt, and Miriam Garrison suggest, in the world of poetry scrapbooking physical clippings could attain an almost talismanic status, which Miss Emaline Knoop expressed in 1935 when she, like Garrison, sent a poem to *Between the Bookends*. "I treasure this little paper as one of my priceless possessions," Knoop explains. "You being, 'My Friend,' I gladly trust it in your care for a few days."[47] In such a world, as Helen Glass indicates in a note upbraiding the host of *Bookends* that same year, friendships could be made and unmade by the treatment such possessions were given. "I sent you in August some poems of mine taken from my Scrap Book of years standing," a furious Glass writes: "and found out later my grievous error in not sending you copies. . . . Why couldn't you have sent in the original which I sent you that I might replace it in my scrapbook? This mimeographed thing marked copy would have certainly sufficed for your collection. Every one of mine has a meaning for me. . . . You know, Mr. Malone, you didn't sound like some one who would so utterly and completely let a person down. Please give this your very personal attention—and send me back my original verses."[48]

When I suggest we can use the word poaching in the context of poetry scrapbooking, then, it is not in any way a metaphorical concept, as scrapbooks worked to essentially train people in the conversion of common property to private property, and thus clippings could be stolen, and were perceived to be stolen, through simple misunderstandings about, or outright disrespect for, the boundaries between public and private property. In fact, as Cather's use of the poetry-reading tramp might indicate, American literature from John Steinbeck to Jack Kerouac, Ralph Ellison, Nelson Algren, Sylvia Plath, Elizabeth Bishop, Paule Marshall, and Sandra Cisneros has regularly associated the individual scrap, clipping, or set of clippings with people who in some way or another fail at the project of acquiring and keeping property and thus become social or cultural others who intentionally or unintentionally move across—or get evicted from or confined to—lands belonging to someone else.[49] That is, the scrap often becomes literary shorthand for figuring capitalism's dispossessed: the physically, geographically, institutionally, or literarily homeless person who doesn't have a blank book but only a pocket in which to store and maintain the literary capital of modern life. This association was perpetuated in the popular press as well. Consider the following clipping—pasted in a cluster of items, which together articulate that album's raison d'être, on page 1 of a large, 160-page scrapbook assembled in the 1930s—in which the discourses of scraps, scrapbooking, poetry, homelessness, and personal property converge (see figure 1.10):

> Mrs. William F. Davenport, Box 205, Big Ranch Rd., Napa, California, in starting her scrapbook nearly 60 years ago put this verse on the first page with this notation underneath it: "The words of a man whose life is but a scrap of what it might have been." In explanation Mrs. Davenport tells us that it was written by one calling himself a tramp, who worked in a town for a while and then disappeared—suddenly, as he had come. He gave the verse to the young woman who later became Mrs. Edwin Markham, who passed it on to our contributor. We are grateful for both the verse and its story.

SCRAPS

Days are but scraps in the pattern of years.
    Years but scrapwork in the mantle of time.
Scraps are we all in the mystical plan
    That tunes the song of the spheres into rhyme.
The cradle and bier are scraps of a life.
    Infantile dreams and heartbroken cries
Are but scraps of the anthem and dirge
    That anchor the earth to faith in the skies.
Despair's but a scrap of joy that has flown;
    Love's but a scrap of fate's bitter curse.
Ah! Life's but a scrapbook, dog-eared and filled
    With pages of prose and fragments of verse.

If a threat of homelessness or disenfranchisement inhered in the individual scrap—here, that threat is doubly present in the metonymic relationship between the tramp and the verse he carried *and* in the potentially fragmented set of life experiences made coherent only by the poem's metaphysical album—then the comparatively permanent space of the codex helped

FIGURE 1.10. Page 1 of a two-thousand-poem scrapbook assembled by an anonymous woman living near Denver, Colorado, in the 1930s and 1940s. Author's collection.

Americans to manage and even reform the anxiety that the scrap represented and produced. Providing what de Certeau calls "a 'proper' (a spatial or institutional localization),"[50] the scrapbook didn't just offer American readers a literary analogue for a physical home—it was, as Elizabeth Bishop wrote in her short story about a scrap-collecting beach comber, "more like an idea of a house than a real one"—but it then encouraged those readers to view the accumulation of private property as the cure to their existential or metaphysical conundrums as well.[51]

It is ironic that poetry, a genre somewhat exempted from copyright enforcement and representing for many people a discourse not entirely subject to capital, should ultimately figure so crucially in the ideological function of the scrapbook, but that is often how ideology works: the things that appear to be least central to its operation—what Antonio Gramsci regularly called "common sense,"[52] and what Lauren Berlant has studied as "silly objects"—are in actuality sites of intense, if complex, discipline and supervision.[53] The association between private property, scrapbooking, and poetry became so strong around the turn of the century, in fact, that on at least one occasion, as folklorist Lois Karen Baldwin has recorded, "the stairwell walls" of an actual house in Pennsylvania "were papered with . . . newsprint poems" in an act that collapsed the distinction between poem-property and building-property almost entirely; people could literally live inside their poetry scrapbooks.[54] The effects of these associations were far reaching, shaping what Raymond Williams has called a new and modern "structure of feeling," in which the intentional, sustained reading of poetry and the making of poetry scrapbooks came to be viewed within popular culture as a distinctly domestic and feminine activity on par with housekeeping.[55] As a result it was devalued or disparaged by more masculinist discourses even as it served as a site of particular discipline and training in private property accumulation and administration— a dialectic that worked to hide both its ideological aspects and the counterhegemonic intellectual, creative, and critical activities that sometimes went on between its covers (or behind closed doors, if we want to continue the domestic analogy), which I want to illustrate in the next part of this chapter.

Joyce Fitzgerald's Poetry Workshop

In 1919 Odell Shepard's poem "A Nun" appeared in *The Second Book of Modern Verse*, the expanded and revised version of Jessie Rittenhouse's 1917 collection, *The Little Book of Modern Verse*:[56]

> One glance and I had lost her in the riot
>   Of tangled cries.
> She trod the clamor with a cloistral quiet
>   Deep in her eyes
> As though she heard the muted music only
>   That silence makes
> Among dim mountain summits and on lonely
>   Deserted lakes.

There is some broken song her heart remembers
　　From long ago,
Some love lies buried deep, some passion's embers
　　Smothered in snow,
Far voices of a joy that sought and missed her
　　Fail now, and cease . . .
And this has given the deep eyes of God's sister
　　Their dreadful peace.

"A Nun" was first published in the March 1917 issue of *Poetry*—which featured eighteen poems by Amy Lowell, verse by Joyce Kilmer, Ford Maddox Ford, and others, and prose by Pound, Harriet Monroe, and John Gould Fletcher. Shepard (1884–1967) would then include the poem in *A Lonely Flute* (1917), the only book of poems he published in an otherwise long and successful academic and publishing career. Around the same time he would collect the poem in an additional format as well, cutting it out of *Poetry* and pasting it down about two-thirds of the way through the poetry scrapbook that he had started keeping near the end of World War I.

By the time "A Nun" was collected in *The Second Book of Modern Verse* as part of Rittenhouse's effort to define and illustrate modern poetry, Shepard was well on his way to becoming a professional man of letters if not a professional poet. He had attended Northwestern University, the University of Chicago, and Harvard. He had taught at the University of Southern California, Harvard, and Radcliffe, and in 1917 he had been installed as the James J. Goodwin Professor of English Literature at Trinity College in Hartford, Connecticut—a post he would hold until 1946, when, in a move reported on by *Time* magazine, he resigned to protest the increasing corporatization of Trinity's administration.[57] Over the course of his career Shepard would write or edit novels and books of essays as well as two college literature textbooks. He produced well-received editions of Thoreau and Longfellow and cofounded, and served as president for, both the College English Association and the Thoreau Society of America. Known later to some as "Connecticut's Thoreau," he would serve one term as lieutenant governor of Connecticut (1941–1943). And in 1937 his biography of Bronson Alcott, *Pedlar's Progress*, would win the Pulitzer Prize.

The 113 boxes of papers that now comprise the Odell Shepard Collection at Trinity College's Watkinson Library don't include his poetry scrapbook, which I purchased myself on eBay several years ago. At 144 pages long, it contains 245 poems by 150 or so poets, many of whom appeared in the Rittenhouse collections or in the first edition of Louis Untermeyer's 1919 rival anthology, *Modern American Poetry*.[58] Five of the poets Shepard collected would serve as poet laureate. Nine would eventually win either the Pulitzer Prize or the Columbia University Prize for Poetry (the Pulitzer's direct antecedent funded by the Poetry Society of America).[59] Like the album beginning with "Scraps" pictured in figure 1.10, Shepard's scrapbook opens with a mission-statement page—a combination of poem-clippings by Clinton Scollard ("My Library"), Ralph Hodgson ("My Books"), and William Alexander Percy ("Song")—that focuses the project's literary ambitions and that also, in the poems' repetition of the first-person possessive pronoun "my," reveals the impulse to private accumulation discussed earlier (see figure 1.11). The album closes with a typewritten copy of Robert Frost's "For Once, Then Something" pasted inside the back cover. Scattered in between are not just poems by other contemporary writers but also seventy-two of Shepard's own, so that the completed scrapbook feels like a cross between a personal filing system and a modern poetry anthology.

Read in relation to how people publicly collected and presented poems in modern America—in magazines like *Poetry*, anthologies like Rittenhouse's and Untermeyer's, and in single-author books like *A Lonely Flute*—Shepard's scrapbook and "A Nun" underscore at least two things we already know about the intersection of modern poetry and anthologies.[60] First, as the publication of "A Nun" in both *Poetry* and *The Second Book of Modern Verse* should make clear, the meaning of the term "modern" was in a near constant state of flux at this time (who today would call Shepard's poem modern?), and thus collections like Shepard's or Doris Ashley's might well be read as barometers of what "modern" represented for different people. Second, and more pertinent to the present inquiry, such collections remind us that many people expected anthologies to do more than simply file, collate, preserve, and present materials for private, individual-based ways of reading or thinking. Rather, they were expected to also be community-building mechanisms that produced and united readers and writers around concepts like modern poetry, political causes like organized labor (see, for example, the IWW's *Little Red Songbook*), and regional pride (see *The Midland*, run out of the University of Iowa from 1915–1933). The same could be said for Shepard's anthology, for while it remained unpublished and was a project he pursued in private, I would argue that the process of physically positioning, mapping, and reading his

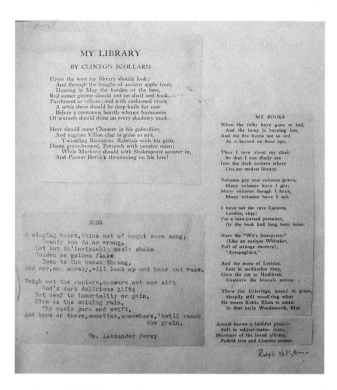

FIGURE 1.11. Page 1 of Odell Shepard's scrapbook, circa 1918–1920. Author's collection.

work in relation to other modern poets materialized something similar to what Benedict Anderson has called an "imagined community" of literary colleagues, peers, and associates. Assembled at the start of an academic career that relocated him away from centers of modern writing where he had once lived (Chicago and Harvard), the scrapbook mixed his verse with other modern poems to create what Anderson describes as an "image of their communion" that continued to tie him to those centers, allowing him to identify and surround himself with other writers, and thus helping to drive and sustain his work.[61]

I like the term "workshop" to describe Shepard's scrapbook. Not only did Shepard actually perform small pencil edits on a few of the clippings he collected, but in the time before what Mark McGurl has called the "program era"—the period after World War II when poets and aspiring poets increasingly were brought to college and university campuses to teach and study in creative writing programs—Shepard more or less created a virtual classroom (even a virtual bohemia) where he could study his own writing, bring peer writers together, and compare their work to his own. Calling his album a workshop also develops an unexpected but not inappropriate aspect of the extended metaphor that encouraged people to conceptualize scrapbooking as a type of homemaking activity. As with Shepard, who also had a physical study (or office) in which to do his work, scrapbooks offered readers and aspiring writers—especially people who had less access to a physical space, not to mention fewer opportunities in higher education—a text-based workshop that Virginia Woolf might have described as a room of one's own.

Such is the case, I would argue, with Joyce Fitzgerald's album, an anthology she used not only to map a tradition of women's writing and identify a contemporary generation of women writers but also to establish an authorial subject position for herself that resisted what she felt were the limiting and outdated values of a World War II-era literary establishment. Unfortunately, I know much less about Fitzgerald than I do about Shepard; other than the material in her scrapbook, and her name written in pencil on the album's inside front cover, nothing indicates who Fitzgerald was or who she went on to become.[62] That her collection survived is remarkable in its own right. Even more remarkable, though, is how it stages the creation of an imaginary workshop as an act of literary expression. The result is an album that is not just indexical or social in nature but artistic as well—an extended composition that relies on, reacts to, and incorporates its various influences to imagine a set of new ethical and social imperatives for contemporary poetry. While Fitzgerald's album is a unique literary text that can be measured and appreciated by the traditional tools of literary analysis, in presenting it here I want to suggest that it is, to some extent—along with the scrapbooks by Ashley and Eckert—also a representative text standing in for the types of literary expression that such projects could at times acquire in the hands of ordinary poetry readers and writers who have, as yet, been afforded little physical or discursive space in the history and archives of American poetry.

Sometime between 1942 and 1943 Fitzgerald, probably in her late teens, began assembling her poetry collection in the "Authorized Edition" of a spiral-bound Shirley Temple Scrap Book that features a color cover portrait of the child star complete with dimples, golden hair, pink bonnet, and frilly white blouse—quite a contrast to the stately, hardcover, olive-green album with a spare modern floral design motif that Shepard used for his album. Like Shepard, though, Fitzgerald would identify and collect poetry by noted writers including a number of past and future Pulitzer Prize winners.[63] Judging by the eight Robert P. Tristram Coffin poems in the scrapbook, the 1936 Pulitzer winner—a Princeton- and Oxford-educated author of more than three dozen works, and a onetime teacher at Wells and Bowdoin Colleges— was especially important to her. In fact, she pasted an autograph from him on its own page near the center of the album, showcasing his little pen-and-ink drawing of two pine trees and an inscription that reads, "For Joyce / Fellow Author / With Best Wishes / Robert P. Tristram Coffin" (see figure 1.12).

An initial look at the collection, however, hardly suggests Fitzgerald as the "fellow author" of Coffin's address. The scrapbook opens with a large reproduction of *Child with Cherries*, a crayon pastel drawing by the eighteenth-century British portrait painter John Russell in which a seated, angelic young

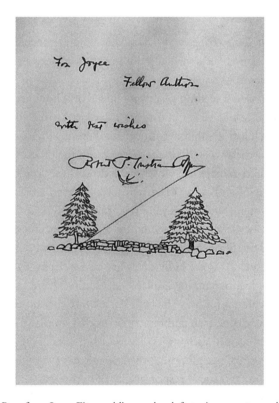

FIGURE 1.12. Page from Joyce Fitzgerald's scrapbook featuring an autograph from Robert P. Tristram Coffin addressed, "For Joyce, Fellow Author," circa World War II. Author's collection.

girl holds aloft for the viewer's consideration a pair of cherries from a basketful of the same that she holds in her lap—an opening paragraph of sorts that, in its clear rhyme with the portrait of Temple on the book's cover, might suggest that the figure of an innocent or naïf, and not an author, resonated particularly strongly with Fitzgerald (see figure 1.13). Below the reproduction of Russell's drawing, Fitzgerald then pasted three poems of what many would call dubious literary merit, including Una Phyllis Dod's three-stanza "Snippity-Snee."[64] With its near baby-talk rhyming, Dod's poem would seem to confirm an initial impression that this scrapbook was little more than a childhood pastime:

> Doggy and Pony and me
> Met in a field of clover;
> We met a lambkin by a tree,
> When the day was over.

In fact, a second *Shirley Temple Scrap Book* I have found pursues this childhood motif entirely, as it collects virtually nothing but nursery rhymes and huge pictures of babies in its pages.

A more considered reading of Fitzgerald's work, however, finds it to be less a child's garden of verses and more a project carried out by someone working to establish a subject position for herself as a young, politically minded woman writer in early 1940s America. In the process of carving out this position—and perhaps even in order to do so—the scrapbook identifies, dramatically stages, and even violently resolves a set of anxieties about, and strong disagreements with, a prevailing culture of professional male writing and associated social values that the figure of Coffin, however ambivalently, comes to represent. Susan Miller has described eighteenth-century commonplace books as "places where individuals hail themselves into specific identities, where people move among available ideologies,"[65] and I think that reading Fitzgerald's album for how she hails herself into the subject position of a new generation of American authors confirms that, in the twentieth century as well as the eighteenth, such projects were also "material sites that produced cultural property."[66] Once glimpsed, the struggle over the meaning, production, distribution, and social responsibility of authorship as both a cultural good and political act in a changing America shows itself in the material, thematic, and even psychological aspects of this album.

Reproduced from the original painting in the Louvre, Paris

"CHILD WITH CHERRIES"—By John Russell

LOVE, RAKE THE ASHES
By WADE OLIVER

Love, rake the ashes over the dying fire;
Conserve for a blacker night the last, least gleam;
Now let us drowse; the sparks of old desire
Under their ashy blanket breathe and dream.
And then to bed; with creak and counter-creak
Compose our worn bones till the stab of dawn,
When we must rise to candles guttering weak,
And robes of immortality put on.

And if upon the midmost verge of dark
I hear the lean cold clicking at the latch,
And, rising in the bitter stillness, mark
The death-ticks' chitter through the frozen thatch,
Yet will my heart dance to a faster rhyme,
Knowing we've had our world k< in our time!

SATIRE ON A SATIRIST
By HELENE MULLINS

May you have all the good and pleasant things
    You could be wanting or be thinking of;
Every good song that every poet sings,
    And fame and power and fighting skill and love.
May all your roads be soft and smoot and flat,
    And you the friend of king, poet and paint,
And may you have a hard time after that.
    Finding a reason for a just complaint.

SNIPPITY-SNEE
By UNA PHYLLIS DOD

Doggy and Pony and me
Met in a field of clover;
We met a lambkin by a tree,
When the day was over.

"Doggy, where has your puppy tail gone?"
"They cut it off, snippity-snee!"
"And Pony, where is the mane you had on!"
"They cut it off, snippity-snee!"

"Lambkin, where is your soft white wool?"
"They cut it off, snippity-snee!"
"And little girl, where are your yellow curls?"
"Well—they did the same to me!"

FIGURE 1.13. Page 1 of Joyce Fitzgerald's scrapbook featuring a crayon pastel by John Russell and poems by Wade Oliver, Helene Mullins, and Una Phyllis Dod.

Fitzgerald's scrapbook is ultimately unified by her interest in locating a community of women writers—especially other young women poets—whom Fitzgerald imagines as a set of her own "fellow authors." Roughly two-thirds of the poems with bylines in the collection, including pieces by Christina Rossetti ("A Birthday" and "A Christmas Carol"), Emily Dickinson ("'Tis so much joy!"), and Edna St. Vincent Millay ("God's World," which Shepard included in his album as well), were written by women, an editorial rubric that mattered enough to Fitzgerald that when she accidentally cut off a byline on one occasion, she was sure to print the author's name in ink above the poem (the only handwriting in the entire album). The presence of Rossetti, Dickinson, and Millay is striking—as Fitzgerald identifies poets who would become central figures in the early academic canon of women's writing—but not as striking as Fitzgerald's attempt to create a circle of contemporary women writers, the presence of Coffin's eight poems and autograph notwithstanding.[67] Several of the bylines on the collection's poems include their respective authors' ages—all are sixteen or seventeen years old—and, in what is one of the album's more telling features, Fitzgerald devoted entire pages to three of these writers, whose pictures appeared alongside their poems when they were first published. Jan Struther, Barbara Jean Olson, and Carolyn Kizer stare out of the scrapbook, creating a series of girlish images that continues the motif established by the Shirley Temple cover and Russell's *Child with Cherries*. Indeed, the scalloped lace collar of the blouse Olson is wearing, and the similar lace designs near her shoulders, are particularly consistent with the outfits on Temple and *Child with Cherries*.

If Fitzgerald was using the album to identify a community of poets, she was also using the scrapbook's compositional possibilities to put their poems in dialogue with each other and with poems by men. In fact, if Fitzgerald's coterie of women writers seems to outnumber and even overwhelm a male tradition represented by Coffin, Untermeyer, University of Iowa Writers' Workshop director Paul Engle, and Ogden Nash, it is because Fitzgerald doesn't just put men and women writers together but sometimes pits them against each other. When we come across Coffin's "The Way to Know a Father" pasted just above Clare Kemper's "Woman with Child," it is difficult not to see the general ethos of the album in miniature, as the gender-neutral language of Kemper's piece (she refers to her child as "this joy," "new life," and "another heart" but never to the child's sex) stands in stark contrast to Coffin's confidently gendered declaration, "No man knows his father till he sees / His father in the son upon his knees." A thematic reading of the scrapbook's poems confirms that the male-female dialogue had a particular interest for Fitzgerald, for while there is an ample supply of poems about housework, mothers and daughters, childbirth, dating, and marriage that might have interested young women of the time, the young photographed poets whom Fitzgerald showcases and with whom she appears to have identified most strongly—Struther, Olson, and Kizer—all engage expressly with, and respond critically to, male speakers in their poems. In "The American Way of Life," for example, Struther relates an encounter with "an old man" who preaches "His own particular / Hymn of Hate," in which he argues that "Helping the Russians / And helping the Jews" is a threat to

Our own,
Known,
Sure,
Secure
Great American Way of Life.

Undeterred by the old man's vituperative, twenty-seven-line "burst of hail," Struther's narrator—revealing her own status as "a guest / From across the sea"—counters his argument with a response twice as long that claims to know the "True American Way of Life": that even though America's founders "ached / From their own day's labors, / They were never too tired / To help their neighbors."

In responding to the masculine discourse of isolation and hate, Struther appeals to, and finds her moral center in, that aspect of American political and social thought that imagines the female voice as the nation's conscience speaking on behalf of peace, kindness, and love. That same center motivates Barbara Jean Olson's untitled poem from *Ladies' Home Journal* as well, except that, as Fitzgerald's album reveals, Olson didn't have to invent a straw man or imagine a "hymn of hate" with whom and which to disagree; instead, she wrote in direct response to real-life writer Struthers Burt and the anthem for wartime hatred that he published in the *Journal* as "Forbearance," which has as its refrain, "Now—and I shall not hesitate— / I will hate." Fitzgerald tracks this poetic argument by pasting Burt's poem and Olson's riposte (about the moral force of love) on the same page, provocatively separated only by Louise Owen's "American Biography" (see figure 1.14). Headlined "Nix on Forbearance,"

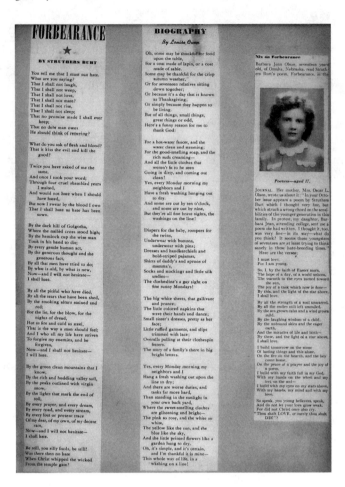

FIGURE 1.14. Page from Joyce Fitzgerald's scrapbook with poems by Struthers Burt, Louise Owen, and Barbara Jean Olson.

the prose introduction to Olson's poem opens with a few words from the *Journal*'s editor and then an explanation from Olson's mother, who submitted Barbara Jean's poem for publication. "In your October issue appears a poem by Struthers Burt," Mrs. Oscar L. Olson writes, "which I thought very fine, but which struck a wrong chord on the sensibilities of the younger generation in this family. In protest, my daughter, Barbara Jean, attending college, sent me a poem *she* had written. . . . It seems these youngsters of seventeen are at least trying to think sanely in these hate-breeding times" (italics in original). A revealing partnership of literary-agent mother, poetess daughter, and the *Journal* editor who gave space to their views, the publication and

collection of Olson's poem not only testify to the sort of moral literary econ-
omy binding communities of women readers and writers (and mothers and
daughters) together—an economy in which, through her album, Fitzgerald
participates as a sort of literary sister—but also suggest how thinking "sanely,"
articulating oneself politically, writing poetry, and the moral and intellectual
activity of scrapbooking were perceived to go hand in hand.

Fitzgerald affirms her moral, political, and literary allegiances across
gender lines as well, with poems like Carl Sumner Knopf's "Conscientious
Objector" and the Rev. Dr. George Stewart's "Prayers for the Day" that are
only marginally connected to the project that Shirley Temple and *Child with
Cherries* seem to begin.[68] And when Fitzgerald's thematic concerns begin to
shift—poems such as "Letters to a Soldier" (Grace Maddock Miller) and "A
Marine to His Girl" (Lt. S. P. Wright) register U.S. intervention in World
War II, for example—those concerns are no sooner raised than they are tied
to, and become part of, the analysis of gender, the activity of writing, and the
challenges of contemporary authorship. I am particularly taken by Miller's
poem, which not only identifies one of the predicaments—even a poetics—
binding women writers together across generations, but which also begins
to explain why the Shirley Temple–like images of innocence figure so promi-
nently in Fitzgerald's album. Here is "Letters to a Soldier" in full:

> Each day she writes. My memory knows the way
> Her pen, though dipped in seething loneliness,
> Contrives an interlude so warmly gay
> That he, in reading, will not ever guess
> The emptiness beneath. Her pages tell
> Those small familiar things that mean, "All's well!"
>
> I know the way her mind and pen conspire
> To etch the picture of a heart serene
> While outer worlds grow livid with the fire
> Of war, to spin a thread of love between
> Their lives now harshly separate—for I knew
> Another war, and I wrote letters, too.

Compared to the socially engaged, historically aware, up-to-the-minute
poems by Fitzgerald's peers, Mullin included, Coffin's eight verses—the
strongest representation of any author in the album—seem out of touch

or stuck in the past, relevant, perhaps, only for the fantasy of an untroubled history that gives "The Almanac," "Young Farmers," "Joy Meets Boy," "Reunion," "I Still Look Up," "The Bonfires," "The Way to Know a Father," and "Late Christmas" their effect.

Indeed, we only have to read the scrapbook forward in history—especially toward Carolyn Kizer's politically active and award-winning career, not to mention Kizer's own receipt of the Pulitzer Prize for poetry in 1985—to see the established male literary tradition that Coffin represents being supplanted by a younger generation of socially active women poets. A rewriting of "The Star Spangled Banner," Kizer's poem "Stars Through the Perilous Night" (also first published in *Ladies' Home Journal*) is aggressively progressive, "written," its prefatory note explains, "for high-school history class" but attempting to make history in the process. "We see the kind of a world we want to live in," Kizer writes:

> the kind of a
> world we can build,
> the kind of a dream we can make,
> the kind of a song we can utter,
> the kind of a dawn that will break
> in the land of the free and the
> home of the brave.

Katriel and Farrell have described scrapbooking as a "practice of life review"[69] that presents an individual's "life as *perfected*, as 'well-lived'"[70]—an idealized (and ideologically pressured) narrative "of growing up as a fun-filled journey through episodic time, subordinating most memories of pain and tribulation that might characterize a more comprehensive description of the growing-up process."[71] While it could be argued that the pictures of Shirley Temple and *Child with Cherries* orient Fitzgerald's scrapbook in relation to the retrospective life narratives that Katriel and Farrell describe, content like Kizer's poem—with its insistent preview of a time yet to come—suggests that this album is not so much about the act of preserving, documenting, or fantasizing about a finished self as it is a workshop space in which to think through, revise, and practice a newer one. That is, rather than imagining life as finished and "perfected," Fitzgerald's album imagines it in a more utopian way as something that might—personally, culturally, politically, and literarily—*be* perfected. In thus reworking the retrospective logic of the scrapbook as a cultural form, Fitzgerald not only writes her life in a different way but imagines the writing life differently as well, as the scrapbook's progressive narrative no doubt tropes—if not produces—an idea of literary history that is also not perfected but open to change. In this context the "we" of Kizer's collective narrator takes on additional resonance, as it is not solely a rhetorical strategy of the poem, but of the scrapbook as well; it is the very "we" that Fitzgerald identifies and assembles over the course of the album—a forward-looking, intergenerational feminist community of women writers ready to supplant Coffin and the literary and social nostalgia in which his authority is steeped and that his poetry comes to represent.

Working counterculturally within a culturally approved space, this material is made even more provocative for how it ultimately absorbs the Shirley Temple cover and *Child with Cherries* image into its feminist literary project. For while the scrapbook tends toward respectful, controlled rhetoric and ethical feminine virtue, those discourses barely manage a resentment and will to violence that Fitzgerald bears toward masculinist literary culture and that the latent content in Temple and *Child with Cherries* enables her to express. If we read the collection for this nearly repressed aspect—one that the conflicted letter writer in Miller's "Letters to a Soldier" dramatizes with her own elaborate façade of "All's well!"—then the album acquires a Janus-faced character, displaying the hallmarks of feminine peace and innocence on one hand ("warmly gay" writing that presents "a heart serene"), and a distinct, if sublimated, agonism ("seething loneliness") on the other. Seeing this component of Fitzgerald's editing helps us understand the possible range of expressive, even therapeutic, ends that scrapbooking might have served, as the material creation of a women's literary tradition and feminist political consciousness also offered a way for Fitzgerald to articulate and balance an otherwise potentially disabling psychological anger.

Child with Cherries is part of a rococo tradition that regularly eroticizes the young subjects of its artwork, and, despite how the metonymic relationship with Temple encourages us to see only the innocence in Russell's portrait, the presence of cherries introduces an indisputable sexual content that might, for some readers, recall "The bough of cherries some officious fool / Broke in the orchard" in Robert Browning's "My Last Duchess." Indeed, while the leaf and pair of cherries that the child holds aloft might signify a young girl's virginity (an association suggested by the basket of fruit placed in her lap), the phallic resonance of the cherries in the girl's hand—looking like a penis and dangling testicles—suggests the presence of a predatory sexuality operating under the guise of childhood naïveté as well. As Russell's child displays the trophy she has picked, the portrait signifies doubly, her angelic virginity twinned with the triumph of having emasculated an unpictured male. In this context Una Phyllis Dod's childhood baby-talk poem "Snippity-Snee," which Fitzgerald pasted immediately below Russell's portrait, acquires a similarly twinned character as *Child with Cherries*, as Dod's insistence on cutting—"'Doggy, where has your puppy tail gone?' / 'They cut it off, snippety-snee!'"—resonates strongly with its surrounding materials.

A history of academic artwork that gives us pieces of the same title and subject as Russell's drawing (see various children with cherries by Salomon de Bray, Adolphe William Bougureau, and Edouard Manet, among others) encourages us to view the "cutting" implied by Russell's generic piece as not purely sexual but as a way of representing the anxiety and agonism of working in an artistic tradition as well—the very anxiety that Fitzgerald's scrapbook exhibits in relation to masculinist authorial practices and their associated cultural values of hate and war. Under the cover of girlish innocence and moral virtue, then, the page-one combination of *Child with Cherries* and "Snippity-Snee" expresses an anger that the rest of the album works to process. In fact, if we read the scrapbook backward from Russell's drawing and Dod's poem toward the cover of Shirley Temple, we might find the same latent content there as well, as the child star capitalized on her perceived innocence to carve out a significant and much-imitated position of influence in the mass media of Fitzgerald's America. Equal parts naïf and aggressor, child and power broker, Temple thus becomes an exemplary figure for the young American woman seeking authorship (if not an "Authorized Edition") in a man's world—a *Child with Cherries* retrofitted for Hollywood or, in the case of Fitzgerald's collection, American belles lettres.

The psychological drama that the first page initiates is woven throughout, and surely drives, the conversation that Fitzgerald establishes between male and female authors and their ethics and politics. This conversation reaches a crescendo in a two-page spread featuring Robb Bentley Leonard's poem "Grant Us Wisdom . . . for the living of these days" and its corresponding graphic (also by Leonard), a three-quarters charcoal drawing of a standing World War I soldier in the process of dropping his pistol in front of him, nearly into the reader's lap (figure 1.15). A farewell to a father headed off to war, the poem, like Miller's "Letters to a Soldier," expresses the ambivalence that results from having to support a soldier leaving for the front while simultaneously questioning the use of military force—used in "the same old silly way"—as a means of achieving lasting peace. "To be brave seems not enough," Leonard's speaker, echoing both the moral center from which the women in Fitzgerald's album speak as well as the future tense of Kizer's poem, concludes:

> I wonder . . .
> Will we some day learn
> How to attain the things we prize?
> Though we be brave,
> We must—we must be wise.

The poem's final two words, "'Bye, Dad," link the poem to the image; the same words appear, printed in a child's hand, in the drawing's right-hand corner. In an immediate context the phrase bids farewell to a soldier, but we might easily read it as glossing the desire of Fitzgerald's scrapbook as well, as she bids farewell ('bye, Dad) to a tradition of male writing and male cultural values that she has been challenging from the start. Indeed, Leonard's positioning of the soldier's pistol—pointed impotently downward, immediately in front of the figure's crotch—is consistent with Fitzgerald's narrative, rhyming with the emasculation in Russell's portrait and indulging the need for wish fulfillment present throughout the album. Reading the collection in this fashion helps to explain what might otherwise appear to be curious or inconsistent poem selections on Fitzgerald's part. The anonymous poem "Somebody's Boy," published as a public service announcement by the Maine Highway Safety Campaign, for example, tells the gruesome story of a child killed by an automobile while crossing the street and is accompanied by an even more gruesome picture of a young boy lying facedown on the concrete beneath a car tire; read between *Child with Cherries* and Leonard's flaccid soldier, the tragedy of "Somebody's Boy" exhibits just how grimly Fitzgerald's anger can find expression (see figure 1.16).

Despite the deeply individual way that Fitzgerald's anger is given voice, the inclusion of pieces like Barbara Jean Olson's response to Struthers Burt, Miller's "Letters to a Soldier," and Carolyn Kizer's "Stars Through the Perilous Night" encourages us to read the scrapbook in a broader literary historical context and not simply as the product of an isolated reader. In viewing Fitzgerald's

"GRANT US
WISDOM . . .

*for the living
of these days*"

(Poem and drawing by
Robb Bentley Leonard)

You grinned, Dad,
As the train pulled out—
That brave grin
I loved so well—
And called, "'Bye, Son,"
Although you knew,
You who had been to war,
That war is hell.

I grinned, too,
Although I felt like crying.
It seemed so stupid
Still to be trying
The same old silly way—
As if we didn't know
The things you fought for
Might be gained,
But not held,
Merely by brave men
Bravely dying.

To be brave seems not enough.
I wonder . . .
Will we some day learn
How to attain the things we prize?
Though we be brave,
We must—we must be wise.

—'Bye, Dad.

FIGURE 1.15. Page spread from Joyce Fitzgerald's scrapbook featuring a poem and a charcoal image by Robb Bentley Leonard.

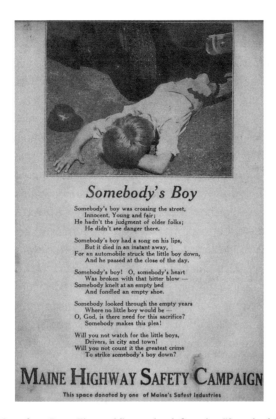

FIGURE 1.16. Page from Joyce Fitzgerald's scrapbook featuring "Somebody's Boy," written for the Maine Highway Safety Campaign.

work next to some of her more celebrated contemporaries—Kizer, Adrienne Rich, and Sylvia Plath, for example—what emerges is not a series of disconnected psychic or emotional "problems" that exceptional individual talents overcome or transform into poetry. Rather, we see the mark of a generation of "fellow authors" from mid-twentieth-century America who struggled individually, in common, and in workshop settings, with how to imagine and configure their relationships with male authority figures, toward whom they felt a mixture of admiration and resentment—relationships that these writers would go on to use as a way of articulating their broader critiques of patriarchy, politics, and the practice of literary history and criticism. Indeed, for the Coffin-Fitzgerald relationship at the core of the *Shirley Temple Scrap Book*, we might very well substitute one or more of the celebrated and studied male-female poetry relationships, such as that between Kizer and her University of Washington writing workshop teacher Theodore Roethke; Adrienne Rich and W. H. Auden, who selected Rich's first book as winner of the 1951 Yale Series of Younger Poets competition; and Sylvia Plath and Ted Hughes. In fact, in an anecdote that nearly collapses the distance between Fitzgerald's scrapbook and Kizer's career entirely, Kizer recalls Roethke urging her to get serious about her poetry by saying, "When are you going to lose your cherry, honey?"[72]

When today's poetry critics stop at the intersection of poetry and popular culture, they often do so to demonstrate how literary writers either critique popular culture or somehow transform its baser, raw materials into art; while certainly legitimate, both approaches tend to illuminate the sophistication, social engagement, and appeal of the "literary" text at the expense of the popular. In citing Kizer, Rich, and Plath in relation to Fitzgerald here, I certainly do want to suggest that scrapbooks like Fitzgerald's can help illuminate the workings of literary writing, but I also want to suggest that reversing that critical logic is not just possible but merited as well—that scholars might study how popular audiences interface with, process, and transform the influences of literary culture (as Ashley, Eckert, and Fitzgerald have done in their albums), and that we might use the work of literary artists to help identify, illuminate, and explain the intelligence of popular activity. Kizer's multifaceted career is a good case in point. As Roethke's student, as founder of *Poetry Northwest*, as the first literature director at the National Endowment for the Arts, as a representative for the U.S. State Department in Pakistan, and as a university teacher and Pulitzer Prize recipient, Kizer has been able to act in many of the spheres that Fitzgerald's album locates as central to the capital of twentieth-century authorship—writing, anthology making, editing, educational training, the distribution of financial support and awards, and even foreign affairs—often foregrounding the subject of gender and a strong sense of how the personal is politically meaningful. Thus, Kizer's millennial anthology *100 Great Poems by Women* (2000) looks a lot like Fitzgerald's, and includes work by Dickinson, Millay, and Rossetti, plus selections from Plath and Rich, who function in *100 Great Poems* partly the way that Kizer and Olsen function in Fitzgerald's collection; one might say that Kizer is publicizing the imagined community that Fitzgerald and other readers and writers were shaping sixty years earlier.

Not content to be one of "the sad sonneteers, toast-and-teasdales we loved at thirteen," Kizer—also like Plath, Rich, and Fitzgerald—has had to situate a politicized notion of women's authorship in relation to the simultaneously enabling and oppressive aspects of father figures in the home, workshop, workplace, and the literary tradition she has inherited.[73] Thus, her poetry can help us better understand the mixture of respect and rage that produced Fitzgerald's album. Kizer's "Thrall" (1984), for example, is about a woman's relationship to a biological father who ignored her childhood, who "drilled [her] in silence and duty," but who was also a first contact for the literary tradition she would later study and write in:

You read aloud to him
"La Belle Dame sans Merci."
You feed him his medicine.
You tell him you love him.

You wait for his eyes to close at last
So you may write this poem.[74]

As with Fitzgerald, Kizer's authorship is purchased by the death or loss of a father ('bye, Dad), literal and literary, and it is the ghost of that tragedy that haunts—and connects—not just their work but their generation.

How much Kizer's poem "Stars Through the Perilous Night" affected her career is difficult to know for sure, but it was cut out from *Ladies' Home Journal* and pasted into at least one other album—a large two-hundred-page, nine-hundred-poem collection kept in the early 1940s by someone I believe to have been a public school teacher in or near Wichita, Kansas. Although substantially larger than Fitzgerald's scrapbook, it nonetheless contains many of the same poets, and while its mixture of typed, handwritten, and printed poems recalls Ashley's album, its nine hundred poems (plus clippings stashed inside the front and back covers) make it feel more like a poetry encyclopedia than an expressive or communicative project.[75] Judging by a number of clippings headlined "Poets Every Teacher Should Know," I suspect the scrapbook served as a teaching resource—or curriculum workshop—as much as anything else, even though not all of the poets included could be called "schoolroom poets."

Ordinarily, I would hesitate to single out this album for special attention, except that more than sixty of its pages have been devoted to collecting a *Good*

Housekeeping poetry feature from the 1940s called "Between the Bookends" (see figure 1.17). Presented by *Good Housekeeping* poetry editor Ted Malone, these full-page features—which were sometimes designed or illustrated to look like scrapbook pages—are actually print adaptations or print renditions of a popular and nationally broadcast radio poetry show of the same name that Malone had been hosting for more than a decade, since 1929; his trademark radio sign-on "Hello there," often followed by a few words of introduction

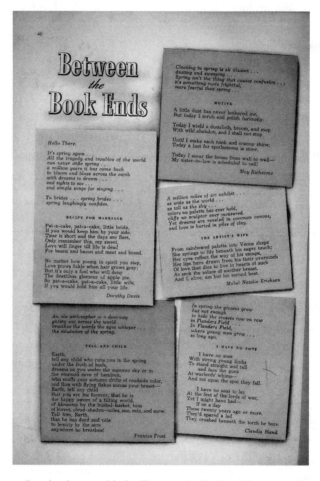

FIGURE 1.17. Scrapbook page with the "Between the Bookends" magazine feature taken from *Good Housekeeping*, circa 1940s. Author's collection.

or conclusion in the way of a presentation context, provides an editorial framework for the poems appearing in print. This reverse remediation—that is, the attempt to back-translate Malone's on-air success to an older media form—is interesting for a number of reasons, not the least of which is the role that poetry is asked to play in facilitating the synergistic efficiency of the Hearst Corporation's multimedia communications conglomerate (which purchased *Good Housekeeping* in 1911).

More pertinent here, however, is how, as the "clippings" in *Good Housekeeping* perhaps suggest, Malone first styled his radio show as an on-air poetry scrapbook. By inviting listeners to send in their favorite poems for potential broadcast, this format not only offered first-generation radio listeners a model by which to understand the dynamics of the new medium—especially the feedback loop between consumer and producer that would become central to mass media's success—but it also worked to route the largely independent poetry-reading and community-making practices of American scrapbookers through the commercial apparatus of the culture industries. How this happened, how audiences responded, and thus how the culture of popular poetry affected the development of twentieth-century mass cultural communications networks is what I would like to explore next.

CHAPTER 2

Invisible Audiences

I very seldom listen in, not being a radio fan. But it has been borne in
upon me in various ways of late, that the poets of quality and standing are
not being broadcast, while numerous impossibles are reading their maudlin
verses to invisible audiences of millions.
—Harriet Monroe, *Poetry*

On Wednesday, February 14, 1940, Ted Malone, host of NBC's pop-
ular daily radio poetry show *Between the Bookends*, invited his listen-
ers to contribute poems to a growing, two-ton "Valentine" that he
had delivered to his alma mater, William Jewell College, the year before. His
lengthy description of, or sales pitch for, what he deemed to be "the most
unique collection of poetry ever started"[1] kicked off a two-part broadcast that,
as usual, concluded with the reading of several poems written or requested by
listeners—on this occasion, all Valentine's Day–linked verses that were sent
out into what some people were still calling the "ether" and that anticipated
the long-distance dedications that Casey Kasem would begin attaching to
songs via the *American Top 40* in 1978. Because almost no one reading this
book has heard Malone's Valentine's Day program, and because it is one of
the few transcripts I have found of what was a long-lived and extremely well-
known but not well-recorded and thus largely inaccessible poetry show, I
want to print the majority of the broadcast here, beginning with Malone's
description of a collection that "is open to any person who wishes to become
part of it" and that he anticipates "will grow to represent every class and race
of people in every corner of America."

Last year on February fourteenth I sent a Valentine to William Jewell that weighed two tons. It was some twenty-six big cases of poetry gathered over the last ten years from . . . from all over America. Boxes of poetry—poems written by housewives, shopkeepers, mayors, governors, teachers, artists, professional people, young loves swayed by the ardor of their devotions, and old grandmothers dipping into their memories. We even had one poem written by a radio announcer named Jerry Burns. I can't remember whether we kept that or not. Poems written by someone who awoke suddenly out of a deep sleep, reached for a pencil, and scribbled a few lines in the semi-darkness. That must have been Jerry; he's always in a deep sleep. Poems written and re-written, changed and refined for a dozen years by some purist who insists that every line be exactly correct. There are books of poems published a hundred years ago on a little press in New England, and the old covers now are worn, and some of the pages are yellowed. Poems carried in stagecoaches out across the prairies to California; kept in scrapbooks through the years and now sent to me and passed on to be a part of this unique collection.

Liberty, Missouri, where William Jewell stands in a haze of rich memories and a legion of legends. Liberty, Missouri, is the historic old Missouri town where the wagon trains were outfitted for the California gold rush. That was a great adventure—to plunge into a new world, new horizons, new lands. Today, on the old hill, we are launching a new caravan in the world of poetry to plunge into the distant future, and save for tomorrow those examples of poetry written in these present years.

You see, this is a unique collection. It's open to any person who wishes to become a part of it. Poems and books contributed to this collection are permanently preserved for the study of students of contemporary poetry. Already, some of the students and scholars are making surveys to determine the themes people write about. What do you think the most people in America write about? Love? Children? Home? Nature? Do you think they'd rather read a serious poem or a funny one? What do you think most folks like? By surveys through these thousands of poems, we'll know the most popular themes and the manner in which each one is most frequently treated.

There are more than a hundred thousand pieces of manuscript poetry in the collection, but in addition to this, there are also copies of all the poetry magazines being published—little literary journals issued by poetry groups in California, Maine, Florida, Oregon, New York, and right here in Cincinnati. Then, of course, volumes of modern and ancient poetry. But I mustn't give you the impression that the collection is in . . . in any sense, complete. Actually, it's . . . it's hardly been started. Even the sheets of manuscripts already gathered are only a small number of what will grow to fill the room in the months and years to come. It is our hope to establish there at William Jewell College the most complete collection of poetry, preserving it for . . . [recording here is indiscernible] . . . but with your help I think we can make it possible.

When you write a poem and want it stored in the archives, preserving it for posterity; or when you've filled the old scrapbook and don't know just what you'll want to do with it, but you'd like to have it saved, I hope you'll send it along so we can pass it on to the collection at William Jewell. I should add that these poems will remain your property. They will not be released for publication without your permission, so that you take no risk or make no sacrifice by sending in these poems, although they may be original to you. You simply procure for yourself an assurance that your poem will be preserved permanently in this poetry collection.

Yes, out on the old hill today—there by the heart of America—they're opening a Valentine containing not one poem, but a vast collection of poems, a collection containing the simple secret hopes and dreams of a half million lives. They're the stories that people live by—the stories that people live each day. People you know. People like you. And once in a while they transcribed them to paper, and the world remembers them as poems.[2]

This collection—which in rhetoric, practice, and result anticipates by more than a half century the Favorite Poem Project initiated by former U.S. poet laureate Robert Pinsky in 1997—is remarkable for many reasons, not the least of which are the twinned, antimodernist documentary and critical impulses at what Malone would probably appreciate me calling its heart.[3] While its documentary motive is easily understood in the context of Depression-era America, which saw extensive preservationist efforts in photography, film, literature, and history, Malone's project hinges on an editorial rubric of inclusivity that figures uneasily in many discussions of poetry and that certainly ran counter to the exclusionary rhetoric of modernism, with which listeners were quite familiar after what Joseph Harrington calls the "poetry wars" of the 1930s.[4] Yet it is precisely the Valentine's inclusivity—measured by "some twenty-six big cases" of verse—that allows Malone's antimodernist collection to at least partially wrestle the cultural distinction of originality away from modernism. Twice during the broadcast he emphasizes that the collection is "unique," not because it is limited to a few contributors working in what Pierre Bourdieu would call a "restricted" field of cultural production[5], but because "it's open to any person who wishes to become a part of it." In calling his Valentine "the most unique collection of poetry ever started," Malone in a sense "outmodernisms" modernism, and he's got two tons of poetry sitting in Liberty, Missouri, to substantiate his claim.

At the same time that the project serves, time capsule–like, to document "examples of poetry written in these present years," Malone sees it having academic value as well. "Already," he claims, "some of the students and scholars are making surveys to determine the themes people write about." However, as with the hospitality of his editorial method, the way he suggests the collection will be studied is also antimodernist in nature. Rather than propose the close reading of individual poems, as advocated by what John Crowe Ransom would call the New Criticism in his book of that title the following year, Malone proposes that his Valentine will aid scholars in what Franco Moretti has more recently called "distant reading," which looks at groups of texts for "a sharper sense of their overall connection. Shapes, relations, structures. Forms. Models."[6] This is exactly how Malone prompts his listeners to imagine the project. "What do you think the most people in America write about?" he asks, "Love? Children? Home? Nature? Do you think they'd rather read a serious poem or a funny one? What do you think most folk like? By surveys through these thousands of poems, we'll know the most popular themes and the manner in which each one is most frequently treated." Like modernist writers and the New Critics, Malone is interested in taste ("what do you think most folk like?"), but unlike modernist writers and the New Critics, the scholarship he imagines will not attempt to legislate but study it.

These two aspects of Malone's antimodernist literary-critical method—an editorial rubric that values every text as special, but then reads texts distantly and not for their singularity or individual merit—seem contradictory in the abstract, but that contradiction is more or less accounted for by the rest of the broadcast's framework. Contributed by writers from coast to coast (New England, California, Maine, Florida, Oregon, New York, and Ohio) and located in the conveniently named town of Liberty at the geographical center of the nation, Malone's Valentine represents the heart of America itself, and thus its collection and study balances if not expresses the tension between the individual and the collective that many people believe constitutes, or is at the heart of, U.S. national identity. What goes unstated but not unperformed in Malone's conceit, however, is that this poetic expression of a national heart "with veins [Whitman would say] full of poetical stuff" is ultimately facilitated if not engendered by *corporate* radio—not public, independent, underground, or pirate radio—which, in its coast-to-coast reach, links the needs of the individual, even isolated listener to a national community of listeners. In an era when radio was a new technology and not imagined to be inevitably commercial or national in formation, Malone's project presents corporate broadcasting and its regulatory structures as what radio historian Michele Hilmes has called "a natural outgrowth of the 'American way.'"[7] One might say that while Malone's *Between the Bookends* did not have sponsors like Froz-Ann ice cream or Spry vegetable shortening (both of which approached Malone about sponsorship), it was hardly removed from the business of selling. It, and the America it brought into being, helped to sell the idea of corporate radio itself.

This sleight of hand—in which Malone regularly made corporate radio's modern and American but antimodernist character a main undercurrent of the show—worked very well. At the height of its popularity in the mid 1930s, then airing on CBS, *Bookends* received more than twenty thousand fan letters per month which was, *News-Week* reported, "more fan mail than any other unsponsored performer on any network"[8] and an amount deemed high "even in radio circles, where astronomical figures are the usual thing."[9] And yet, despite a level of success that saw Malone employ a full-time secretarial staff just to keep up with answering fan mail, stations regularly changed the show's broadcast time from what Malone regularly called "long about half past," and some dropped *Bookends* from their roster of shows entirely. Invariably, torrents of angry letters from listeners restored what the *Los Angeles Times* called "radio's vox pop" to the air, but it is nevertheless worth asking why Malone didn't have more job security than he did.[10] It wasn't, I'd like to claim, that Malone was doing his job poorly, but that the second half of his program—the part that relied on listener-generated poetry for its content—was capturing and keeping his audience's attention too well. By granting listeners a high level of participation by which they became active collaborators and not just passive listeners, the innovative format of *Bookends* made early corporate radio uncomfortable; not only wasn't the show "programmed" enough, it also wasn't always easy to make the collaboration between Malone and his listeners neatly dovetail with corporate interests. Consider, as an example, the second half of Malone's 1940 Valentine's Day broadcast, which I quote below and which on this day included four poems pasted together by Malone's commentary:

> If we were there today, you and I, I would hunt through the files of the poems for the manuscripts of several that are my favorites. Today, on Valentine's Day, we might call them Valentines—to someone, somewhere, who will understand.
>
> For someone well along in years, Ina Draper DeFoe's Valentine: "A Prayer for a Girl No Longer Young":

> Autumn, be kind to her. Slow your arrival.
> Summer, be good to her. Let the revival
> Of spring in her body be passionate, heady.
> Love may yet come to her. Let her be ready.
> Chilled were desires in the spring's mating season;
> Shadows pursued her without a good reason.
> Lately, I noticed her, after fresh grooming,
> Almost, she's pretty now, wistfully blooming.
> Let her have blossom time, white petals flying,
> Making a bridal bed smooth for her lying.
> Spring, with your magic touch lulling the senses,
> Stay, while she joyfully hurdles Love's fences.

> "Prayer for a Little Girl with a Braid": a Valentine to a little girl by Beryl Holdren:

> Dear Lord, I'm not complaining much;
> At least, I hope not much.
> But since you've made the crippled walk

Without the aid of crutch,
And given sight unto the blind,
Well, I've a small request.
It seems so very much to me;
I'm sure it's for the best;
But couldn't you let me have
(You can't, I'm so afraid)
A lovely, long and shining curl
In place of this old braid?

A Valentine we never send—the first poem in our collection. It's by
Lawley Williams. A Valentine for a little girl who isn't with us any-
more—a little girl called Elsie, my little sister. Out in Colorado Springs,
Colorado . . . out on the east side of town, there's a large park and a
small, white stone for a little girl named Elsie. A Valentine to one who
died young:

You believed with childhood magnitude
And all was well. You never saw the feud
When old ideals encounter world's demands
And come to dust. Your artless, chubby hands
Will never strangle hope, nor nurture greed.
You'll never know the time that gods recede.
How good a thing it is. Those candid eyes
That saw truth as truth and lies as lies,
Will never see the taint of compromise.
You'll never be a part of sorrows past.
Here rests the dream.
Here rests the fate, intact.

Then, one more poem—a Valentine to you:

I wish you happiness—
Not just the kind that bubbles up,
But happiness that is a quiet peace
within your heart.
Trials will come. They always do,

But somehow they'll always go away
Because that peace of happiness is there.
I wish you faith—
Not the fair-weather kind of faith,
But the faith that faces the blackest sky
And says, "I trust."
My wishes for you—
I do not wish you fame, or power, or gold,
But I think what share of these comes your way
Will be the brighter and the dearer
And still more sweet, because
These other three belong to you.

Goodbye.

(Organ music—"Somewhere a Voice Is Calling")[11]

From a station manager's perspective, this part of *Bookends* is a potentially confusing mess, and not only because Malone shortened the final poem (possibly for time reasons) so that its final line "These other three belong to you" lacks a complete referent.[12] First, considering how Malone was probably swimming in seas of love poetry, his selections make for an unexpected if not inappropriate Valentine's Day broadcast: a voyeuristic poem about a spinster's unrequited sexual desire; a prayer from a little girl who wants curly hair; an elegy for a dead child; and a redacted greeting card poem about abstract values of happiness and faith. At least three of the four verses were written by women for other women—although here, importantly, they are voiced and delivered by a man on the radio—and none of them have any of the conventionally romantic, heterosexual relationship content commercially associated with, and celebrated by, Valentine's Day. Second, the narrative map that Malone constructs from poem to poem, which takes his audience backward from the loneliness of advanced age to a child better-off dead than alive, is not just puzzling holiday material but seems likely to elicit anxiety from a listener more than anything else and certainly not the "soothing and comforting" experience that the program's promotional materials regularly boasted *Bookends* would produce.[13] Certainly, some of this jumble is part of the show's desired effect if not its thrill—by selecting verses from what audiences themselves provided, Malone induces anxiety in the listener and then, in the final poem, perhaps works to dispel it—but the rest of the show doesn't particularly champion or operate according to commercial logics, including the specific interests of advertising sponsors delivering the daytime shows being played on either side of the "public service," not-for-profit oasis that *Bookends* was said to provide.[14]

What Malone creates in relationship with his listeners, however, is a sort of queered wireless space that, in the context of the Valentine's Day broadcast, centers on the redefinition, equitable distribution, and thus counterhegemonic force of love. By dedicating poems to people who wouldn't under prevailing logics receive Valentines much less be featured as the faces of the day's rituals, he not only redefines what a Valentine does (thereby enfranchising the day's dispossessed) but effectively calls for, and performs, a reallocation of Valentine's Day capital (love) as well. He can get away with the implications of this performance for a range of reasons: by enfranchising new audiences, he perhaps expands the customer base for Valentine's Day; he expresses these sentiments through poetry that, as I explained in chapter 1, was an effectively managed public discourse for the expression of potentially noncapitalist values; and he again associates corporate radio with values that aren't entirely commercial. However, the position that Malone strikes with listeners not only acknowledges but also gives expression to potentially disruptive, even utopian impulses without entirely managing or repressing them as Fredric Jameson has argued other mass-cultural products do.[15] In fact, rather than repressing the egalitarian spirit of a Valentine economy, *Bookends* actually uses it to further institutionalize the expression of nondominant views, providing a regular means of publication for listener poems—often written or contributed by women, shut-ins, workers, and other people feeling isolated, lost, or voiceless during the Depression—sanctioned by a male voice that no doubt worked to legitimize those views; by reading three poems about intimate, painful, taboo, or possibly embarrassing subjects that people might not expect to be part of public discourse (a spinster's desire, a prayer, a dead sister), he encourages listeners to speak out rather than stay quiet. As I hope to show later in this chapter, this dynamic opened up a forum that both male and female audiences valued and that Malone and other broadcasters like him had to then negotiate with corporate authority in complex ways.

Between the Bookends was perhaps the most successful but hardly the only poetry show airing on the commercial networks in the 1930s and 1940s. In 1930 *Poetry* magazine editor Harriet Monroe would dismiss them in toto as "numerous impossibles reading their maudlin verses to invisible audiences of millions"[16]; twenty years later Randall Jarrell would echo her discontent by criticizing people for "reciting one-syllable poems over the radio."[17] Although there is much to be said about the broadcasting of poetry on national and local airwaves during this time, a comprehensive history of the phenomenon (what we might call a study of wireless "bardcasting") has not been written since Milton Allen Kaplan's *Radio and Poetry* in 1949.[18] In such a history both *Between the Bookends* and *R Yuh Listenin'?*—the latter program hosted by Tony Wons, who, despite a popularity that at times rivaled Malone's, seemed to also change jobs frequently—would have to figure prominently not only because of their wide appeal and longevity (Malone kept his audience for nearly twenty years) but also for how their success helped to drive the participatory dynamic of mass culture as it emerged from, and yet stayed closely connected to, newspaper, periodical, and other print formats.

In this chapter I want to approach radio poetry from two vantage points along the feedback loop of that participatory dynamic: the radio host who served as an interface between public and corporate interests, and the audience with whom he was in constant dialogue if not collaboration. As I have already suggested, figures like Malone and Wons were forced to balance relationships with various stakeholders—most prominently home audiences, on one hand, and corporate radio's commercial infrastructure on the other—whose interests and needs did not necessarily synchronize. As poetry's middlemen they had to therefore present different but equally credible or legible personalities to both sets of stakeholders, often at the same time. Their solutions to this predicament took various forms, but for the purposes of this book I want to trace how a guiding metaphor of poetry scrapbooking, in conjunction with the poetics of abstraction or vagueness at the center of a lot of popular poetry, specifically enabled them to do so. In approaching radio poetry from this direction, I hope to offer an example of how, as N. Katherine Hayles has explained, new media "emerge by partially replicating and partially innovating upon what came before," while also showcasing the unexpected role that poetry played in the development of American mass-media practices.[19] In so doing I also want to show the usefulness and appeal that now critically dismissed vague or abstract verse had for many people in an age when a central (and now academically privileged) discourse of modernism emphasized the concrete image and poetry based on what William Carlos Williams famously described as "no ideas / but in things."[20]

Secondly, by turning to an archive of fan letters that are now part of the Arthur B. Church Papers at Iowa State University, I want to put something of a face to the "invisible audiences of millions" that Monroe described in her 1930 *Poetry* essay "The Radio and the Poets," which is the source of this chapter's epigraph. Saved by Malone's original "home" station, KMBC in Kansas City, while Malone was in a three-month, work-related transition between the Midwest and New York, these letters offer us an unusual glimpse into listener reactions and suggest how audiences did not absorb the poetry on Malone's show passively or uncritically, but used it as an entry point into engaging and coping with the history of their time. Unfortunately, the actual poems that listeners sent or addressed have been detached from the letters (very possibly for inclusion in Malone's Valentine collection), but the extant writing about, or commentary on, both those poems and Malone's broadcasting practices nevertheless reveals how people were taking what appear to have been ahistorical or vague, inspirational poems and applying them to the specific historical and social conditions of the Great Depression. Read in aggregate—that is, read distantly as Malone or Moretti would suggest they might be read—this fan mail produces what Cary Nelson has elsewhere described as "a distinctive sort of textual microhistory . . . a partial window on ordinary life gained by way of discontinuous recovered voices."[21] Those voices can be quite stunning—in part for how some bear witness to the effective, nearly hypnotic effects of the culture industries, but also for how others look to popular poetry as a way of processing or expressing their fears, anger, and despair with the Depression and as a way of challenging commercial radio and imagining an alternative to what Theodor Adorno has described as consumer capitalism's "hostile, distant, cold, and oppressive" nature and its "overpowering force of material things."[22]

Middlemen

Listeners could be forgiven if they imagined Malone's Valentine's Day collection as a giant scrapbook—even a scrapbook made up of other scrapbooks—and not only because Malone mentions poetry scrapbooking twice in his broadcast. In fact, like many other radio hosts dating back to the emergence of commercial networks in the late 1920s, he had been framing *Bookends* as an on-air version of scrapbooking for over a decade, both imitating and setting the pace for an eclectic set of radio hosts and their shows, including Wons on *R Yuh Listenin'?*, Ted White broadcasting as "New England's Favorite Philosopher" on several stations in the northeast, country vocalist Gene Lowery on WIBC (Indianapolis), Dr. John Holland preaching for the Little Brown Church of the Air on WLS (Chicago), and Ray Zaner, "the poet scout," who featured solely student work as a "distinctly public service" on WSBA (York, Pennsylvania).[23] All of these programs published print companions that made explicit the scrapbook model on which they were based: *Ted Malone's Scrap Book* was published annually well into the 1940s; *Tony's Scrap Book*, featuring a few "gems which proved most popular on the air," also came out yearly for a decade in the late 1920s and 1930s; White published *From My Scrapbook*; Lowery issued a *Radio Album* of songs, poems, and pictures; the Little Brown Church of the Air (for whom Wons at one time worked) sponsored *John Holland's Scrap Book*; and Zaner put together *My Poetry Scrap-Book*, containing five year's worth of student verse. Even during World War II, when rationing made resources scarce, this trend continued. In introducing *Jim and Bob's Victory Album of Poems* from locally run KMA (Shenandoah, Iowa) in 1943, for example, "Uncle" Russ Davis of sponsoring Spark-O-Lite Company apologized to the "many thousands of pairs of eyes [that] will scan these pages" for the wait, explaining that "today's publishing world is a different world from that of a year ago" and expressing his belief that "the quality of the poems contributed by our good friends and listeners will more than offset the little delay you have experienced"[24] (see figure 2.1).

No doubt the appeal to print scrapbooking offered first-generation radio audiences an analogy by which to better understand the dynamics of what we tend to forget was once a new, confusing, and even threatening medium—an analogy that Hayles calls a "skeuomorph" and that helped novice listeners conceptualize and acclimate to the disembodied acoustics of a wireless age.[25] Radio's potentially disorienting or difficult acoustic overlaps, juxtapositions, and samplings, its varying types of material, shifts in tone, idiosyncratic editorial styles, and multiple, often uncited sources were simply—or so the metaphor would have it—an on-air version of physical scrapbooking. Radio historian Susan Douglas argues that first-generation audiences needed coaching along these lines, as people were apt to find the medium's "blend of talk, music, and static" plus "interference, often in the form of cross talk, overlapping voices and music, or noise" to be challenging if not off-putting experiences,[26] to say nothing of the new and "different modes of listening"

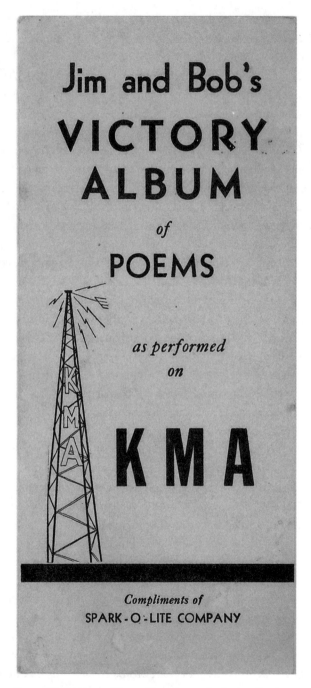

FIGURE 2.1. *Jim and Bob's Victory Album of Poems*, 1943. Author's collection.

that such auditory endeavors demanded.[27] If a 1933 postcard from Tony Wons is any indication, broadcasters regularly and casually mixed their print and acoustic vocabularies to both explain and interest audiences in the scrapbook-like overlaps, blendings, and generic juxtapositions that Douglas describes, and to also offer a model for how listeners might personally contribute to that process.[28] "Thank you sincerely for your friendly note and fine contribution to the *scrapbook pages*—" Wons writes, "only regret *programs* are necessarily prepared too far in advance to permit making a definite date at this time for the *broadcasting* of your selections" (emphasis added; see figure 2.2).[29] This is precisely the sort of responsibility, Michele Hilmes argues, that hosts were expected to fulfill. "The radio 'host' spoke directly to his audience," she explains, "guiding them through the unfamiliar listening experience, organizing and making sense of a potpourri of entertainment . . . [and providing] neophyte radio listeners with a framework for this new knowledge, a guide for interpretation."[30]

I'd like to suggest, however, that in the case of radio poetry scrapbookers like Malone and Wons, this was only half the story. Certainly, such hosts served the needs of listeners: they hailed listeners as acoustic subjects, they facilitated audience experiences and encouraged people to contribute, and they appealed to listeners as individual people, not just an undifferentiated mass. At the same time Malone and Wons recognized that they were working in a culture of what Walter Ong has called "secondary orality," in which electronic media trigger and cultivate the "living"[31] or "situational" (ibid., 51) aspects of real-time communication between humans but are ultimately "dominated by a sense of closure which is the heritage of print" and thus "do not tolerate a show of open antagonism" (137).[32] "Programs," as Wons explains in his postcard message, "are necessarily prepared . . . far in advance." These hosts therefore developed the scrapbook metaphor in another direction, emphasizing the role of the scrapbook maker—not reader or contributor—to give corporate interests a framework for understanding how potentially antagonistic feedback loop dynamics were not essentially disruptive or destabilizing phenomena. Casting the host as the show's final editor or composer culling appropriate material for broadcast and presenting it within industry-friendly frameworks, they illustrated how radio could elicit and involve but not be held hostage to audience response. The resulting compromise position—which invited listeners to contribute their material and labor but then surrender their editorial agency to a corporate structure shielded or

FIGURE 2.2. Postcard from Tony Wons, 1933. Author's collection.

even made largely invisible by someone like Malone or Wons—established a role for the letter-fielding, poetry-reading radio host as middle management or petty bourgeoisie.

The conflicting interests of that subject position needed to be regularly resolved, however, so a fair amount of each program and its supporting print apparatus worked toward that end. Take, for example, "Tony at Work," the frontispiece from a commercially published 1930 edition of *Tony's Scrap Book* (see figure 2.3). An elaborate pen-and-ink drawing that is part caricature, part cartoon, and part portrait, the image shows Wons sitting at his desk and assembling (perhaps broadcasting) material for *R Yuh Listenin'?* by reading through a scrapbook. Most printed radio scrapbooks included a frontispiece of some sort—it put a face to an otherwise disembodied speaking voice and assured first-generation audiences that the voice they heard matched up with a respectable real-life source—but those images ranged widely in appearance from charcoal sketches to glossy black-and-white publicity headshots and scrapbooklike montages such as "Tony at Work and Play," from another 1930 (self-published) edition of *Tony's Scrap Book* (see figure 2.4).[33] While this variety suggests the multiple identities radio hosts were trying to cultivate, the commercially produced "Tony at Work" efficiently—even remarkably—fuses them into a single polysemantic image that articulates and manages competing sets of corporate and audience interests without putting them in conflict with one another. As his place at the center of the drawing no doubt suggests, Tony is the perfect middleman.

The combination of cultural signifiers in "Tony at Work" suggests that, like Malone's broadcast on Valentine's Day, this drawing is partly tasked with legitimizing radio as a natural expression of American entertainment and communication formats: the shelves of books, bust of Shakespeare, theatrical curtain, and the grotesque minstrel reference argue for network radio as an extension or amalgamation of recognizable cultural forms. It also, and more importantly I think, gives listeners a sort of duck-rabbit gestalt optical illusion by which to help conceptualize the magical dynamics of Tony's participatory show in particular. At the same time that it offers a glimpse of the usually invisible man behind the screen—the curtain thus promises a transparent listening experience in a medium otherwise characterized by a potentially unsettling obscurity—it also offers, by way of the six portraits arranged around the frame, a view of the broader and usually just as invisible *home* audience. The simultaneous and perhaps even generous reveal of

FIGURE 2.3. "Tony at Work," frontispiece from commercially published edition of *Tony's Scrap Book*, 1930.

radio's unseen participants not only has the effect of dissolving lines between the public and private—showing the normally public Tony as he works in private, and showing the normally private audience listening in public—but also establishes an "objective" third party perspective for the reader of "Tony at Work"; occupying an outside, three-dimensional space in relation to the two-dimensional drama taking place on the page, the reader witnesses if not studies the dynamic by which radio's otherwise imagined community works. He or she sees how Tony, like Malone, values and preserves the individual listener's feedback, as well as how the listener's participation makes the magic of radio broadcasts possible; as suggested by the drawing's geometrical motif

Copyright 1930 by
Anthony Wons

Published by
Anthony Wons
New York, N. Y.

TONY AT WORK AND PLAY

FIGURE 2.4. "Tony at Work and Play," frontispiece from self-published edition of *Tony's Scrap Book*, 1930.

that tracks audience contributions via a sequence of rectangles—the rectangular frame around audience members' portraits tropes the rectangular letters they send, the scraps Tony collects, the shape of his album, the books stacked behind him, and the rectangular shape of the "Tony at Work" drawing as a whole—the show would not function without active listener involvement. When Tony is at work, the image suggests, he is working to facilitate radio as a space for public expression.

And yet, for as much as it speaks to audience interests, "Tony at Work" signifies doubly, seemingly constructed as much or more for the purpose of instructing corporate interests how the participatory formats of write-in (and later call-in) programs don't necessarily have to derail the networks' authority. For just as the drawing's curtain may be seen to reveal the individual figure of Tony in his studio and thus promise transparency, it also serves to conceal or disguise the real ghost in the machine and thereby promises that the underlying administrative, economic, and ideological structures of mass media will remain invisible, untouched, and unexamined. Furthermore, while "Tony at Work" makes the scene of Tony's studio publicly accessible, it ultimately holds its listeners at a distance, providing them an opportunity to contribute to the making of their own entertainment but nevertheless situating them on the margins and giving them no access to the means of production that other (underground, pirate, public) forms of radio might in fact have encouraged. As with the duck-rabbit illusion, the visual field of the drawing can manifest only one party (either duck or rabbit, Tony or the audience) in the given space at any one time, a phenomenon that further works to keep home audiences out of Tony's workplace even as they help constitute it. As a result not only are listeners not encouraged to take up the microphone themselves, but as they sit passively in orbit around Tony, they are encouraged to cede their own creative and individual scrapbook-making practices as well. For his part Tony transforms the carnivalesque jumble of envelopes representing listeners' uncoordinated and situational responses into an ordered album where everything is fixed in place. While the scissors in his studio gesture to scrapbook making, they hang unused from the desk, as Tony doesn't specialize in cutting things up but in the more industry-friendly activity of standardizing and homogenizing individual feedback—of effectively separating the raw material of poems from their listeners' comments, just as Malone did with the fan letters now contained in the Arthur B. Church collection. This is not to say that "Tony at Work" doesn't show Tony at work; on the contrary, in this version of the drawing he is working very much on behalf of corporate interests.

If one element in "Tony at Work" represents Tony the radio host, it is the open paste pot that overlaps with his right hand, a detail suggesting that, more than anything else, Tony is the adhesive or right-hand man who glues competing interests together. As middle management he not only occupies the middle of the page but, located neither in an actual recording studio nor in an actual home, he also occupies a middle ground from which space (as suggested by the bust of Shakespeare, the sophisticated-looking books, the scrapbook, and the minstrel entertainment) he broadcasts middlebrow entertainment. Such a result is not unexpected; Ong writes that in a regime of secondary orality where "electronic media do not tolerate a show of open antagonism. . . . Genteel, literate domesticity is rampant."[34] That Tony is thus tasked with providing something for everyone does not go unacknowledged; he concludes his scrapbook's foreword by explaining, "Here will be found good cheer for those who are sad; hope for those who are ill; praise for the winner; encouragement for the loser; inspiration for the young; tranquility of mind for the old, and a smile for everyone." In fact, in the event that the poetry collection that follows—containing verses ranging from Ben Jonson to Goethe, Elizabeth Barrett Browning, A. E. Housman, Ella Wheeler Wilcox, Elbert Hubbard, Walt Mason, Carl Sandburg, and individual listeners like Roscoe Gilmore Stott and Miss Will Allen Dromgoole—is not inclusive enough, the book ends with ten to fifteen blank pages reserved "For Your Selections." The opportunity to personalize Tony's anthology in this manner comes with one seemingly contradictory condition: that a reader trade his or her individual scrapbooking practices for Tony's standardized format. As a case in point consider the specific copy of *Tony's Scrap Book* that I've been working with, which was once owned by Annie L. Blake of Bangor, Maine. Blake accepted Tony's invitation by writing, pasting, and straight-pinning her own selections in the blank pages until she ran out of space, at which time she began writing, pasting, and straight-pinning other clippings inside the front and back covers and on blank spaces in the book's front matter (see figure 2.5). When she ran out of space yet again—one newspaper article is dated March 6, 1960, thirty years after this edition was issued—she started storing clippings between individual pages and inside the book's front and back covers. I don't know whether Blake kept a separate album of her own design that might have accommodated her scrapbooking needs more comfortably, but her fidelity to this particular edition and its material constraints suggests just how successful Tony's standardizing activities could be.

Given his ability to perform for different interests, it is worth noting that Wons was actually born Anthony Snow (Wons spelled backwards), and thus his on-air personality was a performance from the start. Ted Malone was fictional as well—a personality that Frank Alden Russell invented on the spur of the moment in 1929 when conscripted to fill an unexpected gap in the programming schedule at KMBC, the station where he had gotten his start in radio several years earlier, before he had graduated from college.[35] Russell would later claim that he used the pseudonym to save him the ignominy of being a "sissy" associated with poetry, though the multiple identities he would cultivate for audiences, employers, and media outlets later in his career suggests—as I will explain in a moment—that we consider this claim with some degree of skepticism.[36] In subsequently organizing *Between the Bookends* around listener contributions, however, Malone stumbled onto a hit, becoming so successful that by 1931 *Bookends* was airing three times per week on KMBC and once on the Columbia Blue network. By 1935 KMBC had expanded from three to eighty employees in part to deal with the increase

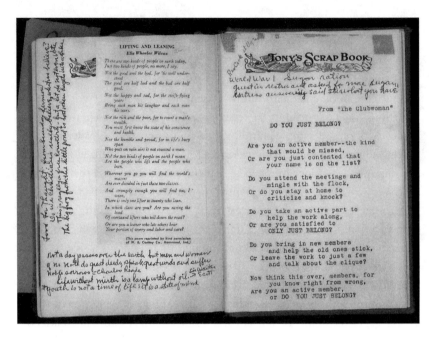

FIGURE 2.5. *Tony's Scrap Book* (commercial edition) used as a scrapbook, circa 1930–1960. Author's collection.

in traffic *Bookends* stimulated, and Russell was broadcasting nationally on CBS and receiving upwards of twenty thousand fan letters per month, all of which were answered by the full-time secretarial staff working for what *Book-ends* stationery at one point called "Radio's Most Intimate Program." On the strength of this following, Malone would go on to serve as poetry editor of the *Pictorial Review* (1937–1939) and *Good Housekeeping* (1940–1944), and in 1939 he parlayed his reputation as "Radio's poetaster"[37] into a two-year stint at NBC developing and hosting *Pilgrimage of Poetry*, a program that visited "poetic shrines" around the country and that ultimately moved U.S. poet laureate Joseph Auslander and the Library of Congress Poetry Division to designate Malone as "The Voice of Poetry."[38]

As his success indicates, Malone was a savvy performer both on and off the air, cultivating various radio and real-life personae to cast himself, sometimes simultaneously, as an on-air cupid, romantic confidante, confessor, surrogate father, salesman, businessman, poetry advocate, huckster, industry insider, marital therapist, and more. On air he was what Joan Shelley Rubin has called "a master of the simulated intimate encounter,"[39] beginning each themed show with an informal "Hello there" and a segment of friendly chit-chat delivered in what was called the "coziest parlor voice in U.S. radio nowadays" (*Time*, "Pilgrim"). "May I come in?" he began one broadcast, "I see you are alone. . . . Now I'll just take this rocker here by the radio and chat awhile. . . . What lovely new curtains" (ibid.). Malone's crossing of the ether into people's living rooms recalls the imagery from "Tony at Work," but whereas Wons appeals almost exclusively to print culture for his model of audience comportment (Tony reads at a desk, there are stacks of books behind him, his listeners write letters), Malone also worked in reference to what would have been, in real life and the cultural imaginary, a social site of oral exchange, performance, singing, and reading: the living room and fireside.[40] "Now, it's Monday, and we're back in New York City, and I can't tell you what kind of weather we're having, but we're certainly having it," he explained, for example, on January 19, 1942. "So . . . we'll just sit down here and tell you that if we had our choice on a day like this, we'd build a big fire in the fireplace, and take off our shoes, put on some leather slippers . . . and we'd . . . read poems."[41] By anchoring his authority in a modernized hearth space as well as the world of print, Malone (broadcasting here nearly a decade after President Franklin Roosevelt's first Fireside Chats) installs himself as an idealized head of radio's national household—a role that not only worked to explain the show's participatory aspect in terms that both corporate and audience interests could understand, but that also hailed audience members into a wide range of possible partnership roles evoked by the fireplace and living-room setting.

Journalists reporting on *Bookends* marveled at Malone's success and especially at the effect he was said to have on female members of this "radio family." Russell's obituary in the *New York Times*, for example, remembers Malone as a broadcaster who "had millions of fans, particularly housewives and schoolgirls who deluged him with love letters and odes,"[42] and a 1939 feature in *Time* magazine reports that "when Ted Malone comes visiting, the average U.S. woman-of-the-house finds herself as politely helpless as when the gadabout from down the street calls." "To folks thus beguiled," the feature continues: "Ted Malone is Shelley, Prince Charming, Don Juan, Galahad in one. One woman has been wiring him daily and hopefully for six months, seeking a rendezvous. From Missouri, where Ted used to visit in the evening, a once-misunderstood wife confessed to curling up in her nightie in front of the radio, listening to Indian Love Lyrics, being then & there cured forever of the 'coldness' of which her husband had complained. A one-armed girl once sent him a silk hanky with his name embroidered on it with her toes."[43] Even though such reports contain only anecdotal evidence (often planted by Malone himself) that the *Bookends* audience consisted primarily of solitary, needy, and overreacting women, they were believable, despite the hyperbole, in part because such reports played to a larger discourse about mass-cultural audiences wherein, as Andreas Huyssen has explained, "woman . . . is positioned as reader of inferior literature—subjective, emotional and passive— while man . . . emerges as writer of genuine, authentic literature—objective, ironic, and in control of his aesthetic means."[44]

But if coverage of *Bookends* tended to feminize and disparage radio audiences (and thus also radio as a medium), reports about Malone himself and his complicity in this phenomenon are more complicated, in part because he played to the second aspect of Huyssen's analytic—the level of objective, ironic control it was assumed he could exercise. Reporters seemed to have enjoyed outing the physical Malone as an "earnest, balding, fattish young man with a blonde mustache [and] rumpled pants" and not the "glamour boy"[45] or heart throb with "long, flowing, snow white hair as you've probably imagined"[46] (see figure 2.6). Exposing this disconnect no doubt worked to cast even more aspersions on radio as a less-than-credible medium (Malone was a fraud—a relatively harmless fraud, but a fraud nonetheless), but it also had the effect of outing the "tear-drawing" program host as an admirably shrewd, calculating, and even cynical operator knowingly and capably exploiting the advantages that radio had on print. "I never address [the audience] as 'ladies and gentlemen,' or as 'folks'—but always as a single person," he explained to *News-Week* in 1935. "Sometimes I play games with them. Sometimes I make love. For instance, if I blow softly across the microphone, their eardrums will vibrate just as though I'd blown into their ears."[47] Objective, ironic, and entirely in control of his aesthetic means, Malone not only distances himself from the imagined hysteria that powered his success but manages via this performance to get *News-Week* to admire his work. "In proof of his tear-drawing powers," *News-Week* writes, "Malone gets more fan mail than any other unsponsored performer on any network—from 4,000 to 20,000 letters a month. As a businessman, he draws an unsentimental conclusion: Make 'em cry, they're sure to buy."[48]

Most of the time, though, Malone wasn't asking people to buy much more than the services of radio itself. The important part of *News-Week's*

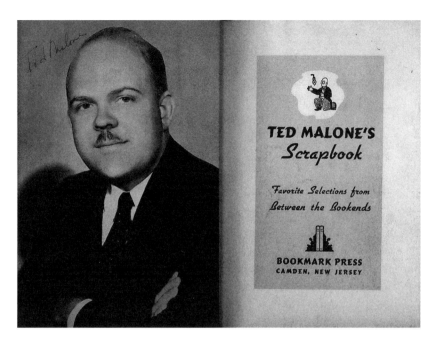

FIGURE 2.6. Autographed frontispiece and title page from *Ted Malone's Scrapbook* (Camden, N.J.: Bookmark Press, 1941).

assessment has less to with his commercial abilities and more with the lack of Malone's sentimentality, which effectively excuses the close company he was keeping with listeners and poetry alike. As with Tony his reasonable, masculine control in the face of hysterical audiences and over a genre he initially feared would tag him as a "sissy" helped purchase the program's feedback loop, which was essential to the show's success but which Malone likely knew would elicit a more diverse set of audience responses than the industry and its press coverage were willing to imagine—or stomach. This diversity was not an inevitable consequence of simply inviting listeners to contribute to *Bookends*, however, but was the product of a wide range of subject positions that he invited listeners to occupy through his appeals to the fireside and other social spaces of the home; listeners could be children, spouses, relatives, friends, neighbors, colleagues, or suitors, and they could therefore find in the invisible Malone a parent, sibling, suitor, beloved, relative, confidante, friend, sympathizer, spouse, and more. Participating in *Bookends*, therefore, meant not just sending poems to Malone but first imagining who he was and thus—as the next part of this chapter will explore in greater depth—thinking about who one was as a listener, and who one wanted to be.

As much as Malone's semantic availability was powered by the scrapbooking and domestic metaphors built into the show, it was cued and made especially possible by a type of poetry often at the center of *Bookends* and common in popular culture more generally—the abstract, non-image-based verse styles like the two poems Malone uses to close his Valentine's Day broadcast. Trucking in words like "hope," "truth," "greed," "happiness," "faith," and "power" (and phrases like "childhood magnitude," "how good a thing is," "the taint of compromise," "sorrows past," "a quiet peace within your heart," and "the faith that faces the blackest sky"), none of which are anchored by the concrete specifics Pound called for when he urged writers to "go in fear of abstractions,"[49] this aesthetic of abstraction may result in bad imagist poetry but nonetheless made and makes for widely applicable and useful poetry; hermeneutically underdetermined, it was easily adapted to a wide range of presentation contexts and, acting as what Marshall McLuhan would call a "cool" or low-definition medium like television or comics rather than a "hot" medium like radio or film, relied on readers to participate by supplying specifics, thus hailing them as collaborators if not coauthors.[50]

Consider, for example, the following poem "It Can Be Done":

Somebody said that it couldn't be done,
    But he with a chuckle replied,
Maybe it couldn't, but he would be one
    That wouldn't say so till he tried.
So he buckled right in with a bit of a grin
    On his face; if he worried he hid it.
He started to sing as he tackled the thing
    That couldn't be done, and he did it.

There are thousands to tell you it cannot be done.
    There are thousands to mock and to rail you.
There are thousands to point out to you one by one
    The dangers that lurk to assail you.
But just buckle right in with a bit of a grin,
    Take off your coat and go to it.
Start in to sing as you tackle the thing
    That cannot be done, and you'll do it.

This is a two-stanza version of Edgar Guest's popular three-stanza poem of the same title, which is currently offered to high school students as a performance option for competing in "Poetry Out Loud," the national recitation contest sponsored by the National Endowment for the Arts and the Poetry Foundation.[51] (Both the NEA and the Poetry Foundation have apparently recognized that the generic message of self-reliance, hard work, and persistence in the face of adversity would be as meaningful to diverse audiences today as it was seventy or eighty years ago.)[52] There are some slight changes in wording from Guest's original, the second stanza has been removed, and—in a move that suggests the spirit of public poetry ownership that I discussed in chapter 1—Guest's name has been completely omitted from the byline, which now reads "McZigas" (possibly the person who sent it to the newspaper that reprinted it). As if taking a cue from how the protagonist hides his worry from onlookers in stanza 1, what we might describe as an otherwise "accessible" poem is nonetheless propelled by a certain obscurity or lack of access, refusing to stipulate what "it" is, who the thousands of detractors are, what dangers "lurk to assail you," and how, exactly, "it" eventually got done (except through the protagonist's force of character). That set of materials is supplied by the reader.

I found this version of Guest's poem in the 160-page, two-thousand-poem scrapbook that opens in part with the poem "Scraps" and that I discuss in chapter 1. "It Can Be Done" appears on page 4 of that album, grouped with twelve other inspirational, motivational verses of Progressive-era uplift, all of which are vague and abstract in the way that "It Can Be Done" is vague and abstract, all of which trade in a similar set of truisms, proverbs, and generalities that make such verse widely applicable and easily cited, and all of which have similarly vague titles like "Keep Moving," "Keep a-Hopin'," "Keep At It," "The Things That Count" and "Be the Best, Whatever You Are" (see figure 2.7). Without using many concrete details—and without following the "show, don't tell" maxim of postwar creative writing programs—these poems mostly celebrate commonplace activities and encourage a positive outlook on life, but for all of that, they don't value the status quo or encourage complacency or self-satisfaction so much as create a discursive field that promotes learning, hope, persistence, and faith in the progressive if incremental nature of change. Anyone who can "Keep Moving" or "Keep At It" is a potential audience for these poems, which provide abstract but not unidentifiable templates or analytics for users to apply to and test against the specific realities of their own lives. This scrapbook page is itself an excellent case in point.

Here the scrapbook maker pastes a single, postage-stamp-sized image captioned "to Washington on business" in the middle of the page, using the black-and-white drawing of a modern woman carrying a briefcase and striding confidently in front of the U.S. Capitol to clearly articulate the surrounding poems' subjects (hope for social change, optimism, persistence, etc.) to a women's rights agenda (see figure 2.8). In this scrapbook "it" might very well have meant women's suffrage.

It is worthwhile rereading this page for the range of meanings made possible or even authored by forces external to the poems themselves. I'm especially intrigued, for example, by how the women's rights content of the "to Washington on business" image inflects Janice Blanchard's poem "Ripples Spread," which is pasted in two parts along the right side of the page's upper right quadrant—

He cast a stone into the lake
    And watched the ripples spread;
The near ones ended at the shore,
    The far went on instead.

He tossed his laughter toward a friend
    Who flashed it back again;
The fragments that the crowd took up
    Were heard by countless men.

—but I need to return to my regularly scheduled programming about Ted Malone, Tony Wons, and their audiences. As I suggested earlier, Malone's semantic openness is a function of his use of the scrapbooking metaphor and his appeal to the social life of domestic spaces, but it is especially made possible by his connection to a style of poetry and a culture of poetry reading that relied on readers to supply contexts and details, if not an entire surround of other texts, in order to make verses meaningful. Ted and Tony knew that as radio's first middlemen, they needed to cultivate an aspect of this in themselves as well, and so they worked—on air, off air, in print, in fan-letter responses, and elsewhere—to make themselves abstract or vague, and therefore as readable by, and useful to, as many people and interests as possible. In a sense they became popular poems in their own right, and it is how they were subsequently interpreted and used by their listeners that I want to turn to next.

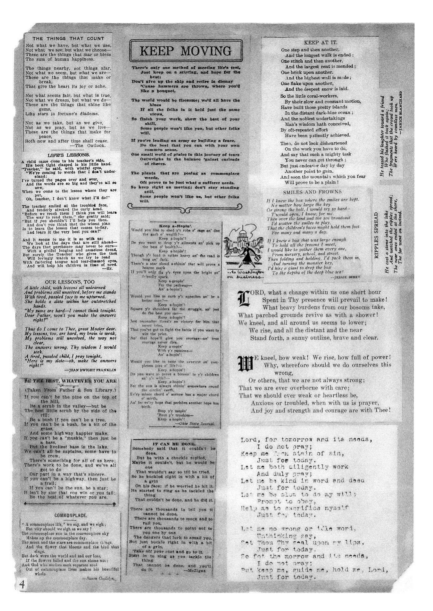

FIGURE 2.7. Page from a two-thousand-page poetry scrapbook featuring inspirational and motivational poems, circa 1930s and 1940s. Author's collection.

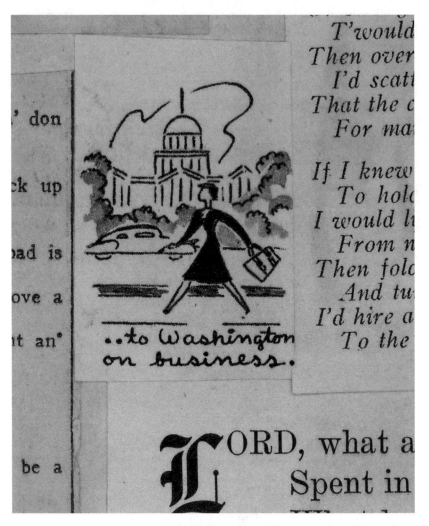

FIGURE 2.8. Detail of image (captioned, "to Washington on business") from scrapbook page pictured in figure 2.7.

If the World Is Mad, That's Just When It Needs Poetry

On November 4, 1935, Afton Clegg, a student at Brigham Young University in Provo, Utah, wrote a four-page letter to Malone requesting a copy of "The Perfect Gift," which Malone had read on air that same day.[53] Here is the beginning of that letter:

Dear Ted Malone,

I liked you so well today—I just had to tell you about it. You were more like yourself. You know, I wrote to you a couple of weeks ago— and asked you to please go home. I missed the little priceless moments of intimacy that seemed to go so well with Kansas City. Of course you didn't receive the letter. I didn't send it. But today, you were so nice— and you read the grandest poems. And you were my old friend again. And all of a sudden I wanted to write to you.

I liked the very first poem you read today. The one about "The Perfect Gift—your Friendship—" I think it's beautiful—and I should like to give it to someone. May I tell you about him? He's my very dearest friend and he's going away to Germany on the 18th of this month. He won't be back for three years. Imagine—three years! It seems like forever. I'm going to miss him terribly—we have such good times together. Last summer we took long walks in the mountains— and talked—we understood each other. He likes poetry and beautiful things. He says poetry isn't only verses and rhymes—it's everywhere— it's all the beauty in the world—beautiful thoughts, beautiful souls. He's right, isn't he.

Mr. Malone, would you please send me a copy of that poem? I must have it for him. His eyes are the color of amber, and are kind and searching. Oh you've no idea what his eyes are like.[54]

Clegg goes on to further describe her friend, how he has promised to keep in touch by sending her German poetry, how hopeless the recent snowfall makes her feel, how she appreciates a poem by Ruth Carroll, and how she hopes that one day Malone might read a poem for her. Then, in her final paragraph, she writes:

I'm enjoying school this year even more than last. I belong to a National Honorary Journalistic Fraternity—Omega Nu. And I'm on the staff of the Y [Brigham Young University] News (college weekly) and co-editor of the Y Literary Magazine. I don't have much time for poems—just now and then. My friend asked me—why didn't I write more poems? And I said, "There's no place for poetry in this mad world." He said, "If the world is mad, that's just when it needs poetry."[55]

For the purposes of framing a consideration of fan responses to *Bookends*, I want to highlight three aspects of Clegg's letter that are common to many of the letters listeners sent to Malone in 1935. First, motivated by the program's simulated immediacy of oral communication, Clegg writes immediately after hearing Malone's broadcast, reciprocating as best she can with the type of real-time response that Ong says electronic media are designed to trigger but ultimately frustrate.[56] She not only responds in terms of what Ong calls "a real existential present"—citing the recent snowfall, her emotional state, her activities at school, and, of course, the impending departure of her friend for Germany—but does so via the "close, empathetic, communal identification"[57] that keeps meaning situational in spoken contexts and thus "close to the human lifeworld."[58] Second, despite admitting that she has little time for poetry in her life, Clegg gives us a partial window onto the real and symbolic values associated with poems as they were exchanged and circulated between people and thus embedded in, and made meaningful by, social relationships of many types. Here she not only credits poetry with the ability to sustain relationships in a world conspiring to break them apart, but she then voices the notion, through her male friend, that poetry offers a critical tool by which to gauge and repair the madness of the world. Unlike the media coverage of *Bookends*, which cast audience enthusiasm for poetry, along with the desire to belong to a community of poetry fans, as unreliable and unreasonably emotional responses, Clegg's friend views poetry as a logical and natural corrective to an otherwise irrational world.

As Clegg's letter also shows, however—and this is the third aspect that I want to highlight from her response—listeners were certainly interested in, but not duped or "beguiled" or rendered "politely helpless" by, Malone's show of intimacy and apparent connection to the value systems poetry represented. As the first paragraph of her letter indicates, Clegg's affection for Malone is conditional upon his faithful or authentic representation of her values, which are not necessarily values she shares with commercial radio. While she appears to have forgiven him for the temporary personality changes she suspects were brought on by his move from Kansas to New York, her expression of discontent, and her rather formal use of Malone's full name in her salutation, suggests she is not only keeping a watchful distance but sending him something of a warning as well; next time he falters, she insinuates, in what seems to be a minor case of blackmail, she really *will* send the letter of disapproval she wrote a couple of weeks earlier. In fact, despite the emotional candor of her writing, which neatly returns Malone's own performance of sincerity, Clegg's request for "The Perfect Gift" sounds a little like a test to see whether Malone will actually participate in the real-life gifting of poems he encourages and facilitates but from which he is nonetheless removed by virtue of the medium as well as his location in a network studio located a continent away.

These three elements—people's desire to communicate with as little mediation as possible in relation to the particulars of their experiences, their belief in the power of poetry to repair human beings and human relationships damaged by modern life, and their enthusiastic but nonetheless guarded and sometimes critical assessment of Malone's motives—are present in many, though certainly not all, of the letters Malone received. Reading such responses in aggregate doesn't just help to correct the skewed portrait of radio audiences disseminated by *Time*, *News-Week*, *Poetry*, and even Malone himself but also reveals how poetry was in fact a vehicle, source, and symbol for beliefs, hopes, values, and other emotional experiences that were neither acknowledged nor particularly accounted for by dominant and impersonal ideological rubrics. That Malone fielded such an outpouring during the worst years of the Great Depression is especially telling. For even though *Bookends* was pitched and even described by audiences as a "soothing" radio experience, correspondent after correspondent wrote of economic hardship, insufficient social services, the need to travel for work, and the separation of parents from children, spouse from spouse, and lover from lover that their hardship entailed; other letters come from, and describe, the physical or emotional living conditions of the old, geographically and socially isolated, sick, mentally ill, and disabled "living on borrowed time" in cramped quarters and institutions. Here are a few examples:

> I'm young yet (or so my friends tell me), but I'm somewhat whipped, Ted. I am out of work, discouraged and often wonder why I even try to carry on at all . . . I've been terribly hurt by the loss of my position but my pride keeps me from expressing myself about myself.[59]

> All summer in the heat there are men to prepare huge meals for and canning and fighting my miserable, painful arthritis . . . I long to be carefree, to take the hands of my three children and romp in the water and along the woodsy roads, forgetful of sweeping and dusting, and washing and ironing and cooking over a stove. I am quite domestic by necessity, but oh, the struggle it costs me thru the years.[60]

We want to get married but can't because I'm unlucky enough to be one of the many unemployed. It doesn't seem to matter how hard I try, everything just seems to go against me. Gee but it is really heartbreaking.[61]

I went to work, doing as best I could with such limited experiences, in a business career, being both, father, Mother, Wife, pal, and companion, it just didn't work out, with a husband who was making a mere sum of eight and ten dollars per week. . . . One day, while I was at work, he left Los Angeles, taking our baby girl of seven years, can you imagine what a living blackness I went though. . . . Night after night, I bury my head in the pillow to stifle sobs.[62]

Because single, isolated examples of audience responses—like *Time*'s account of the one-armed girl who sent Malone a hanky with his name embroidered on it, or the woman who was cured of her frigidity after hearing his show—tend to cast listener reactions as idiosyncratic and perhaps even pathological (at any rate, certainly not cultural), I want to continue accessing listeners' responses in direct relation to each other as I've just done here. By reading them together as a sort of composite narrative about how popular verse enabled Malone's audiences to not merely survive the potentially debilitating psychological and emotional effects of the Depression but actively respond to forces they felt were rationalizing, standardizing, or otherwise damaging their lives, I want to read in a way that Malone and the networks would have *not* wanted me to read but that can, as a result, tell a story about the cultural power of popular poetry that would be largely invisible in just one or two letters.[63]

For many people, as Clegg's letter perhaps suggests, responding to *Bookends* offered a way to rehearse and keep alive the language and ritual displays of emotion required by real-life personal and social relationships but frequently oversimplified in the media and disparaged as "emotional slither" by modernist writers striving for a poetics of impersonality and detachment.[64] Because the language of affect describes subjective experiences that are difficult to calibrate in relation to other people's experiences, it needs—much like the popular verse I discussed earlier—to be vague, semantically capacious, and perhaps even as unoriginal as possible if it is to have any substantial communicative value. Thus semantic taxonomies of affect are complex and rare: grief may

have multiple stages, but they are all ultimately "grief"; love has many mani-
festations, all of which are ultimately "love"; and hope has many referents but
is always "hope." At the same time, this otherwise unspecific semantic quality
makes it difficult to name one's emotions exactly—to "express myself about
myself" exactly, as Glasselle Adams, the first letter writer, puts it in the list of
quotations—so that even as they want to communicate, Malone's correspon-
dents wrestle with the inability of language to describe what they feel; they
are "somewhat whipped," "terribly hurt," "long[ing] to be carefree," and liv-
ing through "terrible blackness." This struggle to name their lived emotions is
part of what makes these passages especially moving and more than cathartic;
in asking Malone to "imagine what a living blackness I went though," the
fourth letter writer realizes that only empathy, not words, can make someone
understand her actual situation. Thus when she writes, "Night after night, I
bury my head in the pillow to stifle sobs," her suffering is in fact partly *pro-
duced* by, as well as registered (in the form of inarticulate sobs) as, a failure of
language to articulate her particular emotional state.

In order for *Bookends* audiences to communicate their emotional lows in
the imprecise language of affect, they resort to real-life examples (like sobbing
into a pillow) that help clarify or put a face to the terms they use; seventy-five
years later we grasp what "somewhat whipped" and "really heartbreaking"
mean not by any quality inherent in the terms themselves but by virtue of
their proximity to the human lifeworld (Adams lost a job, Benson was forced
to labor, Allen couldn't get married, Avera lost her child) that each writer
uses to narrow down the possible semantic field of his or her communica-
tion. During the Depression there was a surplus of such reference points by
which to express the nature of despair, isolation, loneliness, and grief, but this
was not the case with the experience or expression of emotional highs, which
were in short supply in people's daily lives but which *Bookends* nevertheless
appears to have regularly elicited. Correspondent after correspondent writes
about listening to the presentation of poetry on *Bookends* as a transformative,
rapturous, even ecstatic experience, using in the process a language of joy,
hope, love, sympathy, and passion that is remarkable for its rhetorical excess
and that got cartooned in the press as hysterical or unreasonably romantic in
orientation. Consider, in the way of an example, the final two paragraphs of
a typewritten letter that Ruth Carroll—possibly the Ruth Carroll named in
Clegg's letter—sent to Malone from Berkeley, California, on October 13, 1935,
after hearing him read the poem "Eternity":

Today surpassed breathlessness. The madcap thrill, the tumult of rejoic-
ing, the feeling that my heart must break—from happiness—were
merged into a sublime, reverent attitude of waiting, of listening. For
faintly in my soul new untouched dreams were stirring, fragile with
birth. Awakened dreams bring a surge of peace together with their tem-
pestuousness, a feeling soft as snow and as white. And as I listened, a
warm quiet flowed over me, a knowledge that you felt me there.

And my tears were a consecration of a moment of hush from out
eternity, a star-soft moment when one soul looked into the heart of
another and saw itself reflected there.[65]

Instead of agreeing with the media that such responses are the voices of would-
be lovers captivated by Malone's spell, I want to take this type of reaction more
seriously—and not just because Carroll closes her letter (in the final sentence
quoted here) with an embedded reference to the very poem ("Eternity") that
prompted her writing in the first place. Rather, I want to suggest that *Book-
ends* and its poetry offered audiences like Carroll a regular opportunity ("long
about half past") to practice the expression of happiness, joy, hope, love, and
passion that the Depression did not occasion on a regular basis. This rehearsal,
prompted by Malone's own shows of compassion, not only kept the prospects
of positive human experience on the emotional horizon but also helped to sus-
tain or keep in shape a linguistic and emotional skill set foundational for empa-
thetic human relations and capable of moving people to creative and political
action that Afton Clegg's friend believes poetry makes possible.

Carroll's letter, for example, certainly employs a conventional language of
romantic experience ("breathlessness," "the tumult of rejoicing," "the mad-
cap thrill," "my heart must break") but makes clear—both by naming her
emotion and separating it with dashes from the heartbreak and sublimity on
either side of it—that her subject is in fact happiness and not love.[66] Troping
the intensity of feeling most frequently articulated in terms of romantic love
allows Carroll to perform a heightened expression of happiness that not only
becomes a creative process insofar as it brings "new untouched dreams" into
being but that, through her imagined relationship with Malone, models an
act of human empathy as well. By its conclusion the letter transcends the
specific listener-host relationship prompted by *Bookends* by finding a more
universal human "moment when one soul looked into the heart of another
and saw itself reflected there"; this is no longer (if it ever was) a letter about

Malone. In a sense, Carroll's excessive rhetorical display of happiness enables her to write empathetic human relations *into* existence.[67]

This language of emotional awakening or rebirth is not unique to Carroll, or to women correspondents. T. E. Kalas of Oakland, California, writes to *Bookends* identifying himself as "a man, a strong man" who has "been called 'hard' and 'cold' by people" and who has seen "some very strange and very horrible things" in the world.[68] Nevertheless, and acknowledging in the way of a disclaimer that his experience might "sound like a lot of 'rot' to you," Kalas describes how he heard a poem on Malone's show and "actually felt 'wet inside.'" "Now that is something," he remarks of the tears that then came to his eyes, "that has not happened since I was a little boy. And believe me there were lots of times since when a tear or two would not have been out of place." Similarly, author and bodybuilder Earl E. Liederman, "America's Leading Director of Physical Education" and one-time mentor to Charles Atlas, writes on professional letterhead (which features a bare-chested, crew-cut Liederman showing off his sculpted pecs and six-pack) to say that "the soulfulness and pathos" of the poem "Little Boy" "created a lasting impression."[69] For Kalas and Liederman the activity of listening to *Bookends*, and then of writing about that experience, serves to expand or facilitate, rather than shut down or limit, the range of emotional subject positions they feel capable of occupying or expressing in their lives as American men.

There are many more examples, but, for the sake of the larger argument, I want to illustrate how audiences not only used *Bookends* as a simulated environment for the practice of emotional expression and empathetic display but then used the poems they heard to broker, conduct, formalize, and articulate emotional and social connections in real life as well. As Clegg's letter to Malone indicates, the exchange of poems from one person to another was, and still is, both a communicative and symbolic act of affiliation and emotional involvement that created and sustained relationships. This is sometimes evident in personal poetry collections—like the "to Washington on business" scrapbook—that rarely preserve and record the standard bibliographic information (publication name, date, and copyright notice) anchoring poems in commercial communication networks, but instead employ alternative bibliographic systems that record this information in terms of specific poems' origins in noncommercial social networks. The scrapbook maker I refer to, for example, uses handwritten annotations —"Esther sent me this 1946" (on "Life's Afternoon," by Margaret A. Shea); "From Mrs. Alma Carlson

Garfield, Kan 1935" (on "Lean Hard," author unknown); "I mailed copy to Anna Underwood 1938" (on "The Personal Touch," by Zella Pauline Patterson); and "Sent from Santa Cruz by Esther July 1948" (on "Grandmother's Quilt Speaks," by Rhea Sheldon)—to distinguish poems of social adhesion from the nearly two thousand other verses she collects.

By airing audience contributions and anonymously dedicating poems to individual listeners ("for someone well along in years," for example), Malone positioned *Bookends* as a key relay point in this exchange economy. His audiences, therefore, wrote not just to contribute and hear him read their long-distance dedications but to also request copies that, like Clegg, they then used to facilitate their real-life relationships. On November 15, 1935, for example, Mrs. Francis Golemon wrote from Bayou La Batre, Alabama:

> In your collection of poems what have you that I may get a copy of a poem for a lady Principle [*sic*] of a school. I want a poem some thing real good. I have been appointed one room mother from the Teacher of my little girls room. And I am to present a token to the Principle. . . . She has been there as Principle for 20 years. This is the first time I have ever taken part in any thing, so I want to make a good start. Do you have any poems written by J. Edward Jones, the board [*sic*] of the Kuskokwin Anchorage, Alaska? I'll exchange one or two with you. I used to write him several years ago after I married lost track of him.[70]

Charged with presenting an unspecified "token" to the principal, Goleman decides on, and then emphasizes that she wants, a poem (and not, say, a plaque, a book, or a gift certificate), because poems build and confirm emotional and social connective tissues in ways other tokens do not. For Golemon, who has "[n]ever taken part in any thing," this connectivity seems especially important, as her token selection not only promises to confirm the legitimacy of her appointment as room mother—something that, given her spelling and grammar, might have been simultaneously empowering and anxiety producing for her—but to also embed her in a social and institutional network of women (the "lady Principle," probably the teacher, other room mothers, and her little girl) at school, home, and, given the town's small size, probably the larger community.

What is especially noteworthy about Golemon's letter to *Bookends*, however, is that despite her anxieties about the social relationships she feels are hinging on her selection, she shows little hesitation about approaching Malone or about how to traffic in poems. Hardly beguiled, and certainly not rendered politely helpless, she establishes herself as an equal partner in trade by proposing the terms (two of Jones's poems for one of Malone's) of a fair exchange which is mutually beneficial and in which neither party is subordinate or left owing the other. Moreover, her letter suggests that a poem's value in this exchange economy has less to do with the quantity or quality of verse changing hands than with the social relations that come attached to or even embedded within it. When Golemon introduces her pen-pal relationship with Jones, it is not to increase her own legitimacy as a trading partner, but to establish and certify the value of her goods via their provenance. In such a trade Golemon doesn't just seek a suitable poem to present to her principal, but, since that poem was acquired from *Book-ends*, she seeks to offer the principal a place in a social network two degrees removed from Ted Malone as well—a "token" that would have undoubt-edly increased Golemon's prestige as that social network's capable and con-nected administrator. In return Malone is promised a poetic good of mea-surably equal value; he doesn't just get a poem written by Jones, which he might have found simply by reading a newspaper or magazine, but he also gets placed in a new social network two degrees removed from "the board of the Kuskokwin."

Poems were thus not without value. They could be traded, gifted, bestowed, and converted to and from various forms of capital—although, as the exchanges presented here suggest, such transactions rarely operated according to the logic of the commodity, which gets measured in terms of qualities thought to be inherent to it (i.e., what the New Critics called the "poem itself"), which converts to cash currency, and which is thus separated from the human lifeworld of social relations.[71] This isn't to say, however, that poems weren't fetishized. On the contrary, because of the emotional lives, empathetic relations, and social ties they represented and secured, poems became especially charged sites of value that had more in common with the fetish logic of precapitalist societies in which value, Michael Taussig writes, "arises from the sense of organic unity between persons and their products" and not "from the split between persons and the thing that they produce and exchange."[72] On October 14, 1935, for example, Miriam Garrison of Attica, Kansas, sent *Bookends* a set of poems that she hoped Malone would read on air. "For several years," she writes:

I've collected these poems, and have lived them in my imagination until they have become so real that I feel almost reverent on hearing them or reading them. My poem notebook is my hobby and my most treasured literary possession. . . . I wonder if I might enclose another favorite poem—also by Helen Welshimer. It has been my favorite since one rainy night when I was away at college. I couldn't sleep so I turned on the light and read it through till it became fixed in my mind and I have spoken it to the moon and stars many times since.[73]

In describing a collegiate scene of reading that almost eerily recalls Whitman's "When I Heard the Learn'd Astronomer,"[74] Garrison's letter illustrates the organic unity between people and things that Taussig describes—Welshimer's poem is fetishized by virtue of its connection to the specifics of Garrison's lived experience (college, her sleeplessness, the weather) and thus, unlike the commodity, loses its ability to signify independently. The letter suggests how a poem's value changes in relation to this unity as well; Garrison confirms and even increases the value of Welshimer's poem with every recital, so that its value goes up the more frequently it is used. In fact, if it sounds from this letter like poems depend on users for their existence, Garrison might agree; as she explains in the opening of her passage, it is her imagination, and not some objective measure or quality, that brings them into being and makes them "real."

Even though poems sent to and from *Bookends* were routinely invested with value through their connection to the human lifeworld, they hardly circulated in a single exchange economy. Rather, as the correspondence from Golemon, Garrison, and Clegg suggests, they were swapped (Golemon to Malone), given (Clegg to her friend), extorted (Clegg of Malone), shared (Garrison with Malone), and presented (Golemon to her principal) as real, emotional, or symbolic capital in barter, prestige, token, gift, and other such economies where the logic of the commodity was insufficient much less paramount. All of these economies are worth further examination in the context of radio and especially within the culture of popular poetry more generally, but, given the set of responses elicited by *Bookends* and now in the Arthur B. Church Papers, I want to extend particular attention to the gift economies that Malone (perhaps unknowingly) tapped into and that, ultimately, proved to be a cause of suspicion if not a site of conflict for his audiences. It is not surprising—given the unsponsored nature of the show, the displays of affect it stimulated, its "free" publication of listener contributions, and people's desire to locate a logic by which to reorganize and sustain relationships damaged by the Depression's economic failure—that listeners would frequently find the logic and language of gifting suitable for understanding *Bookends*; the show offered the possibility of, if not promised, what Lewis Hyde has described as a gift economy's "equilibrium and coherence, a kind of anarchist stability"[75] that anyone could participate in and that seemed a partial remedy for unstable economic times if not for a culture in which, as William J. Hodges wrote from Tampa, Florida, "we are in such a hurry to get our particular job done . . . that we don't often have time to stop and look for the beauties of this world about us."[76] Nor is it surprising—given what Hyde and others have observed about the complex structures of gift economies— that the various obligations, manifestations, and assumptions of differing gift logics would be impossible for Malone to recognize and respond to in kind.[77] Thus, as a result of encouraging and appealing to varying gift economy logics, but then failing to live up to or honor them each from within the nationalizing and homogenizing framework of network radio, Malone sometimes found himself in breach of his promise and subject to listener feedback that was not only skeptical of his motives but then sought to correct or discipline his behavior. That is, the very enthusiasm for the type of human exchange he was promoting as part of the recipe for *Bookends*' success came back as a legitimate critique that he was not actually promoting that type of exchange.

As Hyde, Marcel Mauss, and others have observed, not all gift economies are alike, and the differences between them—which not only keep them living but also difficult for capitalism to incorporate—were undoubtedly hard for Malone (and his secretarial staff) to ascertain much less respond to on the basis of individual letters. Consider Lucille D. Angell of Oneida, New York, who sent the following request to *Bookends*. "I would appreciate your telling me of some books of poems," she writes. "Not the old poets, seems as I have all of them. I have 1500 of Edgar Guest's poems and several other Scrap Books. My mother thinks it's an awful hobby but I send them to friends and copy several for 'Shut Ins' there's not a day that passes but that I try to do something for someone."[78] Understanding that the gift, as Hyde writes, "move[s] from plenty to emptiness," Angell appeals to Malone, who no doubt has more poems than she;[79] by writing she invites him to participate in a gift economy that not only reallocates poetic wealth but that, in so doing, helps stitch together the fabric of a community likely torn by the logic of the commodity. As she assumes the same role in her community that Malone occupies on air—that of middleman facilitating the circulation of poems—Angell is right to approach Malone as a kindred spirit, and the set of obligations structuring her request is fairly clear: in being called out Malone is obliged to contribute, lest he break the gift economy's contract by keeping all the poems for himself, and in accepting his gift Angell is obliged to make sure that it keeps circulating—proof of which ability she provides in her letter, not just by citing her daily commitment to do something for someone, but also by explaining how she continues to do so in spite of her mother's disapproval.

Now compare the logic of Angell's gift economy to that evinced by Helen Glass's angry November 12, 1935, letter to Malone, which I quote in chapter 1:

> I sent you in August some poems of mine taken from my Scrap Book of years standing and found out later my grievous error in not sending you copies—I have felt so disillusioned about the sincerity behind your readings that I simply haven't any desire to listen in any more. . . . You finally sent me a copy of "If I cry Release." Why couldn't you have sent in the original which I sent you that I might replace it in my scrapbook? This mimeographed thing marked copy would have certainly sufficed for your collection. Every one of mine has a meaning for me. . . . You know, Mr. Malone, you didn't sound like some one who would so utterly and completely let a person down. Please give this your very personal attention—and send me back my original verses.[80]

Unlike Angell's letter, this is not an invitation to enter into a gift economy but a response to a specific breach of its rules. But while the communication happens at a different point in the gift exchange process and thus has a different tone, it also presupposes an entirely different gift economy logic. Unlike Angell's, which requires that a gift circulate from plenty to scarcity, Glass's logic recalls some Native American gift economies requiring that a gift, when accepted, must then be given back to the giver (a source of frustration for the English, who called such behavior "Indian giving"). In failing to understand his obligation to reciprocate in this manner, Malone commits a number of other missteps: he fails to respond in an appropriate amount of time; he misapprehends the value of the original poem and substitutes Sarah-Elizabeth Rodger's "If I Cry Release," which has no meaning for Glass; and he sends a mimeograph instead of an original clipping. Four times betrayed, Glass is probably even more infuriated by having to articulate for Malone the very assumptions he led her to believe he understood.

When Miss Emaline Knoop sent a poem to *Bookends* from Dayton, Kentucky, on December 29, 1935, she wrote, "I treasure this little paper as one of my priceless possessions. You being 'My Friend,' I gladly trust it in your care for a few days."[81] Like Garrison, she states the value of her clipping—one that, in its pricelessness, can't be converted to cash and thus made into a commodity—but, unlike Glass, Knoop takes care to craft a little contract that lays out the conditions of her contribution: her gift is both the loan of a poem to Malone and her placement of trust in him; the poem must be promptly returned; and their friendship is contingent upon full acceptance and fulfillment of these terms. Knoop wasn't the only listener encouraged by Malone's performance but made suspicious enough of his motives to take pains to either protect herself or her poems and to make explicit the nature of her engagement with *Bookends*—a rhetoric, I think, that not only suggests how *un*beguiled audiences were by Malone, but that we might read as an attempt, sometimes disguised as positive reinforcement, to discipline Malone lest he treat poems and readers with the disrespect of radio's commercial logic. Vivian Barritt of Los Angeles thus spells out the nature of her exchange, emphasizing that Malone is obligated to keep poems moving, as Angell does, and providing a copy of a favorite poem (not the original as Glass did): "I'm enclosing a stamped envelope for the copies of the two poems you read today and said we might have," Barritt explains. "In return for this kindness, I am sending you a copy of a favorite poem of mine . . . and pass them along to others who may enjoy them."[82] Myrtle Braaten, an aspiring writer of nineteen from Cathlamet, Washington, echoes this statement of reciprocity. "It seems only fair," she writes, "that I, too, should share something with you, so I'm including copies of a few poems found between my book-ends."[83] In reminding him of his obligations to people, poetry, and the values poetry represented and expressed in its circulation, such responses made Malone accountable to the public and not just to network management—a dynamic that not only kept *Bookends* operating in partial service of a human lifeworld, but that also suggests what poetry and its readers could do in a world gone mad.

Postscript: Breaking News

As far as I can determine, Malone's 1940 Valentine project collected more than a thousand books and pamphlets plus tens—possibly hundreds—of thousands of original poems submitted by *Bookends* audiences around the country. That was in addition to the "twenty-six big cases" of verse Malone claimed to have packaged up and sent to William Jewell College a year earlier. For years, however, most of this collection—along with a thousand unidentified reel-to-reel recordings and fourteen bankers' boxes of radio scripts that Malone would later add—remained virtually untouched and unopened, stored in the archives of William Jewell's Curry Library, which didn't have the research or support staff, the external scholarly demand, or even (more recently) the playback technology to make it more accessible.

In December 2010 the bulk of this collection was transferred to the University of Missouri's Miller Nichols Library twenty miles away in Kansas City, the city where, in 1929, *Bookends* debuted on KMBC. UM-KC's Labudde Special Collections has started what will be a long intake process; a student worker has been assigned the sole task of cataloging and counting the manuscripts of original poetry, which arrived packed in six large crates, each about half the size (I was told) of a standard office desk. This material and its history—let alone the poems, letters, and programming records of other poetry radio shows from the time—is in many ways representative of the treatment popular poetry has received at the hands of literary critics and historians more broadly. As a result, less than seventy-five years after his 1940 broadcast, we are no more able to answer Malone's basic questions than he was. What *did* most people in America write about? If the question gives you pause, then consider that UM-KC's Special Collections has only six of the twenty-six crates that Malone said were delivered. Who knows where the other twenty eventually ended up?

CHAPTER 3

The Business of Rhyming

And it was there I first saw the shaving advertisements that delighted me one little piece on one board and then further on two more words and then further on two more words a whole lively poem. I wish I could remember more of them, they were all lively and pleasing. . . . I wish I could remember them I liked them so much.
—Gertrude Stein, *Everybody's Autobiography*

The "theme" of the *New York Times* crossword puzzle on Wednesday, April 30, 2003, begins with the clue for 17 across: "Start of a roadside verse." That clue and four others—23, 38, 47, and 58 across—link to produce a rhyming answer that staggers through the crossword's grid not unlike the way the Burma-Shave billboards being quoted from were staggered in sets of six along U.S. highways for nearly forty years in the mid-twentieth century, before regulations limiting "visual pollution" helped bring the shaving oeuvre to an end: "THIRTY DAYS / HATH SEPTEMBER / APRIL JUNE AND THE / SPEED OFFENDER / BURMA SHAVE."[1] While the crossword is not exactly what William Zinsser had in mind in 1964 when he claimed that the poems in the then recently discontinued advertising campaign had become part of "the national vocabulary," it is nonetheless a compelling piece of evidence on his behalf. "No sign on the driver's horizon gave more pleasure of anticipation," Zinsser eulogized in the *Saturday Evening Post*. "Roads are no longer for browsing."[2]

From 1926 to 1963, however, roads were for browsing, as the Minnesota-based Burma-Vita Company erected poem after poem along preinterstate highways to promote its brushless, nonaerated shaving cream, Burma-Shave.[3]

In this campaign six billboards were sequenced one hundred feet apart on the roadside with each sign containing part of a single jingle, a rhyme always ending with the product's scripted logo, "Burma-Shave." Humorous, folksy, pun-filled, and usually related to shaving or highway safety, these signs can be powerful sources of nostalgia for Americans of a certain age, as Gertrude Stein suggests in this chapter's epigraph; indeed, after the Philip Morris Companies purchased family-owned Burma-Vita in 1963, a set of billboards was presented to the Smithsonian Institution (see figure 3.1). "Burma-Shave," wrote Robert Dunphy in the *New York Times* in 1970, "made its poetry a pop-art before pop-art was ever heard of."[4] California's *Ventura County Star* claimed in 1997 that "before rap there was Burma-Shave."[5] At the height of the campaign over seven thousand sets of signs using six hundred individual poems were maintained in forty-four states and were seen by untold numbers of drivers; a 1933 *Burma-Shavings* newsletter, sent to farmers whose land the company was renting, boasted, "Over 5,000,000 men read Burma-Shave signs every day in 38 states."[6] It is possible that through the 1920s, the Depression, World War II, and the 1950s, the Burma-Shave poems were the most public, widely read verse in America.

This possibility in itself merits further scrutiny by literary and cultural critics, but the nature of the campaign's ubiquity and longevity will remain secondary, though insistent, topics throughout this chapter, because I want to focus more specifically on what the Burma-Shave poems can reveal about the commodification and for-profit use of poetry in modern America. As much of the material I am presenting in this book suggests, a large amount of popular poetry was explicitly commercial in orientation if not origination, as it was issued on or with a wide variety of consumer and promotional goods ranging across media and products as different as playing cards, postcards, wall hangings, candy boxes, souvenir handkerchiefs, radio shows, decorative plates, trivets, milk bottles, pads of paper, thermometers, small town newspapers, and mass periodicals.[7] Contrary to the prevailing image of the starving, penniless poet slaving away at his or her dying art, some people actually made a more-than-fine living by participating full or part time in the monetized poetry business. Anne Campbell, for example, reportedly earned $10,000 per year off of the poems she wrote for the *Detroit News* (the equivalent of $150,000 today when adjusted for inflation);[8] Edgar Guest, Campbell's better-known crosstown equivalent at the *Detroit Free Press,* possibly made five or even ten times that amount, given the popularity of his books, the radio

FIGURE 3.1. Cover, *The Burma-Shave Signs—A National Institution*, 1938. Author's collection. Burma-Shave ® is a registered trademark of Eveready Battery Company Inc.

shows he anchored, the advertising verse he wrote, and the speaking engagements he accepted. In 1932 *Time* reported that radio poetry broadcaster Tony Wons made an estimated $2,000 per week from his on-air work plus sales of his annual anthology, *Tony's Scrap Book*—an astounding $1.5 million per year when adjusted for inflation.[9] In the 1950s *Ladies' Home Journal* paid $10 per line of poetry, enough that Richard Eberhart was able to pay his entire summer rent when his single forty-six-line poem "The Clam Diggers and Diggers of Sea Worms" was accepted for *LHJ* publication in 1957.[10] And, as Terry Ryan's memoir, *The Prize Winner of Defiance, Ohio: How My Mother Raised 10 Kids on 25 Words or Less* demonstrates, poem- and jingle-writing contests supplemented the incomes of many more, less professionalized writers across the country, as their verse helped to create markets for consumer goods and profits for corporate stakeholders. W. H. Auden was wrong when, in "In Memory of W. B. Yeats," he claimed that "executives / would never want to tamper" with poetry;[11] as the character of Don Draper, creative director at the 1960s Madison Avenue advertising firm of Sterling Cooper on AMC's acclaimed television series *Mad Men* suggests, executives tampered with poetry all the time.[12]

Nowhere is this tampering with poetry more on display than in the history of American advertising, which presents us with the most sustained, overtly commercial use of verse that U.S. culture has produced—what Adorno might have described as the epitome of language "in enforced service . . . of economically organized purposes and goals."[13] In an epithet most fitting for the subject of this chapter, Marjorie Perloff calls this instrumental use of language by consumer capitalist culture "billboard discourse," which is fundamentally opposed, in her calculus, by poetry, or what she characterizes as "that discourse that defers reading."[14] Putting aside for a moment the claim implicit in this binary—that billboard discourse does not defer reading (for it does, as I will demonstrate shortly)—the distinction that Perloff and Adorno make between advertising verse and literary poetry is representative of an anticommercialist discourse in modern poetry and modern poetry criticism that often singles out the poetry of advertising for special critique. Advertising poetry saturated American and British print culture in the nineteenth and early twentieth centuries when it was used to promote nearly every product through trade cards, business cards, posters, streetcar placards, a wide range of promotional giveaways and premiums, postcards, broadsides, newspapers, magazines, pamphlets, booklets, and almanacs. Hart Crane, Charlotte Perkins Gilman, Bret Harte, Elbert Hubbard, and Marianne Moore were connected to the industry at various points in their careers.[15] Long poem sequences advertised shoes, mock epics were written to sell soap, and elaborately illustrated booklets with narrative poems dramatized the purported merits of patent medicines and life insurance. Some of these ads reprinted or appropriated part or all of well-known poems by prominent authors. Other ads featured poetic parodies; Longfellow ("Excelsior"), Poe ("The Raven"), and John Greenleaf Whittier ("Maud Muller") were especially frequent targets. This verse, as well as the incomes it was capable of producing, comprised such a large portion of the literary and commercial landscape around the turn of the century that Ezra Pound sought to define modern poetry in opposition to it, instructing poets in his 1913 *Poetry* tract "A Few Don'ts By an Imagiste" to "consider the way of the scientists rather than the way of an advertising agent for a new soap."[16]

In singling out soap advertising for special notice, Pound wasn't being facetious, as all the major players in the late nineteenth-century's "soap wars" used poems of various lengths, forms, and degrees of literary sophistication in their nationwide ad campaigns.[17] However, not all modernist writers would dismiss what Sinclair Lewis in *Arrowsmith* called "the first of the poetic Compelling Ads."[18] In fact, some came to see in the inventive wordplay, design, and condensed messages of U.S. advertising a particularly American and modern literary form. In 1922, for example—and perhaps alluding to Ivory's famous claim that its soap was "99.44% pure"—Matthew Josephson unironically wrote in the avant-garde publication *Broom: An International Magazine of the Arts* that "the most striking conclusion drawn from a study of specimen advertisements is that the American business man, in the short daily time at his disposal, reads the most daring and ingenuous literature of his age . . . in all cases far more arresting and provocative than 99 per cent of the stuff that passes for poetry in our specialized magazines."[19] Indeed, a growing body of recent scholarship examining the relation between literary writing and advertising suggests how canonical American and British authors—including Pound—were intrigued with the possibilities for artistic expression offered by the marketplace.[20]

Despite this scholarship and the considerable attention paid to advertising in other disciplines, literary critics have been slow to examine the vast amounts of poetry written for advertising and other commercialized purposes.[21] Usually, as is evident in Perloff's dyad, "billboard discourse" is assumed to be a monolithic category of writing that, regardless of style or medium, has been irrevocably corrupted by the ideology of the capitalist marketplace and that, as such, offers little to interest the scholar invested in cultural critique—the critic working in the tradition of the historical avant-garde or the southern agrarian Fugitives, both of which sought to simultaneously protect poetry and promote its potential as a site for oppositional discourse by positioning it on the margins of the consumer economy. So central has this oppositional stance become to the business of rhyming that Jerome McGann has even proposed a direct relationship between it and aesthetic quality. "Much of the best recent American poetry," he writes, "gains its strength by having disconnected itself from highly capitalized means and modes of production."[22]

Sometimes, however, as I have been suggesting throughout this book, commercially oriented poetries, and the culture of popular poetry of which they are more generally a part, are more complex than these critical traditions would have us think, and I want to use the history of the Burma-Vita Company and its advertising poems as a case study to expand those critical approaches in two major ways. First, I want to show that, in at least one significant instance, the distinction many people make between "billboard discourse" and high-art poetry (the "discourse that defers reading") is not a practical one, as the Burma-Shave poems not only cultivated a poetics that foregrounded the materiality of poetic language and in doing so deferred reading but, also, like many of the new poetries of twentieth-century America, experimented with the effects of new technologies on reading practices while self-consciously engaging discourses of modernity. That is, the popularity and market effectiveness of Burma-Shave's sales pitch depended in large part on, and succeeded in popular culture because of, the innovative thickness or ambiguity of its language rather than the transparency that we might otherwise be tempted to attribute to commercial discourses. This is the innovative spirit of advertising that attracted writers like Josephson, Stein, and no doubt others (like William Carlos Williams) whose poems are full of billboards, signs, and other aspects of early American road culture. As a comic strip by Randall Munroe playing on the similarities between Burma-Shave and Twitter communications humorously suggests, it is also a spirit that is contiguous, if not continuous, with more recent transformations in media and social network technologies that present "new" forms of expression even as they anchor users in a history and architecture of brand names and marketplace logic (see figure 3.2).

While the formal aspect of the Burma-Shave campaign suggests how easily linguistic innovation and literary techniques can be pressured into serving the marketplace, the campaign's reception history illustrates how ordinary readers do not always consume commercial poetries as passively or predictably as one might think. Indeed, motorists responded with such enthusiasm to the poetry—and to the company's invitation to participate in the campaign through jingle-writing contests—that they increasingly ignored Burma Vita's signature product in favor of the pleasure, humor, and creative forces of reading and writing poetry. In the late 1950s and early 1960s, in fact, members of Burma-Vita's board of directors accused the rhymes of contributing to the company's declining market share, arguing that Burma-Vita should limit its use of jingles and begin "using prose . . . as simple, direct selling copy" to get sales back on track.[23] These responses not only caution against our characterizing for-profit or commercially used verse as inevitably corrupted or owned by the marketplace but also suggest that readers of popular verse forms are not as easily manipulated or constrained by the culture industries as some people assume. For while Burma-Vita's campaign proved financially successful for a time, helping the company turn a profit throughout the Great Depression, its history shows how poetry created even in the most commercial

FIGURE 3.2. *Twitter* comic strip by Randall Munroe, 2008. Used with permission of the author.

of contexts might come to resist the commodification feared by many canonical writers and critics in the twentieth century.

The Faces of Modernity

Burma-Shave's jingles were unconventional by the prose- and image-heavy advertising standards of the 1920s and 1930s, but they were otherwise fully part of their age—a literary form made possible by a newly mobile American public, the new system of highways on which that public's mobility depended, and the establishment of outdoor advertising as a legitimate (i.e., self-regulating) industry in the United States. The Outdoor Advertising Association of America formed in 1925, one year before the first Burma-Shave signs appeared and midway through the decade that James Fraser calls the "golden age of billboards."[24] A feeling of modernity was in the air—on radio airwaves, in the skies, and in the heights of the first skyscrapers, as well as on and along the new highways—and Burma-Vita viewed itself, its billboards, and its new shaving technologies as participating in the project of its time. "Shaving with Burma-Shave is the Modern Way of Shaving," the company's *Advertising Copy Manual for "Burma-Shave" Road Signs* reads. "Shaving soap and brush belong to the age of the shaving mug, the moustache cup, the ox-team and the beaver hat. Burma-Shave is representative of the age which has produced the safety razor, the airplane, and the radio."[25] Indeed, insofar as it sought to distance itself from shaving soap—a version of the product that Pound singled out in "A Few Don'ts"—Burma-Vita might even be said to have been pursuing a Poundian rhetoric into the mid-twentieth century.

If the Burma-Shave campaign was enabled by specific historical factors, its disappearance is equally historical. By the 1950s men's beards were growing as fast as ever, but while Burma-Vita was managing (for the moment) to keep up with newer shaving technologies like aerated shaving cream and electric razors, it was struggling to meet the challenges of a new medium, television, which was drastically affecting the face of advertising, if not the face of the American man.[26] Company president Allan Odell's *Annual Message* from 1953 mentions the "saturated program of 10-second announcements on TV in Chicago" designed to plug the new "Burma-Shave Bomb," but the company was never able, here or elsewhere, to translate its well-known poems to this (non-inner) tube. The problem was not Burma-Vita's lack of mastery of the medium; in a last-ditch effort to reclaim its market share in the 1960s, the company hired a professional agency to develop television spots, but those failed, too.[27] The experience of reading Burma-Shave poetry—a site-specific temporal, material, and technological experience—just didn't cross over to TV.[28]

In the intervening years, though, what is commonly called America's love affair with the road helped sustain conditions that were right for Burma-Vita's poems. Even so, the campaign's success was more accident than cool calculation. In 1926 the company founder, Clinton M. Odell, resisted his son Allan's idea of using billboards, but in an effort to salvage what was then a failing company, he gave Allan two hundred dollars to experiment with. The signs, which did not start rhyming until 1929, worked better than either could have imagined, capturing motorists' attention so well that Burma-Vita almost immediately began turning a profit and continued doing so during the Depression. Although the company would eventually manufacture other products (including Burma-Shave Spicy After Shave Lotion, Burma-Vita Tooth Powder, B-V Mosquito Cream, razors, and razor blades), which were marketed on the radio and in newspapers, store windows, magazines, ball-parks, and buses, its shaving cream and jingles, like

MUG AND BRUSH
OLD ADAM
HAD 'EM
IS YOUR HUSBAND
LIKE ADAM, MADAM?
BURMA-SHAVE [29]

remained the focus of the company's and the country's attention, even during World War II when tire, gas, and automobile rationing made maintaining signs difficult. In the 1930s and 1940s the poems were described (sometimes tongue in cheek) as "most interesting and unusual," "ubiquitous, whimsical," "deathless," and "roadside Browning," and their initiator, Allan Odell, was dubbed the "Connoisseur of Corn."[30]

In 1930, however, Allan Odell's poetic imagination was beginning to flag, and Burma-Vita began to look for other sources of wit and rhyme. At first, *Life* reported in 1947, "Odell tried to hire big-name poets but found they wanted too much."[31] So, in keeping with his do-it-yourself ethic, Odell started a jingle-writing contest. Offering one hundred dollars for every submission the company chose, the contest proved wildly popular, sometimes fielding fifty thousand entries in a year and meeting the company's copy needs until the 1960s; some people sent in upwards of five hundred jingles in a single package. Not only did Burma-Vita's board of directors affirm the "contin-ued importance [of the contest] to the general welfare of the Company" in 1951, but the popular press responded as well, fascinated by the anonymity of the "shaving cream poets," "those sweet singers of the open road,"[32] and by Odell's claim that he possessed the longest list of jingle writers in America (reportedly over seven hundred names). Odell published a list of winners annually, but by keeping the credit for specific signs secret, he fueled pub-lic speculation about who in fact authored the verses. *Pageant*, for example, tantalizingly claimed that "some well-known poets have paid the rent with Burma-Shave checks," while *Life* accused the contest of letting "loose upon America a torrent of doggerel from the pent-up ambitions of every under-cover poet in the country."[33]

The considerable media commentary the jingle writing elicited suggests that while *Life* might blame the contests for loosening the ambitions of under-cover poets, those same contests outed undercover literary critics, too. And, indeed, just as Burma-Shave imagined itself as the face of modern America, so we can read this critical discourse—one especially concerned with defin-ing, crossing, or policing the lines between high- and lowbrow poetry—as increasingly modern as well. Joan Shelley Rubin characterizes American read-ers from the late nineteenth and early twentieth centuries as "repositories of both the high *and* the popular—aware of, but not constrained by, a shifting boundary between them" (emphasis added).[34] For Mark W. Van Wienen, this shifting boundary in World War I–era classrooms had a "a democratizing effect on the writing of poetry," so that "just about anyone might consider himself or herself fit to read poetry and even called upon to write it."[35] For these audiences the thrill the *Pageant* writer experienced at the thought of well-known or literary poets secretly writing for-profit Burma-Shave verse, as well as the shrillness of *Life*'s pronouncement upon the culturally threatening "doggerel" writers in America, would have made less sense than it did for readers nearing the mid-twentieth century.[36]

The discourse of taste, discrimination, erudition, artifice, and individual artistry presupposed by the comments in *Pageant* and *Life* was produced by what Joseph Harrington calls the "poetry wars" of the late 1920s and the 1930s, the decades when the modernist aesthetic project went public, leap-ing from little magazines to the mainstream press.[37] In the process the dis-cursive category of poetry split into two mutually exclusive halves: serious, academic, and intellectual highbrow poetry endorsed by the moderns, and sentimental, inspirational, popular, and lowbrow poetry of ordinary readers. By 1934, Harrington writes, the resulting "row between popular and elite lit-erary cultures had become an established institution in its own right" and had so much cultural currency that Frank Capra relied on it to write the character of Longfellow Deeds, the small-town poet and hero of Capra's 1936 film, *Mr. Deeds Goes to Town*.[38] When *Printers' Ink* in 1932 felt moved to assess the generic Burma-Shave lyric as "*usually* a jingle that would irritate a highbrow poet beyond measure" (emphasis added),[39] it was registering the increasing pitch of this conversation in U.S. culture. Fifteen years later, in 1947, *Life* would be able to dismiss the entirety of Burma-Shave's jingles as "doggerel," suggesting the extent to which the modernist agenda had by then permeated

mainstream America. But in 1932, in the midst of the poetry wars, *Printers'
Ink* could not be so bold.

By the early 1930s this conversation was writing Burma-Vita from the
inside as well. Founded and operating on the tradition of popular, brow-
crossing reading practices that Rubin and Van Wienen describe, the company
was nevertheless concerned by how to best—and most profitably, no doubt—
imagine and represent its writers, contest, and signature ad campaign. In the
second issue of *Burma-Shavings* (1929), for example, the company unequivo-
cally presented a jingle written by "our poet," and in April 1930 Clinton Odell
wrote to *Burma-Shavings*'s primarily rural audience, "I have no doubt that
among our 3,000 lessors there are many who have real talent in the writing of
verse."[40] Two months later, though, *Burma-Shavings* was careful to distinguish
"among the poets (amateur and professional) of the U.S.A." who were enter-
ing the contests.[41] By 1935 Odell even more carefully qualified his language
by using quotation marks in his description of the contest's entrants. "Each
year," he wrote, "the 'poets' of the United States submit upwards of 50,000
jingles for our next year's sign copy."[42] While he still recognized the shape of
the work his writers produced, Odell's critical standards had adjusted to the
contemporary discourse of poetry in the 1930s; his reluctance to grant his
writers the unqualified cultural authority he previously bestowed is evidence
that he was being written by the very conflict his road signs would come to
represent well after New Criticism consolidated the modernist aesthetic proj-
ect as the privileged poetic discourse in U.S. culture.

The spectacle of *Life's* rhetoric in 1947—long after the culture wars of the
1930s were supposed to have ended—indicates that the tradition of popu-
lar poetry in the United States refused to cede to modernism's agenda and
that American aesthetic hierarchies needed to be continuously policed; this
popular tradition was not just visible in the rearview mirror but was main-
taining its public presence by making millions of readers "giggle, or think, or
laugh out loud."[43] The personal memories collected in Bill Vossler's *Burma-
Shave: The Rhymes, the Signs, the Times* offer plentiful evidence that parents
and children not only looked for and read the signs together but also used
them as occasions for learning to read and write. Other people jotted the
rhymes down in notebooks or scrapbooks. The amount of discursive atten-
tion—from Stein to *Life* to *Printers' Ink*—paid to the Burma-Shave billboards
is nonetheless surprising, and one cannot help wondering why those poems

in particular (and not, for example, the illustrated advertising poetry on bill-boards for Taystee Bread [see figure 3.3]) elicited so much critical anxiety. It is clear that the jingles' popularity touched a cultural nerve, in part because the campaign proved doubly challenging to those policing and enforcing lines between high and low in modern America. For while Burma-Vita's poems were undeniably rooted in a rural, popular, midwestern literature of patriotism and moral edification, they also incorporated and celebrated aspects of modern life, so that if modern poets and critics could claim cultural authority as the writers of a new age, Burma-Vita could as well—and, as it turns out, in literary ways that frustrated the terms of the high-low divide central to modernist and avant-garde identities.

Sign Language

Burma-Vita employed a fleet of trucks to set up and maintain the company's signs, and the people hired to work this job were known as PhDs, or "post-hole diggers." In this playful appropriation of the mark of academic achievement, we can see the company deliberately constructing its identity vis-à-vis American high culture. In a similar way Burma-Shave's poems and their readers had one foot in the conventions of popular nineteenth-century poetry and the other in the spirit of modernism that attended the new poetries. As Cary Nelson makes clear in *Repression and Recovery*, this type of mixture was not uncharacteristic of the period's poetry. The modern-genteel dichotomy frequently made in histories of American poetry is, Nelson argues, more "melo-dramatic" than accurate and obscures the exchanges that actually occurred between traditions. "Indeed," Nelson writes:

> one of the striking things about the gradual emergence of modernist forms in American protest poetry . . . is the lack of a sense of a radical break with the past. The thematic continuities in this hundred-year-old American tradition are so strong that a sense of opening out and diversification, of thematic conservation and formal variation, overrides the adversarial model of modernism wholly rejecting the more formal traditions in American poetry. . . . And the rhetoric of the genteel tradition and the rhetoric of modernism were oftentimes counterpointed in the work of individual poets.[44]

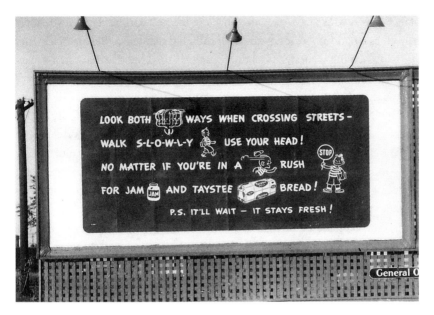

FIGURE 3.3. Indiana billboard advertising Taystee Bread, circa 1930s to 1940s. Reproduced with permission of the Indiana Historical Society.

If Burma-Vita embraced a spirit of modernity in the approach it took to its product, it also embraced a spirit of innovation in its poetry. Allan Odell often referred to the campaign as a set of experiments, and the poems indeed experiment not only with the effect of new technologies on reading practices but also with style and form—an approach to poetry typically attributed to practitioners of literary writing or the avant-garde. In chapter 4 of *Radical Artifice* Perloff explores the strategies of avant-garde poetry in terms of the spatial frameworks proposed by the "billboard culture of the late twentieth century" and especially poets' artistic appropriation and/or redemption of those frameworks.[45] She makes clear she is speaking "by analogy," however, since the particular poems on which she concentrates use the page, not the actual roadside, to achieve their effects.[46] The history of the Burma-Shave poems can eliminate Perloff's need for an analogy by opening up an examination of poetic innovation in the literal terms of her project; in so doing, though, it ends up distressing the discursive divide between mass culture's "billboard discourse" and the redemptive avant-garde on which her critical stance depends. We have become, since the 1920s, a nation of moving readers as well as a nation of readers-on-the-move, and in a sense, Burma-Shave met us there, helping us understand the complexity of a literacy that often occurs away from what Robert Carlton ("Bob") Brown in 1931 called "the arbitrary page" and "the antiquated word-dribbling book."[47]

The Burma-Shave reading experience foregrounded the materiality of language and text: not only did the signs (forty inches long and twelve inches high) dramatically stage the physicality of language in the landscape, but the network of workers and farmers constructing, erecting, maintaining, and replacing them was a constant reminder of the text as a particularly and perpetually produced experience. McGann has praised how in Stephen Crane's work "the capitals, as well as the isolation of each poem on the page, draw one's attention to the poetry's material features, and ultimately to an awareness of poetry as a system of material signifiers."[48] If Crane's work is conscious of this material aspect of language and is to be admired for cultivating it, then we might say that the three-dimensional Burma-Shave poems are hyperconscious of it. Further emphasizing the materiality of this signification, a look at company records and newsletters indicates that individual signs regularly disappeared—the work of vandals or pranksters literally realizing Michel de Certeau's description of reading as "poaching."[49] (Vossler reports that the sign "FIRST CLASS MALE" vanished so frequently, especially in college towns, that the company eventually changed the lineation to destroy the meme's integrity and thus its appeal.[50]) As a result readers regularly encountered gaps in the poems that needed to be—and were—mentally bridged. Additionally, competitors seeking to imitate Burma-Vita's success found their own signs regularly corrected by Burma-Shave loyalists, who covered rival brands' names on the final sign with the "proper" ending, "Burma-Shave"—an instance of what we might call drive-by revision.

The element most central to grounding Burma-Shave's poems in a process of material and temporal signification, however, was the driving encounter, a dynamic that encouraged driver-readers to cruise the text, to read backward as well as forward, and to cocreate the poem—to "write ahead" of it, as John Fiske describes the popular literacy practice[51]—while riding in the white space or extended line breaks between signs that many twentieth-century poets have explored on the page and that McLuhanesque "cool" media comic artists like Munroe (see figure 3.2) and Tom Batiuk and Chuck Ayers (see figure 3.4) have directly associated with the gutter space between

FIGURE 3.4. *Crankshaft* comic strip by Batiuk and Ayers, October 24, 2010. *Crankshaft* (new) © 2010 Mediagraphics Inc. North American Syndicate.

individual comic strip panels.[52] Bruce Andrews has called this type of audience activity "wild reading," describing it as a type of progressive or critical literacy practice that challenges the "paradigms of sense" set up by normative, often linear and school-based literacies. "The job is to go beyond these norms and limits," he explains, "to *read them backward*, to offer up a different refraction of the circumstance."[53]

Were it not for the fact that Andrews uses the notion of wild reading to describe and champion the reading practices sought by the avant-garde Language poets of the 1970s and 1980s, we could very well think he was describing the actual reading of Burma-Shave signs by motorists. The memories in Vossler's history repeatedly describe reading—and reading backward—in the terms Andrews proposes. "The child on the right was assigned to read aloud the forward Burma-Shave signs," one person remembers. "But the older child on the left had the awesome responsibility of reading the backward Burma-Shave signs, sticking them into short-term memory, reconstructing them, and reciting them in the correct order."[54] Someone else remembers having the same arrangement when she rode with her family, except that reconstructing the original message in its "correct order" became at times a goal secondary to the reader's act of coproduction:

> When we got too antsy, daddy would ask us to read the Burma-Shave
> signs aloud to him. Mine were easy . . . they were on my side of the
> road. Sherry's were harder, because she had to read the backwards one.
> They were on the other side of the road, so she had to memorize them
> all backwards, and then read them back to us. . . . Sometimes she would
> start reading backwards, beginning with "Burma-Shave!" and we'd

have to figure out what the rhyme said. Or sometimes she'd pretend she was reading the signs, but she would make up another poem that sounded like a Burma-Shave Rhyme.[55]

It is worth comparing Sherry's reading practices here and those desired by the Language poets—especially since such a comparison suggests how the Burma-Shave poems could become a potential, if counterintuitive, site of disruptive literacy in the architecture of mass culture. Indeed, Juliana Spahr's description of a Language aesthetic almost uncannily describes the energy pulsing through Sherry's family's car: "This work insists that the politics of writing does not reside merely in content or in individual writers, as is often assumed, but in a collective and social attention to language. The aesthetic of these works is not individualistic (there are no genius writers or readers), but rather anarchically communal."[56] "Anarchically communal" might be the last phrase we would use today to describe the 1950s family out for a Sunday drive. Brown might not have been so surprised. "Let's let writing out of books," he encouraged, "give it a chance and see what it does with its liberty."[57]

I realize that comparing the Language movement, and by extension the historical avant-garde, with the commercial poetry of Burma-Shave is provocative, in part because the binaries perpetuated by the former tradition and its scholarly consideration—commercial-anticommercial, innovative-retrograde, oppositional-ideological, high-low, difficult-transparent, avant-quietist—create some of the problems for assessing popular poetries seriously. Precisely because the divide between the two appears to be so great, I would like to pursue the comparison. For not only does the criticism produced by Language writers readily lend itself to the model of the poaching, wild, and popular reader of Burma-Vita's verse, but a consideration of the Burma-Shave poems sheds light on how Language poetry—despite its cultivated difficulty—can lay claim to a populist poetics. Jed Rasula suggests that Language poetry strives for two main goals: "the restoration of the reader as coproducer of the text and an emphasis on the materiality of the signified."[58] Language poetry theorists have already helped us to understand the former (the coproducing reader of Burma-Shave's poems), and they can also illuminate how the formal techniques involved in billboard poetry work to emphasize the latter (the material nature of language).

Writers from Sigmund Freud to Lyn Hejinian have observed that puns, riddles, jokes, and other forms of language play have the effect of defamiliarizing language—of turning words into things and thus reminding us, on one hand, that meaning is not inherent in language (i.e., it is the product of social and material relations), and on the other hand, that language doesn't have final control of meaning (i.e., people can change it and thus also change social relations). The Burma-Shave poems' steady reliance on puns not only presumes and entails a certain level of engagement on the part of motorists but, in pleasurably calling attention to the vagaries of signification, actually redirects the reader's attention away from the commercial message and product being advertised and toward the ambiguity of meaning. Often, as in the following example, the shock of this linguistic redirection registers elsewhere as well; when the transparency of language is unsettled, other normative institutions follow suit:

BEN
MET ANNA
MADE A HIT
NEGLECTED BEARD
BEN-ANNA SPLIT
BURMA-SHAVE[59]

In the space of five lines, this poem turns a budding romance into an ice cream treat. The pun on the characters' names (Ben-Anna/banana) not only is humorous but, in destabilizing transparent signification, also destabilizes a conventional romance narrative. First, the pun ironically locates Ben and Anna's breakup at the culturally recognized site where young love is in fact supposed to blossom—at the ice cream parlor, over a shared dessert (I think of Norman Rockwell's famous 1957 *Saturday Evening Post* cover, *After the Prom*). Then the pun insists on an unlikely union between Ben and Anna, who become joined in the same dessert even as the story has them breaking apart. That is, the "Ben-Anna" pun interrupts signification on the level of the word and then again on the level of narrative. Furthermore, once words and narrative become self-contradictory, the romance plot's conventional gender expectations begin to unravel as well, as the poem subjects Ben's body and grooming habits—not Anna's—to scrutiny. The poem's lack of punctuation even suggests that Anna is more involved in initiating her relationship with Ben than conventional boy-meets-girl stories would have it. While one reading of the first three signs sees Ben making "a hit," another reading, across the line break, suggests the opposite: "ANNA / MADE A HIT." Considering the one hundred feet and three to four seconds a motorist had to drive between signs, the more recent mention of Anna could very well efface the memory of Ben as subject of the sentence and agent of the plot. After all, it is not until line two, where the poem's dimeter is established, that the poem really finds its footing: metrically, as well, the poem places Ben outside, or as prelude to, the narrative while Anna is fully part of it and thus more memorable. By the time the "Burma-Shave" tagline appears, not only has the poem's pun disrupted the transparent signification on which, in Perloff's estimation, the language of the marketplace depends, but it has unsettled the dominant model of heterosexual relationships as well.

The centrality of the individual billboard to the Burma-Shave poem becomes evident in an extended reading of a piece like "Ben-Anna." In the absence of punctuation and in a text written in all capital letters, the individual sign becomes the grammar or prosody particular to the form. Such a grammar orchestrates the relation between individual billboards and the series as well as the relation between billboards and the one hundred feet of space between them. Given so much space, billboards had the potential to signify independent of the series (e.g., "FIRST CLASS MALE"), as this PhD road report from 1930 suggests: "While driving in Ohio last year one of our men observed a car parked beside the road opposite a set of Burma-Shave signs. The occupants of this car were laughing hilariously. Upon looking at our signs it was observed that a gentleman cow was earnestly rubbing his neck on the sign which said 'no rubbing.' Apparently this cow didn't believe in signs."[60]

As a result of this independence the act of integrating individual signs into a series is fraught with the complexity of parataxis—a central strategy of twentieth-century experimental writing that has also interested commercial artists making comics, graphic novels, and related types of sequential art. As Hejinian explains: "One of the results of . . . building a work out of discrete intact units . . . is the creation of sizeable gaps between the units. The reader (and I can say also the writer) must overleap the end stop, the period, and cover the distance to the next sentence. . . . Meanwhile, what stays in the gaps, so to speak, remains crucial and informative. Part of the reading occurs as the recovery of that information (looking behind) and the discovery of newly structured ideas (stepping forward)."[61] Burma-Shave readers delighted in this process—overleaping end stops and staying in gaps, covering distance, looking behind and stepping forward—conjuring between signs a multiplicity of possible meanings inevitably weighed against the final rhyme.

In a 1952 piece for the *Atlantic* titled "Too Late I Read," for example, Scott Corbett jovially recalls the "trouble" such discrete units caused on a trip when he repeatedly caught only parts of the rhymes. When he reads, "'Tee-hee!' said he, / 'That's mine you're pattin'!" Corbett can't help wondering, "'Pattin'. Pattin'. The rhyme was probably 'satin,' I muttered, while imagination ran riot. How racy would our roadside Browning be likely to get?" Later Corbett only sees the signs "When Pa tried / What the signs discussed," and considers how "the whole secret is locked up in the lost opening line. I tested out all the rhymes I could think of for 'discussed': bust, bussed, crust, dust, fussed, gust, disgust, just, lust (which seems unlikely, when you consider the family type of audience they get on the average highway), must, rust, trust. . ."[62] Corbett's process dramatically illustrates how the grammar of the Burma-Shave poems generates possibilities, what Hejinian calls "newly structured ideas (stepping forward)" out of the space between signs. Corbett's article is doubly instructive because it also illustrates how a competing discourse of Puritan family values polices poetic association by intruding on his list of potential rhymes at the objectionable word "lust" and shutting that idea down.

Perhaps the most striking aspect of the process of signification in the Burma-Shave poems does not rest solely in the innovative prosody of the individual billboard but in how that prosody is constantly counterpointed against a second, more familiar form: the rhyme and meter of the traditional ballad. From the time the poems started rhyming, the standard five-line jingle (plus the product name in line 6) almost always extended a four-line ballad stanza over the space of five signs. If the poems unfolded visually—short lines appearing as free verse or prose until clearly made into poetry by the rhyme in line 5 or 6—then they unfolded aurally as well, following a popular form that motorists knew by ear. The resulting tension between how the poems look (free verse) and how they sound (a ballad rhyming *abcb*) creates a structural dialectic producing a verse form perpetually engaged in self-examination. The two prosodic systems do not exist side by side but on top of, within, and even at odds with each other, each erecting hurdles for the other during enunciation—a sort of palimpsest in which each system is continuously erased and rewritten by the other. In terms of the politics of signification this dynamic is crucial, for there is always at least a second way to read or hear a Burma-Shave jingle.

Vossler reports that during the 1996 presidential election, Republicans experimented with Burma-Shave–like signs to promote their candidates:

If you're tired of a White House
That's always smokin' hemp
Vote for our future
Vote Dole-Kemp![63]

This jingle makes clear how central the counterpointed prosodies are to the success of the original Burma-Shave lyrics as innovative texts rather than simple advertising poems. Presented in the form in which the ballad stanza would appear on paper and thus confirming normative literacy practices, the Dole-Kemp signs exhibit no interest in examining their media or in soliciting a participatory, coproducing reader. For them language is secondary to content—language is instrumental and intended to signify transparently—and as a result, the jingle lacks the potentially subversive surprise, pleasure, play, and sophistication of Burma-Vita's rhymes.

The Burma-Shave campaign's cultivation of the ballad's aurality does more than counterpoint the prosody of the printed sign; it also inflects the poems with a history and tradition of the ballad that, as Antony Easthope shows, foregrounds the materiality of the signifier and "collective speech."[64] Compared with the discourse of iambic pentameter—which privileges "individualist, elitist, privatized" reading experiences, casting the text as a "representation of a voice speaking" (ibid., 77)—the oral, four-beat medieval ballad form is rooted in a more heavily accented meter that, Easthope argues, "foregrounds enunciation" (103). Additionally, the ballad's use of repetition (which encourages collective speech) and parataxis (which causes "abrupt and unexplained changes of direction" [92]) results in a work that "is openly presented to the reader in the first place as a poem, as an act of pleasurable speaking" (93). Although the Burma-Shave poems tend to be two- rather than four-beat ballads, the principle holds true:

COLLEGE CUTIE
PIGSKIN HERO
BRISTLY KISS
HERO
ZERO
BURMA-SHAVE[65]

Despite this verse's shortness its paratactic strategies are evident, and the poem obviously foregrounds meter and sign instead of an individual voice. And while the poem is not long enough to display much of the repetition characteristic of oral folk ballads, the final "Burma-Shave" line is indeed a refrain carried from one verse to the next.

Repetition in the ballad is important for Easthope not only because it treats words like things but also because it "makes room for collective speech, for others to join in," which is a response the "Burma-Shave" tagline regularly elicited from motorists (*Poetry as Discourse*, 92). One passenger, for example, remembers how the "kids in the back seat would chant in unison . . . it was a lot of fun to see who could shout the last line, 'Burma-Shave,' the loudest."[66] In a sense Burma-Vita's mnemonic marketing strategy succeeded too well: the refrain of "Burma-Shave" in the context of the ballad form slowly drained the name of its content—a fact that will become evident in this chapter's next section—and turned the company's flagship product into a series of phonetic details or a linguistic thing. Ultimately, Easthope helps us to read the Burma-Shave advertisements not just as isolated verses in which the ballad form makes the mechanisms of signification visible but also as poems situated in the competing ideological discourses of a specific and ongoing Anglo-American literary history.

Poetic Justice

Beginning in 1930 Burma-Vita's jingle-writing contests produced a body of contest literature similar to that of today's literary competitions and professional publishing industry.[67] The company distributed a set of submission guidelines, including postmark deadlines, manuscript formats, and prize amounts, in which it also attempted to articulate its aesthetic criteria. Prospective members of what advertising writer, magazine poet, and crossword puzzle designer Harold T. Bers might have called Burma-Vita's "writing coterie"[68] were encouraged toward "brevity, originality, and interest."[69] They were also instructed in matters more technical: "The jingle form of copy, necessarily means that some of the lines must rhyme, and that the meter of the various rhyming lines must be the same. In the language of the professional verse-writers, the lines must 'scan.'"[70] I don't know whether Bers submitted jingles of his own creation to Odell's contest, but line 13 of his illustrated, antibillboard *Holiday* magazine poem "Sing, O Sing of Billboards" from September 1947 (see figure 3.5) no doubt alludes to Burma-Vita's success in eliciting the "perfect-scanning verses" that company contest literature described:

> Lissome whippets tell you what to "fill 'er up" with;
> Natives name the coffee best to make a cup with;
> Kittens, coy and purring, envy Whatsit's motors;
> Faces full of fervor lure the country's voters;
> Perfect-scanning verses sing of cooler shaving;
> Graceful, rounded numbers calculate the saving;
> Splendid murals, so expansively dimensioned—
> *But where's the lovely valley that the guidebook mentioned?*[71]

Burma-Vita was not the first American company to solicit poetry written by the public; Procter & Gamble conducted nationally known advertising contests for Ivory Soap in the 1890s, and many other companies followed suit. However, the level of participation that Burma-Vita's contests elicited, and the effect of that participation on the company's self-definition, are both noteworthy. For not only did the contests encourage and reward the writing of jingles, but they also created a relationship between the company and the public that—at the company's insistence—moved beyond that of producer and consumer to one of publisher and author, as the following 1947 sign indicates:

AS YOU DRIVE
PLAY THIS GAME
CONSTRUCT
A JINGLE
WITH THIS NAME
BURMA-SHAVE[72]

This standing invitation to write eventually overflowed the discipline of the contest and the company itself, creating a large cohort of poem writers in the United States who were (and still are) motivated to compose Burma-Shave lyrics regardless of market application. Forty years after the company went out of business, the urge to rhyme and play the Burma-Shave way has moved a fairly unlikely group of people—business executives, newspaper headline writers, and even the former senator and presidential candidate Bob Dole—

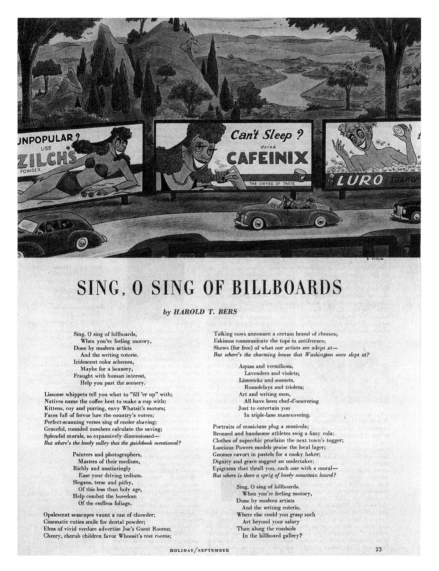

FIGURE 3.5. "Sing, O Sing of Billboards" by Harold T. Bers, from *Holiday* magazine, September 1947.

to try their hands at poetry. This phenomenon not only played a role in the company's ruin but also offers an example of the sort of resistance that the spirit of play and creativity engendered by poetry in popular culture can level against the market, which is frequently thought to inhibit, contain, or corrupt it.

In 1931 Burma-Vita embarked on its first venture into paper publishing, printing a pocket-sized (3-by-2⅛-inch) booklet of jingles intended for promotional use. New rhymes were written as well, appealing to kids and hoping to goad them into convincing dad to buy a jar or two for the free publication:

LITTLE SHAVERS
DON'T OVERLOOK
ILLUSTRATED
JINGLE BOOK
IN EVERY PACKAGE
BURMA-SHAVE[73]

More anthologies would come; I have seen twelve different jingle books issued from 1931 to 1948, the latest identified as volume 12. In shifting from road signs to the more recognizably literary serial format of the *Burma Shave Jingle Book*, the company signaled a change in how it wanted the public to understand the poems. On the road, the rhymes were part of a catchy marketing campaign; published on paper, they became part of an increasingly focused and self-conscious attempt at literary or cultural production. The 1931 booklet indicates that cultural production was at first a secondary goal compared with how the new format could provide another opportunity to plug the product. The first four of the booklet's sixteen pages contain product information and directions for use and are only then followed by a selection of nine poems "contributed by jinglers, amateur and professional."[74] In print each six-line sign sequence has been shortened to a series of four cartoon signs accompanied by a comical illustration (see figures 3.6 and 3.7) and enclosed by a back cover offering a product guarantee and information on "big value sizes" available at drugstores.

Although the jingle book's promotional purpose is clear on reading, its bibliographic codes might suggest otherwise. In fact, the 1936 *Burma-Shave Jingle Book* illustrates the company's increasingly literary ambitions, for while this volume contains much of the same front matter as the 1931 version, that material has been condensed to three pages and is followed by a selection of forty-four numbered poems, printed four to a page and preserving the original six-line format. And while the 1931 cover depicts a trio of barbershop singers surrounded by musical notes, by 1936 those appeals to the nineteenth-century songster form have receded in favor of an abstract, perhaps more

FIGURE 3.6. Cover, *Burma Shave Jingle Book*, no. 1, 1931. Author's collection. Burma-Shave ® is a registered trademark of Eveready Battery Company, Inc.

FIGURE 3.7. Interior pages, *Burma Shave Jingle Book*, no. 1, 1931. Author's collection. Burma-Shave ® is a registered trademark of Eveready Battery Company, Inc.

modern design emphasizing the phrase "jingle book" to signal the publication's heightened literary character (see figures 3.8 and 3.9).

Two years later the company issued another anthology, which displays a self-conscious interest in the prestige of cultural production only hinted at in 1931 and 1936. Titled *The Burma-Shave Signs—A National Institution*, the 5½-by-3½-inch booklet from 1938 is eight pages longer than the 1931 and 1936 editions and barely mentions how to buy or use the company's product; by all appearances the company printing the book produced more poems than shaving cream (see figure 3.1). In this new, self-canonizing booklet the poems are offered, even celebrated, as creative endeavors in their own right, separate from the product they were designed to sell; here they serve the needs of readers, not shavers, and not particularly the market. Even the removal of "jingle" and "jingles" (printed on the 1936 cover) from the front of the 1938 publication suggests this literary reorientation. *The Burma-Shave Signs—A National Institution* contains a history of the signs, a section on the jingle-writing contests and the poets entering them, and a section on the signs' public service messages promoting road safety. Heavily illustrated by cartoons depicting shaving in the lives of various men, including King Henry VIII, the booklet concludes with six pages of testimonials—blurbs from readers extolling not the product's virtues but the virtues of the poems and signs. T. D. of Knoxville, Tennessee, for example, writes, "Just want to tell you that your roadside signs that rhyme do produce results. I get many chuckles from them."[75] The absence of shaving cream here and elsewhere is striking. *The Burma-Shave Signs* also includes an unexpected page of what we might consider "censored" jingles, examples of what Burma-Vita called "pretty good" poems submitted for the contest that the company did not use for fear of offending motorists.[76] Rhetorically, this revelation helps to create an intimate community of readers and writers—a "writing coterie" established on the basis of shared aesthetic principles, not shaving products. It also signals that what is unacceptable for one sphere of the company's attention (generating sales) is entirely acceptable for another (reading and writing poetry), deepening a conflict in purpose at the heart of the company's self-image.

This literary infrastructure not only mediated Burma-Vita's relationship with the public but helped maintain other relationships as well. Both the *Burma-Shavings* newsletter and the employee newsletter, the *Burma Sign Post*, often included jingles or poems written by farmers and employees.

FIGURE 3.8. Cover, *Burma-Shave Jingle Book*, 1936. Author's collection. Burma-Shave ® is a registered trademark of Eveready Battery Company, Inc.

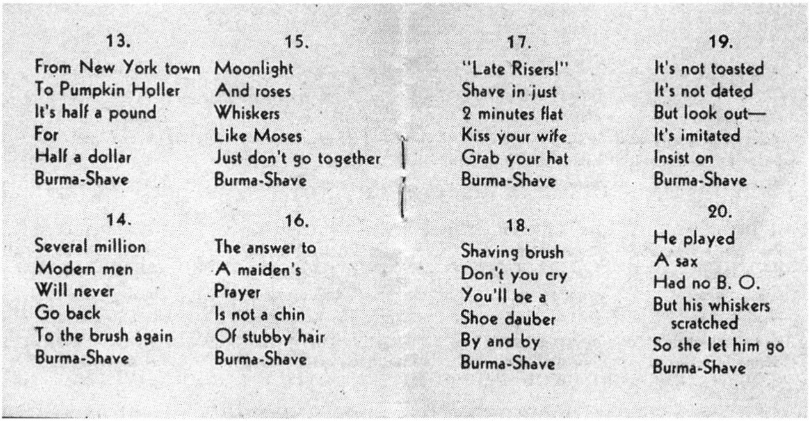

13.
From New York town
To Pumpkin Holler
It's half a pound
For
Half a dollar
Burma-Shave

14.
Several million
Modern men
Will never
Go back
To the brush again
Burma-Shave

15.
Moonlight
And roses
Whiskers
Like Moses
Just don't go together
Burma-Shave

16.
The answer to
A maiden's
Prayer
Is not a chin
Of stubby hair
Burma-Shave

17.
"Late Risers!"
Shave in just
2 minutes flat
Kiss your wife
Grab your hat
Burma-Shave

18.
Shaving brush
Don't you cry
You'll be a
Shoe dauber
By and by
Burma-Shave

19.
It's not toasted
It's not dated
But look out—
It's imitated
Insist on
Burma-Shave

20.
He played
A sax
Had no B. O.
But his whiskers
scratched
So she let him go
Burma-Shave

FIGURE 3.9. Interior pages, *Burma-Shave Jingle Book*, 1936. Author's collection. Burma-Shave ® is a registered trademark of Eveready Battery Company, Inc.

Emma P. Jensen, for example, informs the company in rhyme that the signs on her property have been updated:

Gentlemen:

Your sign was received and put up today
To enlighten the "Shavers" who travel our way.
That the best for the chin wherever they go,
Is Burma-Shave—we use it and know! (says Mr. J.)

Very truly,
(Signed) Mrs. Emma P. Jensen[77]

This is a perplexing moment—what possesses Jensen to make up the rhyme?—but it is not uncommon. From time to time the company responded in rhyme as well, most famously in an exchange with Arliss "Frenchy" French of Appleton, Wisconsin, whose correspondence with Burma-Vita received national press coverage. In response to the 1936 jingle

FREE! FREE!
A TRIP
TO MARS
FOR 900
EMPTY JARS
BURMA-SHAVE[78]

French, owner of a chain of Red Owl supermarkets, informed Burma-Vita that he was starting a jar collection and intended to collect his prize. The company wrote back, "If a trip to Mars you'd earn, / remember, friend, there's no return," to which French responded, "Let's not quibble, / let's not fret, / gather your forces, / I'm all set." Using the opportunity to promote his own business, French hired a publicity manager, placed ads in the local paper asking customers to contribute to his jar collection, set up a "rocket plane" in his store, and, according to Frank Rowsome Jr., who relates the story, put "little green men on the roof firing toy rocket gliders out over the parking lot." When Burma-Vita agreed—writing "Our rockets are ready; / we ain't splitting hairs; / just send us the jars— / and arrange your affairs"—the Odells and

French compromised by selecting the town of Moers, Germany, as French's destination. Dressed in a space suit, French delivered the jars to Burma-Vita in a Brink's truck with the press in tow. Later Leonard Odell would reflect, "It was a real fun kind of thing, and syndicated right across the country."[79]

In fact, the Burma-Shave muse has been long-lived and hard to predict, working its magic in market contexts that have no obvious call for it and little financial reward. The *New York Times*, for example, reported that when the Benton & Bowles advertising agency acquired the Burma-Shave account, the event caused William R. Hesse, agency president, to compose verse. He circulated a memo around his agency that said:

> If a new account
> is what you crave
> Friends, we've now got
> Burma Shave. . . . [80]

Newspaper and magazine headline writers have been similarly inspired to participate in this business of rhyming, as if the very act of reporting on Burma-Vita loosens "the pent-up ambitions" of the poet at every journalist's core. Pages could be filled with examples from nearly every echelon of the publishing world, but the following offer some sense of how contagious—and perhaps gratuitous—the impulse has been: "Perk up, Jack / The Rhymes Are Back"; "Signs of Spring / Make Poets Rave, / Writing Signs / —(For Burma-Shave)!"; "We Still Pine for Those Rhyme Signs"; "For Ad Nostalgia / There Is No Lack; / Burma-Shave Signs / Are on Way Back."[81] When Rowsome Jr.'s history and collection of jingles was reissued in a twenty-fifth anniversary edition in 1990, Bob Dole contributed a foreword, which concludes with a rhyme of his own composition. Individuals and organizations continue to hold Burma-Shave contests as well: Vossler reports on the *Atlantic Monthly*'s 1996 Jingle All the Way contest and on the Richard Nixon Burma-Shave Showdown, a contest intended to malign Nixon for any number of reasons but in only one poetic form. And judging from the overwhelming evidence a Google search elicits, the Burma-Shave lyric has become a widely recognized genre of its own. For instance one Web page containing "verse by Chuck" features three such poems, all rhyming and ending with the right tagline. The bottom of the page, however, displays a link for the uninformed reader: "What is Burmashave?"[82]

As that Web page indicates, the Burma-Shave verse form has flourished but the product name has become, for many, an empty signifier. At some point the company began to recognize that poetry was displacing shaving cream as the focus of consumer attention and took steps to respond. For over a decade magazine advertisements (see figure 3.10) and road signs such as the following attempted to readjust the reader's attention (ironically doing so in rhyme):

WE'RE WIDELY READ
AND OFTEN QUOTED
BUT IT'S SHAVES
NOT SIGNS
FOR WHICH WE'RE NOTED
BURMA-SHAVE[83]

In the early 1950s minutes of Burma-Vita's board of directors meetings began to register anxiety over the place of poetry in the company's mission. At first the records indicate content was the problem, that "serious consideration [should] be given to cutting down the number of safety jingles and substituting a certain amount of serious selling copy."[84] But by April 1952 the issue came to be clearly delineated as poetry versus prose: "Careful consideration was given to Morris B. Mitchell's presentation of the value of using prose on about one-third of our road signs as *simple, direct selling copy*" (emphasis added).[85] The next month, and even into the following year, Mitchell continued to advocate for "the use of prose"—a perspective that probably produced the copy-heavy, hybrid prose-and-poetry ad from the May 1963 *Sports Afield* pictured in figure 3.10—although the board decided to table what was then being called "the question" until sales figures for 1953 were available.[86] Especially noteworthy is Mitchell's insistence that the rhymes (elsewhere called "doggerel," "corn," or "barnyard poetry"[87]) were too complicated to accomplish the job of selling stuff.

Faced with proof—in the form of the contests and the poetry's broad appeal—that the signs were not too complicated for readers, what Mitchell really wanted was to deemphasize the materiality of the advertising language and restore the instrumentality and transparency that he associated with "simple" prose; for him the poems had become too literary, too much an end in and of themselves. It appears he did not get his way, however. For nearly ten years

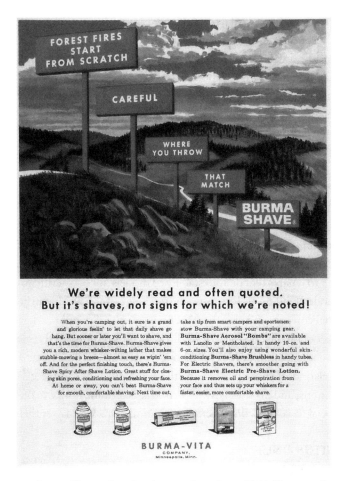

FIGURE 3.10. Burma-Shave print advertisement from *Sports Afield*, May 1963. Burma-Shave ® is a registered trademark of Eveready Battery Company, Inc.

the minutes are silent on the subject, until a February 1962 meeting: "There was a discussion regarding the types of jingles to be used for the coming year, and Morris Mitchell suggested 'hard sell' copy without necessarily using a jingle. President Allan Odell suggested the use of ten year old jingles with a few 'hard sell' new jingles thrown in, and said he would attempt to devise some scheme in the next thirty days."[88] At that point Burma-Vita was running a deficit, and prospects for recovery looked bleak. The "scheme" Odell devised in response to the February meeting may have come to fruition in February 1963, when the company was sold to Philip Morris. As that happened

Burma-Vita bore the scars of its own success; Mitchell still held poetry account-able for those scars, and, as the final excerpt from the minutes above suggests, it was a cause dividing management—executives who, contrary to Auden's statement, had tampered with poetry for nearly forty years. Torn between the family business and the literary form he invented as a young man, Odell could not successfully resolve the conflict and so chose to bow out.

Certainly, a number of factors contributed to Burma-Vita's demise, but I agree with Mitchell that the campaign's poetry—and the popular enthusiasm for rhyming, punning, and collective reading and writing the campaign elic-ited—had an unanticipated role in this demise. Such a possibility should raise a number of questions for literary and cultural scholars, especially for schol-ars investigating the uses of poetry in the nineteenth and twentieth centuries, when enormous amounts of poetry were employed for advertising and other for-profit commercial purposes. What are the literary critic's obligations toward that verse? To what extent do the established models of poetry criticism prohibit us from understanding and assessing the full range of this writing in literary and commercial contexts and elsewhere? Who wrote these poetries, what different business models relied on them, how did audiences respond to them, and what do those audiences' responses say about Americans' "wild" literacy practices and the relation of those practices to the commercial marketplace? These are large questions, and how we answer them will determine how we construct the field of social forces affecting poetry in America. How we answer them—

JUST THIS ONCE
AND JUST FOR FUN
WE'LL LET YOU
FINISH
WHAT WE'VE BEGUN
?   ?   ?[89]

—will also determine how we situate ourselves in relation to those forces and how we thus imagine the relevance of poetry scholarship today.

CHAPTER 4

The Spin Doctor

There was a breezy man,
And he said with a breezy diction,
"En-ar-co Motor Grease
Eliminates all friction."
—*National News Oil Trade Journal*, 1918

The Aquarium is gone. Everywhere,
giant finned cars nose forward like fish;
a savage servility
slides by on grease.
—Robert Lowell, "For the Union Dead"

In 2010 Zach Galbierz of Pontoon Beach, Illinois, was pulled over by a police officer from the Pontoon Beach Police Department who wrote the teenager a $120 ticket—double the cost of a seatbelt violation and twenty dollars less than a speeding ticket—for the "window obstruction" caused by a ninety-nine-cent air freshener hanging from the rearview mirror of the Camaro Galbierz was driving.[1] Galbierz's air freshener was shaped like a maple leaf. The air freshener I hung from the mirror of the first car I regularly drove, an automatic, four-cylinder 1988 Ford Tempo, was yellow and shaped like a pine tree, and its particular olfactory sensation, which the Car Freshner Corporation of Watertown, New York, began marketing in the 1980s, was identified by the portmanteau word "Vanillaroma" printed along the tree's lower boughs.

On its Web site the Car Freshner Corporation explains that in addition to the rearview-mirror design offensive to Illinois state law, it also "offers many other innovative types of air fresheners, from pump sprays to vent clips."[2] However innovative its products might be, the company's method of product naming is not especially innovative, for American road culture has long relied on a speed-reading idiom of which "Vanillaroma" is part and that was produced by the need for consumers to read and remember billboards and other

commercial signage at high speeds while maintaining the type of safety proto-
cols that Galbierz was cited for breaking. From the earliest days of automobile
travel these needs produced a marketplace vernacular that seeks to communi-
cate information quickly and cleverly—I would say poetically—in as few words
as possible. Hence Vanillaroma ("vanilla" plus "aroma"), motel ("motor" plus
"hotel"), and En-ar-co, the phonetically rendered acronym for the National
Refining Company of Cleveland, Ohio, named in the jingle for the company's
motor grease that serves as this chapter's first epigraph. Consider, in the way of
another example, a black and white photograph, probably taken in the 1920s
or 1930s and now in the collection of the Indiana Historical Society, of a Shell
gasoline station complete with several petrol pumps, a billboard advertisement
reading "New SUPER Motor Oil for sustained speed," and the corporate prod-
uct name "Shellubrication" printed in block letters on the building's façade (see
figure 4.1); it is as if, in creating that product name, the "sustained speed" of
a well-oiled ride has overcome the friction keeping the discrete lexical units of
"Shell" and "lubrication" apart and caused the two words to fold, melt, or—to
use the more appropriate petroleum-based word that Robert Lowell uses in his
conclusion to "For the Union Dead"—slide into one. Each of these portman-
teau words is what Marjorie Perloff would call a "'successful' text" by the stan-
dards of the twentieth-century's commercial landscape, each a good example
of the market's language use that "combines high-speed communication with
maximum information" for the purposes of profit and ideological gain.[3]

The emergence of this linguistic phenomenon affected poets, too. Con-
sider Robert Creeley's "I Know a Man," written around 1954 and published
in For Love in 1962, which combines the contracted language ("sd," "yr") and
visual iconography (the ampersand) reminiscent of highway communication
with the site, high speed, and hip, breezy diction of automobile travel in its
final lines, partly to help confuse or blur the sources of the poem's dialogue:

… shall we &
why not, buy a goddamn big car,

drive, he sd, for
christ's sake, look
out where yr going.[4]

Readers have long wondered whether "drive" is "sd" by the poem's nar-
rator or by the narrator's friend—a moment of ambiguity created when

FIGURE 4.1. Indiana Shell gasoline station, circa 1930s to 1940s. Reproduced with permission of the Indiana Historical Society.

both speaking voices slide together in the manner of Vanillaroma and Shellubrication and thus form, out of a superego ("look / out where yr going") and an id ("why not, buy a goddamn big car"), an ego, as the first-person "I" or the contraction "I've" embedded in the word "drive" suggests; one might say that in "I Know a Man," Creeley puts the I (or even eye) in "drive." Or consider the last lines of Elizabeth Bishop's 1965 poem "Filling Station," which engages but stands in contrast to the aforementioned portmanteau words and commercial marketing strategies of automobile culture:

Somebody embroidered the doily.
Somebody waters the plant,
or oils it, maybe. Somebody
arranges the rows of cans
so that they softly say:
ESSO—SO—SO—SO
to high-strung automobiles.
Somebody loves us all.[5]

Vanillaroma and Shellubrication are instances of what Garrett Stewart—whose *Reading Voices: Literature and the Phonotext* I want to take up as this chapter's main theoretical point of reference—calls "that domain of publicly oriented wordplay that capitalizes rhetorically on the very anxiety . . . over linguistic disturbance . . . which it is designed both to induce and then to 'cure.'"[6] Stewart goes on to explain, "As soon as we're 'in' on the sellers' jokes, we are suddenly 'with' them rather than against them; linguistic violence is itself marketable, its assaults converted to seduction" (ibid., 11). Bishop's overlapping oil cans effect a similar type of linguistic violence, but in "Filling Station" that disturbance slows down and breaks *apart*, rather than reaffirms and fuels, the corporate moniker the labels were intended to promote. This breakage happens visually (ESSO—SO—SO—SO) but also sonically, as the sounds of those Esso cans generate a surplus of other meanings as "so" echoes and dissipates throughout Bishop's stanza: forward in the so's of "softly" and "somebody," backward in the /oz/ of "rows," and even, at the far end of what Stewart would call the poem's lexical "echonomics," morphing into "to" and "mo" as the phonemic machinery of "au*tomo*biles" itself (73). As it drives our attention away from the monologic fixity of the commercial signifier ("Esso," a subsidiary of Standard Oil, was, like En-ar-co, a phonetic rendition of the company's initials, S.O.) and into the play of language and production of surplus meaning, "Filling Station" suggests that while such violence is indeed marketable in the commercial landscape, readers nevertheless have the capacity to reverse, misread, slow down, create friction in, or even overlubricate that marketing and give the slip to sellers otherwise intent upon, in Stewart's figuration, a "linguisticommercial" seduction. That is, just as "somebody" arranged or composed the rows of ESSO cans, so somebody else might rearrange or decompose them. Despite being Esso's target audience—a consumer whose short attention span requires the visual display of an entire row of cans to be reached—the reader Elizabeth Bishop does not end up with the sellers at all.

As these examples suggest, there is more than an incidental correspondence between what Stewart calls intra- and interlexical language phenomena and automobility, as the marketing of goods via billboards, roadside posters, road and traffic signs, movie marquees, street banners, neon signs, and moving objects met the newly speedy, or what "Filling Station" calls "highstrung," reader of the twentieth century with a poetic language and media born of Shell's "sustained speed." Along with my discussion of the Burma-

Shave billboards in the previous chapter, the introductory examples in *Reading Voices* suggest the strong historical links between highways, automobile use, and this type of linguistic phenomena even if Stewart himself does not make this linkage his central critical concern:[7] the convenience store chain FASTOP; the "Midwest turnpike franchise parodying the so-called Scandinavian ice cream fad" with its name, Hän Dipped; the automobile ad claiming to put the "'oomph!' back in the Tri*umph* sports car," and others (10). My favorite contemporary example is the Christian nationalist bumper sticker that reads JESUSAVES, its highlighted middle letters cross-lexically making an argument on behalf of an American theocracy in the visual rather than phonetic relations between words.[8]

In 1932, confronting an expanding market for new and used automobiles she felt was threatening to break apart regional identity in the United States, Mary Austin connected this "blurred" language of automobile literacy—or what she might have preferred to call automob*ill*iteracy—with the impending homogenization of American culture and literature, criticizing the new "automobile eye view, something slithering and blurred, nothing so sharply discriminated that it arrests the speed-numbed mind to understand, characters like garish gas stations picked out with electric lights."[9] Robert Lowell's description of "savage servility / slid[ing] by on grease" in the last lines of "For the Union Dead" echoes Austin's concern nearly thirty years later. ("For the Union Dead" was first published in the *Atlantic* in 1960 and is contemporary with "I Know a Man.") Rearview-mirror air fresheners, gas stations, bumper stickers, billboards, oil cans, convenience stores, and commercial signs and slogans: as Austin, Shellubrication, En-ar-co, Vanillaroma, and even the blurred verbiage in a 2004 magazine advertisement for the six-speed Infiniti G35 suggest (see figure 4.2), our literacy and consumption practices have historical roots in the developing transportation and advertising industries of the early twentieth century. Bishop realized this in "Filling Station," and the poetics that enabled her to cite and then split apart the ESSO cans—to frustrate or counter the market by turning its own use of linguistic violence back upon itself in an everyday act of reading—followed a path blazed by William Carlos Williams forty years earlier.

In previous chapters—by linking modernist writers and scrapbooking, for example, or Gertrude Stein and the Burma-Shave jingles—I have suggested that popular culture provided material, models, sets of resources, strategies, opportunities, and even ways of thinking for poets trying to conceptualize

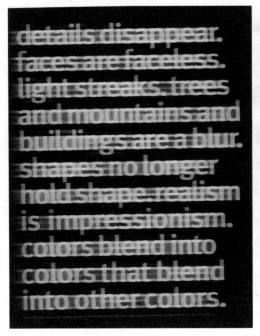

FIGURE 4.2. Infiniti G35 "Enjoy the View" magazine advertisement, 2004. Copyright © 2011 Nissan. Infiniti, Infiniti model names, and the Infiniti logo are registered trademarks of Nissan.

and write "modern" poetry. In this chapter I want to dwell at this intersection more extensively by enlarging and bringing together two usually discrete discussions: one focusing on the relationships between technology, popular literacy, and the commercial landscape of twentieth-century America, and the other seeking to understand Williams's literary goal of capturing everyday American speech—and thus also the commercial vernacular of U.S. culture—in his poetry. There is a tendency in Williams's work toward what Suzanne W. Churchill has called a "restless viewing," and I want to argue that Williams was influenced or pushed toward this viewing practice by the hours he spent driving, reading, and writing in his car while making house calls as a doctor.[10] "My eyes are restless," Williams himself confessed in his 1954 poem "The Host."[11] Immersed in what was, at the height of his career as a physician, a largely unlegislated and chaotic landscape of competing and overlapping billboards and other forms of outdoor advertising—what *The Great American Novel* characterizes as a "Fog of words" that the car "runs through"[12]—Williams recognized the potential for linguistic interference at the heart of that "billboard discourse" and, like Bishop, explored and even cultivated it in his poems. "Words roll, spin, flare up, rumble, trickle, foam—" he wrote, as if thinking of the fragmenting company name on Bishop's ESSO cans. "Slowly they lose momentum. Slowly they cease to stir. At last they break up into their letters."[13]

Ultimately, this recognition enabled Williams to integrate the vernacular of American capitalism into his poetry without simply replicating its commercial and instrumental uses—without advertising the advertising, as it were—and his poems thus offer a model for how readers might engage the "billboard discourse" of American culture while resisting the consumerist subject position that discourse extends. Examples of modernist or avant-garde writing that opposes or critiques American consumer culture are not difficult to find; for many writers and critics, the difficulty, intellectual rigor, and aesthetic complexity of this writing has long represented an alternative or corrective to the products of the culture industries, the "savage servility" those industries try to make desirable, and their increasing standardization and commercialization of U.S. language and culture. I want to argue here, however, that Williams's critical and procedural method—and, by extension, more modernist artistic projects than conventional literary history would have us think—emerges as much from his incorporation and reworking of popular literacy practices as it does from self-consciously intellectual ones.

When one considers the phenomenon of poetry scrapbooking, it is not difficult to understand how that popular practice likely provided a cognitive model for Marianne Moore, who not only kept scrapbooks as a young woman but who, according to Williams's own scrapbooklike 1923 book *Spring and All*, "clips her work into certain shapes" (*The Collected Poems of William Carlos Williams*, 1:230).[14] The same might be said for Williams's own work with "old newspaper files,"[15] which provided him with "a mass of detail to interrelate on a new ground" (ibid., 19). At the very beginning of *Paterson*, in fact, Williams recognizes in scrapbook making the same transgressive aspect that I discuss with regard to "poaching" in chapter 1, as he observes how "clerks in the post- / office ungum rare stamps from / his [Paterson's] packages and steal them for their / childrens' albums" (9). Despite the reasonableness of these two examples—and perhaps due to a general lack of scholarship on the intersections between modernist poetry and popular culture—other modernist incorporation of, or reliance upon, popular practices appears to be comparatively oblique; one can only guess at how Stein's fondness for Burma-Shave signs affected her writing about American cars and highway culture, for instance. I want to argue here that Williams's engagement with the "billboard discourse" of U.S. consumerism offers more evidence of modernism's obscured roots in popular culture, as his readiness and eagerness to split apart the slogans and ESSO-like monikers of commercial culture shares much in common with popular practice itself—what Michel de Certeau would call a "tactic" of everyday reading by which people resist the routine and "efficient" flow of information, and therein frustrate the market's attempt to order and discipline how people read and navigate the textual landscapes through which they move.[16]

Changing Gears

In *Reading Voices* Stewart traces the persistence of a voiced, "phonemic" reading experience in the otherwise silent and visual reading practices encouraged in and by print media. In so doing he keys into "the phonemic counterpart to the spaced lettering of a text" (3) and explores how the reader's "inner ear" produces "sound effects" and "sound defects" (6) that elude or exist in tension with the orderly, graphically enforced word division characteristic of chirographic work since the Middle Ages. "The phonic," Stewart explains, "will not hold fast within the graphic" (4), and what he calls "the phonic merger of contiguous syllables" (18) can create a "lexical fraying and reweaving" (4) that produces an ambivalence in signification between the printed and the aural such as the "sliding of the blank between words" (4) that we hear as the phrase "sound effects" shifts to "sound *de*fects" and back again—or the "leak of acoustic matter from word to word" (27) that we register when "changing gears," the subtitle of this chapter section, drifts to and from the phrase "changing ears." This "locutionary turmoil" (4)—elsewhere described as a "blur" (60) or "spillage of syllables" (27)—creates, Stewart argues, a certain "excrescence, an excess, a surplus, a bonus" (19) of meaning that the scriptural economy's "cultural defense mechanism" (19) of spatially discrete words can't contain. This surplus, he says, is one that "literature, as opposed to other forms of writing, is slow to give up" (19) and thus becomes "one of the very hallmarks of literary language" (12).

Stewart identifies four species of such locutionary turmoil—intra-, inter-, and supralexical effects, as well as the "transegmental drift," which he spends most of his time investigating in *Reading Voices*. Whereas the "least disturbing" of these species, the intralexical transform, "respects most closely the lexical borders, if not the integrity of what they enclose" and "breaks down a word without breaking it open" (such as the contradictory "pen" in the otherwise expansive word "open"), the other three "sound defects" break down word boundaries in increasingly severe ways (55). Of these the transegmental drift is most disruptive, as the inner ear registers "the vanishing act of a single pho- neme . . . in transit from one lexical unit to an adjacent one" in the process of sounding new words or phrases that the written text doesn't admit (58). As he traces the persistence of the transegmental drift through English literary his- tory, Stewart offers plenty of examples, including the one from act 4, scene 5 of Shakespeare's *Troilus and Cressida* that is perhaps most famous: when the Greek soldiers under Agamemnon's command shout, "The Trojans' trumpet!", a call that describes an acoustic event (the stage direction reads, "Trumpet within"), their exclamation is also heard as "the Trojan *str*umpet" and thus also a comment on Cressida, who exited the stage moments earlier (55–58). This double meaning—the disjunction readers register between the visual (trum- pet) and the acoustic (strumpet)—is the "surplus" that drives Stewart's study.

I want to use *Reading Voices* as a reference point for thinking about the "lexical bucklings and permutations" (55) that also happen in the commercial landscape, for if these phenomena constitute, in Stewart's way of thinking, one of the hallmarks of literary language, then they also provide a metric by which to understand a corresponding audible—and visible—literary component of popular culture and especially popular reading practices. As the unvoiced abbreviation "USA" in the aforementioned JESUSAVES bumper sticker sug- gests, the language of the commercial landscape, like the typewriter-influenced poem of the twentieth century, can be as much a graphic as a phonetic affair; both are designed to move the eye as well as the ear. Thus, I don't want to dwell on Stewart's detailed distinctions of and between exclusively phonemic phenomena so much as on how his method of reading and listening within and across words offers a way to more generally identify and understand the production of surplus, even literary, meaning in commercial texts as well.

Despite the high-profile efforts of 1972's *Learning from Las Vegas* to exam- ine how "symbol dominates space" in a commercial landscape that "[commu- nicates] a complexity of meanings through hundreds of associations in few seconds from far away," very little work has been done to theorize the dynam- ics of this ubiquitous and proliferating linguistic space.[17] In offering a tax- onomy of how such language functions (it informs, it advertises, it identifies, it edifies, etc.), Johanna Drucker has rightly claimed that "we cannot dismiss language in the landscape as auxiliary or duplicative."[18] However, discussions of such language use have tended to stop there and are concerned, like much literary criticism, more with the act of textual production than with consumption. Unlike Stewart and de Certeau, both of whom emphasize the creativity at the site of reception and thus the productive agency of the consumer or reader, Perloff depicts ordinary readers or listeners as "vulnerable . . . to prefabricated messages"[19] and "desensitized . . . by the endless billboard discourse around us"[20] rather than as people who are capable of not only surviving but thriving off of what *Learning from Las Vegas* calls the "moving sequences" around them.[21] "It is not an order dominated by the expert and made easy for the eye," Venturi, Brown, and Izenour write in *Learning from Las Vegas*. "The moving eye in the moving body must work to pick out and interpret a variety of changing, juxtaposed orders."[22] The twentieth-century landscape increasingly moved from what Henri Lefebvre has called the symbol to the signal—from "cultural expression" to language that "commands [and] controls behaviour . . . thus forming systems of compulsion."[23] Even so, these systems of compulsion remained (and remain) incomplete in their ability to command and control behavior, and Stewart's ideas about the subordinated but audible meanings in "literary" language can help us see and hear the feedback in, if not resistance to, the linguistic systems that Lefebvre and Perloff perceive as controlling all but the expert.

The potential for experiencing cross-lexical effects brought on by the commercial landscape's breakdown in word division is visible in the maelstrom of competing billboards, posters, and other forms of outdoor advertising from around the turn of the century through the 1930s. Ultimately, legislation passed on behalf of community aesthetics, highway safety, and other issues would help to sort out this maelstrom by separating and isolating discrete messages and thus reducing the possibility of an interbillboard drift; such legislation preserved the integrity, and thus the communicative efficiency, of the commercial message.[24] Before this, however, as Catherine Gudis points out in *Buyways: Billboards, Automobiles, and the American Landscape*, "battles between billposters" regularly resulted in handbills pasted next to, or on top of, each other, creating palimpsest upon palimpsest on just about any surface available. In 1850, she notes, George Foster observed (or made found poetry out of) the strange messages created by competing and overlapping handbills on New York City's Park Theater: "'Steamer Ali—Sugar-Coat—and Pantaloons

for—the Great Anaconda—Whig Nominations—Panorama of Principles—
Democrats Rally to the—American Museum.'"[25] As every available surface
was commandeered in service of the late nineteenth century's advertising
boom, public space became an even greater network of text messages, large
and small, appearing on windows, between windows, between stories, on
building sides and walls, on bridges, public fountains, water towers, along
railroad tracks, and on banners strung in front of buildings and across streets;
sometimes billboards were stacked two or three tiers high on top of buildings,
adding a story or more to the buildings' height. Gudis describes how some
New York architecture—like the content of Web pages that gets covered with
pop-up advertising windows today—"is barely visible beneath the theater
posters and rooftop signs," a textual clutter that, as the photographic record
from these years shows, was common in cities around the country (ibid., 21).

The arrival of the automobile dramatically extended this textual landscape
beyond city limits, as billboards and posters aimed at travelers began to so
thoroughly transform the nonurban American landscape into a textual one
that the issue of "landscape leprosy" (193), "billboard rash," and "litter on a
stick" (233) became a national rallying point—an issue that, as I have indi-
cated, the Burma-Vita Company spent a good deal of time and energy lob-
bying against and that reached its summit in the 1960s with the support of
First Lady Claudia Alta ("Lady Bird") Johnson. Coca-Cola, Gudis writes,
"[plastered] the roadsides throughout the country with small tin, paper, and
painted signs, using every available space on trees, fences, walls and build-
ings under construction, and covering over the layers of existing signs when
space was not available" (110). Elsewhere Gudis details advertising messages
appearing on "white-painted rocks, trees, and bluffs," offering a picture of a
commercialized natural environment that is difficult for us to imagine in our
present age, when such commercial intrusions have become less obvious or
redirected (13). Photographs of the 1920s and 1930s show extensive stretches
of road, sometimes called "billboard alleys," that had long walls of billboards
erected end-to-end and set parallel, rather than perpendicular, to the high-
way, fencing out the natural landscape and literally transforming scenery into
text. Editorial cartoons in Gudis's book show people having to climb over
these walls on ladders in order to view the landscape, and the frontispiece to
Lucius H. Cannon's 1931 antibillboard reference book, *Billboards and Aesthetic
Legislation: New Applications of the Police Power,* features a similar cartoon as its
iconic call to aesthetic arms (see figure 4.3).

SIGNING AWAY YOUR BIRTHRIGHT.
Courtesy of the Saturday Evening Post.

The Offense to the Eye. "So, we have conceded that, of the five senses and the numerous organs of the human body, certain ones are entitled to protection, namely: the sense of hearing and the sense of smell. So your neighbor may not set up an intolerable din upon the next lot after the normal hours of sleep. That would offend the sense of hearing. He may not set up an intolerable stench that would spread over his neighbor's property. But he may offend the eye, he may offend every esthetic sense. He may shut off your view, he may outrage every artistic harmony of the neighborhood. And, in spite of the fact that every other civilized country of the world long ago established laws against that, it would be unconstitutional in the United States to establish, for the eye—or for the soul to which it is the window—those protections which have been established for the ear and the nose."—CHESTER ROWELL. Quoted by C. S. Goodrich in his article, *Billboard Regulation.*

FIGURE 4.3. Frontispiece from Lucius Cannon's 1931 antibillboard reference book, *Billboards and Aesthetic Legislation.*

Foster's 1850 observation about the strange messages created by the Park Theater's overlapping handbills is magnified in the context of billboards and other outdoor advertising in the early twentieth century. A photographic view from one Indianapolis intersection early in the century, for example, shows a building so covered with signs that messages are getting lost and/ or confused; the department store Strauss & Co., for example, appears to be offering "Shoes, Hats, Furnishings . . . and Boys" for sale. No doubt a phrase like "for Girls and" has been interrupted by the competing text as the very structure of the market interferes with or even cannibalizes itself. Indeed, in studying a Walker Evans photo from the 1930s, Bonnie Brennen suggests critics should purposely read like Foster—that we should deliberately "read together" overlapping or adjacent billboards for the cultural narratives they create in sequence.[26]

It is difficult to find hard evidence that people actually read this way in the 1920s and 1930s—though a historical awareness that automobiles were changing perceptions suggests they did, as I will explain shortly—but it is worthwhile considering how frequently people seek out, find, and appreciate such occurrences in the present day, even after considerable regulation of text in the landscape has tried to eliminate the phenomenon. Late-night comedians, for example, feast on a regular diet of inadvertent messages created on signs, as commercial language comes unmoored from its product and signifies multiply, independently, or ambivalently, as in the movie marquees pictured in figures 4.4 and 4.5 and in the following examples:

ALIEN
MEATBALLS
ESCAPE FROM ALCATRAZ

HOWARD STERN'S PRIVATE PARTS
SCREAM
BOOTY CALL

300
WILD HOGS
REIGN OVER ME

THE FLY
GODS MUST BE CRAZY
ALIENS

The college town of Iowa City, Iowa, in which I began writing this chapter, offers many examples of how willing readers and writers are to seek out and reveal such overlaps and unexpected combinations. The *B* from the name of a campus residence hall regularly goes missing, for example, as intralexically (and self-) aware students insist on converting "Burge Hall" into "urge Hall." Equally aware students have converted "Allen Hall" into "Alien Hall," sublexically paying homage to internationally known space scientist James Van Allen by erasing a portion of the second *l* in "Allen" in order to make the lowercase *i* for "Alien." A graffiti skirmish that took place on a wooden fence set up around a campus construction site saw one evangelist's spray-painted message "Beware of God" revised a few nights later with the addition of "iva chocolate," creating the sentence "Beware of Godiva chocolate." The hot-air hand dryers in many men's public bathrooms around the country provide additional evidence of how widespread this phenomenon is. On many of these dryers' instructional panels, words and letters are scratched out by bathroom vandals who regularly convert "towel litter" into "owl litter," "keeps washrooms free of waste" into "keep shrooms free," "Push Button" into "Push Butt," and so on. The phonically rich message created (or revealed) by vandals working in a University of Iowa English Department bathroom (see figure 4.6) is reminiscent of the one Foster saw on the Park Theater over 150 years ago: "You bet - - - We have stalled Poll on arm Air and rye to rot you from the hazards of ease." The clear pleasures—not to mention the authenticity effects—of such linguistic subversion operating outside or in opposition to the official discourse of sign making have even been recognized by commercial artists, such as Matthew Lew, who reveals the word "believe" in a cross section of two juxtaposed commercial fonts for his "american graffiti" print listed at $179 at Crate & Barrel's trendy urban outfit, CB2 (see figure 4.7).

If the foregoing examples are any indication, people in the early twentieth century were not only ready to read in these ways but, given the particular density of the era's advertising, had more than ample opportunity to do so. In fact, being less accustomed to nearly omnipresent advertising and new to the experience of reading in swift-moving automobiles, readers from this time were probably more aware of this type of reading activity than we who experience it daily. Then, the act of driving, which we now assume is second nature for most people, was accused of producing "a state of distraction" (Gudis, *Buyways*, 68), and the simultaneous activity of driving and reading billboards was perceived as an "affront to delicate nerves of eyes" and described as an act of "seizing the eye against one's will" (ibid., 193)— remarks that recall Venturi, Brown, and Izenour's claim in *Learning from Las Vegas* that the strip "is not . . . made easy for the eye."[27] Even the U.S. government's enormous, two-volume 1933 publication *Recent Social Trends in the United States* was moved to acknowledge the singular effect of the automobile on popular communication practices. "It is probable," the authors write in the study's initial words on the motorcar, "that no invention of such far reaching importance was ever diffused with such rapidity or so quickly

FIGURE 4.4. "Erin Brockovich Screwed My Dog Skip," movie marquee, circa 2000.

FIGURE 4.5. "Fantastic 4 Knocked Up Nancy Drew," movie marquee, circa 2007.

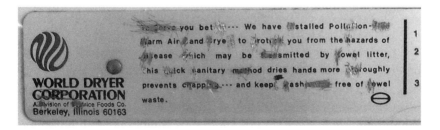

FIGURE 4.6. Hot-air hand-dryer graffiti from men's bathroom at the University of Iowa.

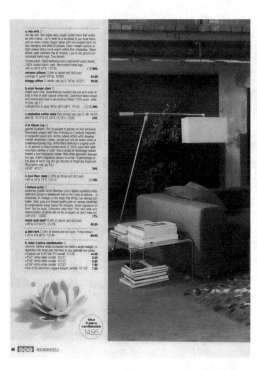

FIGURE 4.7. Pages 46–47 from the Fall 2010 CB2 sales catalog by Alec Hemer, copyright © 2010. Used with permission from the author.

exerted influences that ramified through the national culture, transforming even habits of thought and language."[28]

Advertising designers and copywriters tapped into this new way of reading right away, recognizing both its possibilities and limitations. Early on, the outdoor advertising industry realized the potential for overlapping messages and sought to channel and contain that prospect, encouraging consumers to enjoy and experiment with blurred language within the defined framework of individual signs or individual ads (e.g., Shellubrication, or the National Refining Company's transegmentally drifting kerosene tagline, "National Light Oil makes night toil light toil") but working to prevent the counterproductive practice of creative reading across or between adjacent or overlapping signs. On the one hand, "spaces between billboards along railways are necessary, not only for relief and repose, but for clarity and emphasis of individual signs" writes John B. Opdycke in his 1925 textbook, *The Language of Advertising*.[29] On the other hand, he exhorts his students to "Visualize words.

Fix the arrangement of letters in words by eye"[30] in the manner of William Carlos Williams. In doing so Opdycke offers examples of "common devices ["Combination," "Curtailment," and "Derivation"] employed for forming good advertising words" that result in names like "OILiquid" and "Autolite," many of which, not surprisingly, had to do with automobile or petroleum-based products.[31]

Learning from Las Vegas suggests that, as of the 1970s, this was still the case. In something of a parody or send-up the study summarizes the views of the main social players—the Aesthetician, Legal Statutes, and the Sign Industry—involved in the "Controls and Beautification" debates surrounding the Vegas Strip. While the first two views are articulated without "blurred" language of any sort, the Sign Industry says, "Signs are good, they're good for business, that makes 'um good for H'america too."[32] The run-on sentences, contraction, elided letters, and the strange word "H'america" all suggest that Opdycke's techniques of combination, curtailment, and derivation—and related issues of word or sign spacing and its collapse—are so fundamental to the sign industry's sense of what *Learning from Las Vegas* calls the "autoscape" that they pervade the very language the industry speaks.[33] Suggesting that this is not solely a phenomenon of commercial communication, several of my students have recalled that when they grew too old to play I Spy on family road trips, they played a word game that centered on making riddles that needed to be answered with portmanteau words. What do you get when you cross a Chinese show dog and a destructive ocean wave? A Shihtzunami. And what do you get when you wrap the capitol of Texas in metal? Austin Foil. The fact that my students always played this game in a moving vehicle, and never at home in the living room, is not coincidental but yet another example of how automobility has affected language use in American history.

In understanding the fluidity of commercial language during the early years of speed-reading, it is helpful to reference other discussions about the intersection of modern technologies and visual culture, for they suggest, at least by way of comparison, how the automobile would come to significantly affect American reading practices. Wolfgang Schivelbusch's analysis of European train travel and the emergence of "panoramic viewing" in *The Railway Journey: The Industrialization of Time and Space in the 19th Century* provides a particularly good case in point. For Schivelbusch the development of train travel "introduced [into Europe] a new system of behavior: not only of travel and communication but of thought, of feeling, of expectation" that is analogous to the effects that motorcar travel had in the United States.[34] Schivelbusch argues that European travelers had to learn a new way of seeing as they transitioned from a highly developed system of horse-drawn coach travel to the comparatively speedy train. Unlike the journey by coach, during which the traveler took note of villages, towns, the terrain, and "even details of the material consistency of the pavement of the highway," the velocity of railway transportation denaturalized and desensualized travel, its high speed making close and detailed observation impossible.[35] "The rapid crowding of changing images, the sharp discontinuity in the grasp of a single glance and the unexpectedness of onrushing impressions," Schivelbusch writes, caused a significant amount of anxiety and fatigue in inexperienced or first-generation railway passengers—a discomfort recalling the one expressed by American drivers who complained that billboard reading was an "affront to delicate nerves of eyes"—and thus encouraged an increasingly "panoramic" or horizon-based viewing practice as a means of coping.[36] In a short time, he argues, the railway traveler so "integrated" the "machine and the motion it created . . . into his visual perception" that "he could only see things in motion."[37]

For Schivelbusch these effects were felt mainly in Europe and not the United States, in part because U.S. railway travel didn't supplant an already established system of transportation and thus require the change in seeing practices that Europeans experienced. The emergence of the automobile in the 1920s, however, did demand from Americans the sort of change in seeing that nineteenth-century Europeans experienced in the transition from coach to train. There is a wealth of historical research on the shift from train to automobile travel in the United States, ranging from its effects on mass production to the expansion of the U.S. highway network and the development of the tourist industry, and it is worth repeating that many of those changes—including changes in perception—didn't go unnoticed at the time; Mary Austin wasn't the only one to comment on the new "automobile eye" in U.S. culture. The 1930 *Report of the President's Research Committee on Social Trends* observed in great statistical detail how the railroad was dying out—ridership had fallen to 1900 levels, rural highways had increased over 40 percent from 1904, the mileage of total surfaced roads increased over 330 percent—and that this shift was accompanied by what the report calls a new "automobile psychology"[38] that helped people adjust to the accelerated "tempo of life."[39] It would not be long before American drivers and passengers "could only see things in motion" as well—the language of their landscape included.

People recognized that other technologies were changing language use, too. In "Machinery and English Style," which appeared in the *Atlantic Monthly* in 1904, Robert Lincoln O'Brien concerns himself with how "the veritable maze of devices which have come into widely extended use in recent years"—the typewriter, shorthand, and especially the telegraph—were affecting and complicating reading and writing practices.[40] In particular O'Brien cites the heightened possibility of lexical ambiguity due to inter- and intra-lexical language phenomena taking place in telegraph transmissions (in one of his examples, an order "per [Mr.] Simmons" gets mistaken for "persimmons"), and especially in the use of adverbial phrases that float between sentences in a transegmental fashion.[41] "The adverbial phrase at the beginning of a sentence," O'Brien writes, "is especially dangerous, because it so readily adapts itself to the end of the sentence before, with results that may be amusing or amazing."[42] Such "dangerous" possibilities resulted in new terse and businesslike journalistic writing styles that, as generations of English students have learned, affected the prose style of Ernest Hemingway. For O'Brien the combination of speed and technology at the juncture of scriptural and oral economies engenders a potential for disorder and chaos that threatens to disrupt or derail the very technological practices it makes possible. Many of these telegraphic issues were sorted out by the 1920s and 1930s, but the emergence of the automobile speed-reading through a landscape of already overlapping texts gave rise to a new linguistic danger in American culture—one that Williams recognized and explored in his poems.

Speedy Enunciation

In *William Carlos Williams: A New World Naked* biographer Paul Mariani tries, like critics before and after him, to explain the nature of Williams's "cubist" poems, such as "The Agonized Spires" from 1923's *Spring and All*, in distinctly highbrow and Eurocentric terms. "That poem," Mariani writes, "was more like a Dadaist collage, a composition of overlapping but sharply discrete images, a conflation of the impressions—intellectual, emotional, perceptual—of New York City from the perspective of a multilevel sensibility. The nearest visual image to the kind of thing Williams was attempting here would have been the kinesthetics of a Dadaist film where discrete images followed each other in quick succession without a narrative line or even a subjective eye to hold the images together."[43] While Williams certainly had significant connections to, and was inspired by, the modern art world, I would nevertheless suggest that the "nearest visual image" to the "overlapping but sharply discrete images" of "The Agonized Spires" was not, in fact, European Dadaist film but the competing and often chaotic succession of billboards and other types of outdoor advertising that Williams would have encountered on a daily basis while making his rounds as a doctor on American roads and highways plus, as Mariani indicates, on many trips to New York.

Williams was of that generation of writers and artists who first experienced and registered the effects of a range of new technologies and their attending industries on American culture and perception—radio, x-ray, telegraph, cinema, bicycle, machine gun, airplane, telephone, automobile—and who struggled to figure out what it all meant for their art. In his autobiography Williams remembers, for example, how there were "no sewers, no water supply, no gas, even. Certainly no electricity; no telephone, not even a trolley car" in the New Jersey of his youth.[44] "Then," Mariani writes, "the motorized trolleys came in and ran down Park and all along Ridge Road, jostling noisily with horses and carriages and peddlers' carts, before they in their turn gave way in the 1920s to Buicks and Packards, Dodges and Fords."[45] Writers and artists connected to Williams on both sides of the Atlantic engaged these developments with substantial energy if not always similar opinions. As Wanda Corn argues in *The Great American Thing: Modern Art and National Identity*, artists in Europe were looking to U.S. mass culture, including advertising, for sources of inspiration, and American artists were plumbing those spaces in search of a language and form from which to fashion a "genuine" American art.[46] While some—like Ezra Pound, who advised artists to "consider the way of the scientists rather than the way of an advertising agent for a new soap"[47]—recoiled at the prospect of overtly engaging mass and consumer cultures in his poetry, others such as Matthew Josephson found great promise in it. Admonishing the antibillboard lobby in a 1922 issue of *Broom: An International Magazine of the Arts* (a journal to which Williams contributed), Josephson argued that the urge to "abolish the billposter is ample proof of [that lobby's] failure to understand the unaffected beauty and wisdom of the American *milieu*."[48] For Josephson the American billboard was the stuff of American literature. "The most striking conclusion drawn from a study of specimen advertisements," he claimed, "is that the American business man, in the short daily time at his disposal, reads the most daring and ingenuous literature of his age . . . in all cases far more arresting and provocative than 99 per cent of the stuff that passes for poetry in our specialized magazines."[49] Around the same time Williams's longtime friend, the painter Charles Demuth, tapped into the American billboard genre to come up with designs for the "poster portraits" he was painting, or planning to paint, for friends and associates like Gertrude Stein, Wallace Stevens, Eugene O'Neill, Georgia O'Keeffe, and Arthur Dove. Demuth's most famous of these portraits, *The Figure 5 in Gold* (oil on composition board, 1928), in fact not only uses the cubistlike "overlapping planes and contours" characteristic of advertising along streets and highways to illuminate Williams's poem "The Great Figure" but also includes Williams's familiar first name along the painting's upper edge (as well as "Carlos" in marquee lights shining in the distance), making the poster portrait into a very clever "Bill" board.[50]

As Williams himself was well aware, much of what he saw of the world as a medical professional and working poet he saw from a car window, a fact that has led Robert Pinsky to claim that Williams was "perhaps the first poet to describe the landscape as it looks . . . from a car."[51] While that's a tough case to prove for certain, I want to argue here that his poems, like Hemingway's telegraphic prose, do indeed register—and even cultivate or foster—the effects of that new technology and its cultures on seeing, reading, and writing: not just thematically or compositionally, but at the inter- and intralexical levels of the language as well, in the moments when words and messages drift and overlap, occupying or embodying the spaces between them like the overlaid text of so many competing billboards. Unlike Pound, who dismissed it, Josephson, who embraced it, and Demuth, who used it to make "involuted and complicated . . . intractable"[52] pieces of art as far from mass-produced commodities as possible, Williams seized on the potential for "wild" reading practices he saw in the commercial landscape and not only deployed it to resist or critique commodity culture but then used his poems as a sort of workshop wherein readers were encouraged to pursue the types of literacy practices that the consumer market did not want to happen.[53] "To understand the words as so liberated," he writes in *Spring and All* (which he dedicated to Demuth) "is to understand poetry. That they move independently when set free is the mark of their value" (*The Collected Poems of William Carlos Williams*, 1:234). Such a sensibility, as Stewart suggests, is alert to the linguistic politics of the space—both in the landscape and on the page—that words, like phonemes, move or are moved across. "What else is verse made of but 'words, words, words'?" Williams would thus ask several years later. "Quite literally," he would answer, *"the spaces between the words*, in our modern understanding, which takes with them an equal part in the measure" (emphasis in original).[54] Primed in a culture of automobile literacy and its blurred messages, Williams sees, rather than hears, language being liberated and finds his energy there. We need to "watch, often breathlessly, what [words] *do*," he writes,[55] making the eye, not the breath, the measure as words appear in "an assembly of tides, waves, [and] ripples" that "roll, spin, flare up, rumble, trickle, foam"[56] and rise before our eyes.

While this "modern understanding" made wild reading practices possible, Williams nonetheless registered these moments with caution and ambivalence, as his poems diligently resist endorsing, replicating, or capitulating to the new culture of speed, consumption, and billboard discourse from which they emerge; I hope that the drifting I hear, as this section's subtitle slips back and forth from "Speedy Enunciation" to "Speed *Denunciation*," helps to figure this ambivalence on a phonic level. The man who "put eleven cars through their paces" had good reason for his mixed feelings and for suggesting that his work (here referring to the novelette *January*) "is supposed to portray the wreck that occurs in a physician's life by the tempo of modern times."[57] At the height of Williams's professional and poetic career, as he himself noted and Mariani has emphasized, his medical responsibilities were overwhelming, and he didn't have half the time he wanted to write. "Keep up your courage," he writes in *January*, "Get through with this awful drive . . . it will end soon (in a few years) and then you must write day and night—or as you please forever after."[58] "He was forever in a hurry," Mariani adds. "That was as true of his driving as it was of everything else, and he often drove like a madman to get someplace. He hated traffic with a passion because it wasted time and he would cut out into oncoming traffic to get around some slow-driving bastard, drive up on sidewalks when snow or other cars clogged the roads, race down winding country roads to get someplace just a little faster."[59] Hence the apocalyptic beginning of *Spring and All*'s chapter 13: "Thus, weary of life, in view of the great consummation which awaits us—tomorrow, we rush among our friends. . . . Thoughtless of evil we crush out the marrow of those about us with our heavy cars as we go happily from place to place. . . . Let us hurry! . . . Rushing about, men bump each other into the whirring presses. . . . Children laughingly fling themselves under the wheels of the street cars, airplanes crash gaily to the earth" (*The Collected Poems of William Carlos Williams*, 1:180).

As with much of American culture, the very technologies that made Williams's work easier also made for more of it, and his relationship to cars and the highway was thus fraught with ambivalence and contradiction. His son, William Eric Williams, writes that his father "read with complete sympathy Thorstein Veblen's theory of 'Conspicuous Consumption.' He [WCW] thought 'two cars in every garage' the verbiage of a mind sold out to 'the money boys.'"[60] While letting him "move around more easily," the technologies of modern times came at a price, as the circumstances of his first heart attack—which he suffered while trying to dig his car out of a snow bank in the winter of 1948—dramatically suggest.[61] Thus, while his poems borrow heavily from the experience of wild reading incited by the culture of speed and automobility, that borrowing is selective and tactical, as he used his poetry—like a Jamesonian Marxist, perhaps—to untangle what he identified as potentially progressive practices of modern everyday life from those that he saw capitulating to, or serving, the larger commodity culture. Ultimately, this method allowed him to include an even wider range of the American vernacular in his poems—a major goal of his poetics up through and including his experiments with the variable foot—without replicating the commercial sphere's efficiency and instrumentality, enabling him to demonstrate the process of such reading in his poems and thereby instruct readers in the wild literacy practices of their time.

The Spin Doctor

In reading Williams's canonical modernist work at the intersection of American automobile culture and "billboard literacy," I am taking my cue from two lines of scholarship: a growing body of work that explores more generally the effect of turn-of-the-century technologies on modernist poetry, and another, more established approach to Williams that reads his poetry in particular for the way a cubist—I would like to say billboard—sensibility of overlaps and edges constitutes his poetic praxis.[62] While it is not possible to cite the entire range of this work here, I would call particular attention to Adalaide Morris's *How to Live / What to Do: H. D.'s Cultural Poetics* as an important precedent, not only for the way that it uses Stewart's *Reading Voices* to suggest how developing sound technologies of the early twentieth century affected the phonic qualities of H. D.'s work, but also because the relationship between H. D.'s poetry and sound technologies nicely parallels the relationship between Williams's poetry and the visuality of the American highway and its car culture. "In epics composed, read, recited, and recorded between 1917 and 1960," Morris writes in the process of describing the acoustic equivalent of Austin's "blurred language," "sounds cut in, rise, then fade away as other sounds intrude." The sonic collage that Morris hears in H. D. I both hear *and* see in Williams, especially in *Paterson*, as acoustic pressure points in his poems are accompanied or glossed by a visual and often pedagogical counterpart. For Morris the modernist acoustic experience is "as if we were tapping into a party line on a municipal phone exchange, spinning down a radio dial, or sampling a stack of records." The description is particularly apt for H. D., who had a documented interest in "telephones, radios, microphones, loud-speakers, and talking films."[63] But for the good doctor—who found himself "spinning on the / four wheels of my car" more often than he found himself spinning down a radio dial—that experience of sampling is realized in the visual contexts of the American highway and its textual landscape (*The Collected Poems of William Carlos Williams*, 1:206). If, as Morris suggests, "the acoustical technologies developed in the first half of the twentieth century enticed and enlivened the ear of a print-saturated audience,"[64] then the equally strange and new automobile literacies developing during Williams's lifetime enticed and enlivened the eye as well—that part of the body, Williams wrote, that "always stood first in the poet's equipment."[65]

Both *Al Que Quiere* (1917) and *Sour Grapes* (1921) bustle with the traffic of boats, horses, wagons, carts, streetcars, and trains. And other poems from this period such as "St. Francis Einstein of the Daffodils"—with its medley of compound words like "stonearms," "Venusremembering," "Oldfashioned," "freshturned," and "topbranches"—suggest that Williams was experimenting early on in his career with the possibilities that an overlapping or blurred language could bring to his writing (*The Collected Poems of William Carlos Williams*, 1:130–33).[66] In fact, "St. Francis Einstein" first appeared in the summer of 1921 as the lead-off poem in the "Advertising Number" (no. 4) of the little magazine *Contact*, which he and Robert McAlmon edited, where it was preceded on the page by Williams's send-up of the age's commercialism: a prose paragraph announcing, "Henceforth the writings of William Carlos Williams will be offered for sale at prices fixed by the author. . . . A minimum price of fifty dollars will be charged for all poems, those of most excellence, as in all commercial exchange, being rated higher in price." *Contact*'s cover (see figure 4.8) mined a similar subject matter, as it incorporated a number of text

FIGURE 4.8. Cover of *Contact*, William Carlos Williams and Robert McAlmon, eds., "Advertising Number," special issue, no. 4 (1921).

"ads" or logos, including one for the New Jersey–headquartered Standard Oil Company's petroleum product "Nujol," which William Rockefeller had peddled as a cancer cure in the nineteenth century on the way to carving out space in the market that became the foundation for that family's twentieth-century energy and medical fortunes. As a New Jersey doctor, Williams likely would have known not only that Nujol had been discredited as a cancer treatment but that the company had also refused to pull the product from the shelves, choosing to market it as a laxative instead, since the raw petroleum contents acted as a purgative by coating the intestines and inhibiting the body's absorption of nutrients.

Read alongside the issue's prefatory words by Ezra Pound—"*Pour la Patrie, comme tu veux, mais pour une societe anonyme de Petrole: mourir!*"— Williams's poem (and his parody of marketing language and logic) elaborates the critique that *Contact* as a publication leveled against Standard Oil's business practices: the human body, the body politic (*la Patrie*), bodies of art, and corporate bodies operate according to different definitions of health that are incompatible if not irreconcilable.[67] If Williams's status as a local doctor gave him the authority or legitimacy to indict Standard Oil's health-care claims, I like to think that his qualifications as a poet enabled him to make a similar critique along linguistic lines. As a poet alert to the blurring of language, Williams would have also been aware that the product name "Nujol" was "derived"—to use Opdycke's term from *The Language of Advertising*—by combining the words "New" and "Oil," or possibly "New Jersey" and "Oil." Given *Contact*'s focus on advertising and the commercialization of language, we are thus encouraged to read the litany of compound words in "St. Francis Einstein" as an artistic challenge, provoked by the sobriquet "Nujol," to commercial claims to innovative or "new" language use. Indeed, the poem's desire to move the oil-colored "black boat" of March into the more traditionally poetic landscape of April suggests as much as well.

While the history of "St. Francis Einstein" is suggestive, it wasn't until 1923—during what James Fraser calls the "Golden Age of Billboards," two years before the formation of the Outdoor Advertising Association, and still seven years before New Jersey's first attempts to regulate that industry[68]—that Williams's concerns with automobility and language use came to the fore of his work, just as the automobile was coming to the forefront of American culture. The beginning of 1923's *The Great American Novel*, in fact, appears to dramatize the moment this convergence took place for Williams. "Progress is to get. But how can words get," Williams writes, again raising a question in order to answer it: "—Let them get drunk. Bah. Words are words. Fog of words. The car runs through it. . . . Break the words. Words are indivisible crystals. One cannot break them—Awu tsst grang splith gra pragh og bm—yes, *one can break them*" (my emphasis).[69] *Spring and All*, which also appeared in 1923 and which included "The Agonized Spires," suggests, even in the "missing" letter F of its title, that this breaking of language was becoming a systemic part of Williams's poetics, extending beyond the story of *The Great American Novel* in which, as Williams writes, "a little (female) Ford car falls more or less in love with a Mack truck."[70] Beginning with the first line of poetry, "By the road to the contagious hospital," eight of the twenty-seven poems in *Spring and All* involve cars or their roadways, and Williams positions the view from the car window as one of the book's central tropes from the get-go (*The Collected Poems of*

William Carlos Williams, 1:183). Most famous, perhaps, are poem 11 ("In passing with my mind / on nothing in the world" [ibid., 1:205]) and the mournful conclusion to poem 18 ("The pure products of America / go crazy"), which reads, "No one / to witness / and adjust, no one to drive the car" (1:219). And if the overlapping images of "The Agonized Spires" have, as I suggest, a certain automobile literacy as the guiding compositional rationale, then a poem such as 25 ("Somebody dies every four minutes / in New York State—" [1:231]) confirms that Williams was indeed working in the realm of commercial billboard discourse as much as in the European Dadaist aesthetic that Mariani and others have proposed. Poem 25 not only contains the very signs of the textual landscape as viewed from the "Interborough Rapid Transit" (the alliterative "Cross Crossings Cautiously," for example), but even presents an opportunity to do the sort of wild reading incited by that process:

THE HORSES   black

&

PRANCED   white

(1:232)

Here Williams encourages his reader to read not only right to left and left to right but also up and down, and even diagonally—an experience that eludes the aural and casts this practice as a distinctly visual one.[71]

The most fully realized moment of Williams's billboard poetics in *Spring and All*, however, occurs in poem 8 ("The sunlight in a / yellow plaque upon the / varnished floor" [1:196]) and makes for one of the strangest and most elusive reading moments in a book that can be, generally speaking, as strange and elusive as poetry gets:

And so it comes
to motor cars
which is the son

leaving off the g
of sunlight and grass—

(1:197)

Here, in the context of motor cars, Williams is literally breaking apart the word "song" to reveal an intralexical component ("son")—the exact sort of linguistic disruption that readers experienced in the overlapping commercial or highway signscapes of his time. (In fact, the "Carlos" in Demuth's *The Figure 5 in Gold* really reads "Carlo," as a skyscraper juts in front of, and blocks, the last letter of Williams's middle name.) Stewart explains that, phonically speaking, such an intralexical moment "respects . . . the lexical borders, if not the integrity of what they enclose," and thus "breaks down a word without breaking it open."[72] In what otherwise registers as a relatively docile phonic moment of poem 8, however, Williams reveals that the disruptive nature of modern literacy practices is located in the *visual* experience: in the cut-up language characteristic of the textual landscape, as well as in its literary equivalent, the typographical (rather than acoustic) line break of the modern vers libre poem. As if to further emphasize the visuality at the heart of this disruption, Williams chooses to break the word "song," which has two implications for the poem's phonic life. In breaking "song," not only does he prohibit a word with heavy acoustic content from entering the poem—indeed a word often used to describe poetry itself—but he excludes the potential phonic or phonemic experience of the son/song intralexical event as well; that is, in poem 8 we don't hear the "son" inside of "song" at all. Rather, as the distance between "son" and "g" created by the line break and stanza break indicate, a modern literacy and modern poetics must, like the textual landscape, be experienced with the eye in addition to—or even, as this poem indicates, to the exclusion of—the ear.

By highlighting the visual experience of modern literacy here, I'm not indicating that Williams somehow sought to eschew the phonic in his writing. That would be impossible to do, and in fact the poems do contain stimulating and revealing moments of transegmental drifting even though those moments aren't as common as they are in, say, Morris's reading of H. D.'s *Sea Garden*.[73] At the end of poem 11 ("In passing with my mind"), for example, the words "rail of" in the poem's last line transegmentally drift back and forth between "rail love" and even "real love"; considering the book's emphasis on driving and the rapid transit rail system, the concept of "rail love" as the poet's "real love" that emerges aurally in this line is one that underlies the book's visual poetics as a whole (*The Collected Poems of William Carlos Williams*, 1:206). It's the complex relationship between, or interlacing of, the visual and the aural suggested here that allowed Williams to fully integrate and yet scrutinize the American vernacular in his writing. An exemplary occurrence of this visual and aural interplay happens in poem 12 ("The red paper box / hinged with cloth"), lines 25–26 of which read: "Through its / dial we discover" (ibid., 1:210). Not only is the word "dial" equally associated with aurality (a radio dial) and visuality (a speedometer dial), but the phonetically experienced transegmental drift in these lines happens across the visually registered line break as "its / dial" shifts to become "its style." Williams's style was indeed moving toward the uneasy but complementary interplay of the visual and aural that we experience here; in studying poem 22 ("so much depends / upon") we can thus legitimately listen for the word "read" (the past tense of "to read") in the phrase "red wheel / barrow" to learn how the poem is about a corresponding visual literacy that can register certain sets of modern language phenomena—the broken compound words of the poem, for example, which read not unlike the segmented billboards of a Burma-Shave rhyme—when the ear cannot (1:224).

The operative poetics of *Spring and All* is contingent upon such "intimacies of the eye and ear," as Williams himself explains in the book's prose sections, which describe the imagination and language as "a living current" (1:225) that "creates a new object, a play, a dance" (1:235) as the reader engages in the most modern literacy practice by "moving from one thing to another—as he pleases, unbound" (1:207). These "everyday exercises of the most primitive type" (1:220) would, if slightly veiled, sit at the center of Williams's work for the rest of his career, as he not only sought the "ability to make words" but also looked to popular readings of the everyday commercial landscape to do so (1:207). Driving is regularly entwined with writing, as the lines from the beginning of "The Moon" (1930) indicate:

> driving
> through bedrooms
> makes the car
> ride upon the page
> by virtue of
> the law of sentences. . . .

The "car ride" here assumes particular importance for a writer whose poetry is distinctly "car-eyed" and who regularly makes the car "write" as well as "ride" upon the page (1:326). And the linguistics of commercial signs and advertisements—such as the one for "Lee's Lunch," in which "Lee" and "Lunch" share a single oversized capital L (1:269)—become starting occasions for poems, as Williams seeks to liberate language from those "who betray their trust by allowing the language to be enslaved by its enemies: the philosophers and the venders of manure and all who cry their wares in the street and put up signs: House for sale."[74] His 1923 preparations for *Go-Go*, a pamphlet "to suggest the sense of breakthrough of a poetry of rapid transit,"[75] and the submission of his "Readie Pome" to Bob Brown's anthology of works for the hypothetical speed-reading machine (published by the appropriately named Roving Eye Press), suggest an ongoing interest in the intersection of literacy and technologies that moved the reader through the textual landscape or moved that landscape in front of the reader (*The Collected Poems of William Carlos Williams*, 1:356). I think that his occasional forays into rhyme, unconventional punctuation, and Creeley-like contractions, such as "sh'd," in his less frequently cited work from the 1940s and 1950s stem from what we might legitimately conceptualize as the driving desire to further understand or tap into the blurred languages of popular or vernacular literacy in his work, in order to better resist the commodification of language he saw happening in the larger culture.[76]

If Williams is pedagogical in the prose sections of *Spring and All*, by *Paterson: Book One* he has inserted that pedagogy into the poetry itself, encouraging the reader to continue reading creatively in the modern world and especially from the vantage point of the moving vehicle. As many have noted, *Paterson* as a whole takes its structure from the overlapping of, or blurring between, poetry and prose, creative and found texts, and themes of mind and body, history and present, city and man—"of this, make it of *this*, this / this, this, this this," Williams writes, with a scrapbooker's eye and probably Pound's model of the modern epic as a "rag-bag" in mind (141)—and Williams's "Preface" to the epic encourages us seven times in sixty-four lines to approach this structure as we would see it while "rolling up" in a speeding motorcar (4). Instead of invoking the Muse at some position of remove, Williams drives his reader to the scene—"Rolling in, top up, / under, thrust and recoil, a great clatter"—and establishes a refrain encouraging us to read the poem's juxtaposed prose sections, headlines, letters, and newspaper reports as we would from a highway or automobile lubricated by the oil we hear in "recoil," whose phonemes recirculate even in the word "rolling" (5). If *Book One*, as Williams wrote, "introduces the elemental character of the place" (xiv) of Paterson, then that character has everything to do with the experience of twentieth-century automobility—a sense confirmed by looking at Williams's early efforts writing about the city, such as "Paterson," from 1927, which not only includes bicycles, telephones, a dynamo, and a press but also envisions Mr. Paterson's thoughts "inside the bus" and "his flesh making the traffic" (*The Collected Poems of William Carlos Williams*, 1:264).

By 1946, when *Book One* appeared, the automobile had become such a part of American life that Williams no longer had to name it as forcefully and frequently as he did in *Spring and All* almost twenty-five years earlier. Nevertheless lines such as "Let's take a ride around, to see what the town looks like" serve to remind us that throughout the poem the connection between Williams's poetics and the automobile remains strong (*Paterson*, 106). From the beginning Williams makes these poetics a prime concern. Part 2 of *Book One* thus begins:

> There is no direction. Whither? I
> cannot say. I cannot say
> more than how. The how (the howl) only
> is at my disposal (proposal) :watching—
> colder than stone.
>
> . . . .
>
>   Divorce is
> the sign of knowledge in our time,
> divorce! divorce!
>
>   with the roar of the river
> forever in our ears (arrears)
> inducing sleep and silence. . . .
>
>   (17)

In this passage Williams teaches his reader how to (mis)read by visually illustrating what he means in *Book Four* when he writes, "Kill the explicit sentence, don't you think? and expand our meaning—by verbal sequences. Sentences, but not grammatical sentences: dead-falls set by schoolmen" (188).

He demonstrates the fluidity of those "verbal sequences" by showing us parenthetically how "how," "disposal," and "our ears" shift to become "howl," "proposal," and "arrears." As I've argued earlier, he does so by joining the visual to the aural, laying bare the aural phenomena in visual terms in order to make that process evident to the reader. In identifying the sound effects and sound defects that occur as "our ears" drifts toward "arrears" and back again at the very beginning of his epic, Williams alerts us to the generative possibilities of language that are central to the poem and that find their most elemental form in the surplus of meaning produced when phonemes and lexemes shift and drift.

Thus, encouraged to bring popular reading practices to the literary page, the reader is barraged by the phonotextual experience that follows—a sort of final exam for the lesson conducted in the previous lines. "The heavy air," for example, is followed by "their clear hair," which in turn is followed by "their hair," the words "hair," "air," and "rare" working together to blend body and landscape in the phonetic realization of the poem's main conceit (18). In tempting us to disentangle the word "heir" from this acoustic melee as well, these lines also introduce the theme of inheritance into the poem, which is a subject Williams takes up in later books of *Paterson*, not to mention in the compound word of the title itself, which is formed by a blurring of "father" and "son" that recalls the compound words of "St. Francis Einstein of the Daffodils." The resulting cloud (or fog) of connotations comes to bear shortly in the phrase "unaware of what air supports / us," the passage suggesting not only the aforementioned words "heir" and "hair" but also—in the drift between "what" and "air"—the word "tear" as well, figuring in that word's construction and deconstruction the ongoing rupture between words and generations in a city that burned down only to then be flooded out (23). Just as indentations, punctuation, and type size complicate the visual landscape of *Paterson*, that landscape is as phonetically rich as any of Williams's poetry, and, true to form, Williams insists on lending phonetics the century's visual character as well, whether he is quoting Pound ("Fer got sake" [138] and "IN / Venshun / o.kay" [184]) or using his parentheses to increase the potential for word play in his own phrases, such as "coup de (dis) grace" (183) and "relieved / (relived)" (60).

At times the density of *Paterson*'s visual and aural phenomena can come to feel exhausting and perhaps as overwhelming as the onslaught of commercial messages competing for the attention of drive-by readers in the first part of the twentieth century. What makes Williams's work especially noteworthy, however, is that no matter how intellectually exhausting his poetry may be, its literacy practices are rooted in—or at least cohabitate unexpectedly well with—similar practices that characterize and mark popular responses to mass and automobile cultures, ranging from the found poetry of movie marquees to the Shihtzunamis of car games. Williams didn't respond to the emerging culture of the automobile and automobile literacy with the antagonism of a Mary Austin or an Ezra Pound, nor with the sheer optimism of *Broom's* Matthew Josephson, nor even with the canniness of Demuth, who, like other modernist writers and artists, registered his protest against the larger commodity economy by using its commercial and billboard discourses in pieces of art accessible only to a small circle of friends. Rather, Williams responded to it with a great dexterity that came from recognizing, in the capacity of doctor, poet, and ordinary reader, both the benefits and drawbacks of American technology on everyday life. In 1945, as he was probably putting the finishing touches on, or correcting page proofs for, what would be *Paterson: Book One*, Williams took a break from his work and, for what Mariani calls a "special treat," took his grandson Paul to "a marvelous old-car dump" with "hundreds of junked cars."[77] Surely, for a man who had such a vexed relationship to his automobile, this visit had something of the same ambivalence—both the fulfillment of a longtime fantasy and a reverence for the machine that helped to make his poetics go.

CHAPTER 5

Popular Poetry and the Program Era

On December 4 and 5, 1959, the University of Iowa Writers' Workshop and *Esquire* magazine cosponsored a symposium that brought Ralph Ellison, Mark Harris, Dwight Macdonald, and Norman Mailer to the Iowa City campus, which was then called the State University of Iowa. This was the second such event that *Esquire*—led by founding editor and publisher Arnold Gingrich—had helped to organize. A year earlier Gingrich and *Esquire* had arranged for Saul Bellow, Leslie Fiedler, Wright Morris, and Dorothy Parker to convene at Columbia University in New York in order to discuss "The Position of the Writer in America Today." Under the somewhat narrowed rubric of "The Writer in a Mass Culture," Gingrich and longtime Writers' Workshop director Paul Engle welcomed an estimated audience of fifteen hundred to the Iowa prairie, opening an event that had been pitched to the press in functional, decidedly prosaic language.[1] "Four distinct statements of the problem," the press release read, "will be made by four widely published writers who have faced the constant issues of art and the market place."[2]

Rarely, if ever, did these symposia indicate that mass culture, popular culture, and the consumer marketplace could be anything other than "the problem" for the postwar writer. In New York Morris had complained of the "mindless society" into which he saw authors sending their work, and Harris's leadoff speech in 1959 picked up where Morris left off, with a wholesale denunciation of mass culture from the perspective of highbrow art and literature, which the Workshop, in its capacity as host and by virtue of its reputation for employing celebrated writers who either received or would go on to receive the Pulitzer Prize, was assumed to endorse.[3] "Most Americans would rather eat than read," Harris began. He continued:

> Let us no longer quibble over the question of whether our country men can receive or appreciate literature of the first rank. The fact is that they cannot. Art and mass distribution are simply incompatible. The writer has no business reaching for a mass audience and the serious reader has no business distracting the writer by discussing with him possible methods of bridging the gulf between the writer and the mass—it cannot be bridged.[4]

Harris went on to make several proposals that he felt would improve the situation of the literary arts in the United States, including a drastic reduction in the number of books published each year, the subsidizing of presses by wealthy foundations, and "the creation of a bureau of pure books and standards, whose role would not be censorship nor repression, but education and clarification" (Symposium transcript, "The Writer in a Mass Culture," box 11, 6). It is possible, I suppose, to interpret this performance as a Stephen Colbert–like send-up, but I don't think it was. Nor was Harris above naming names. "Let us declare once and forever," he implored, singling out the nationally syndicated "people's poet" of the *Detroit Free Press*, "Edgar Guest was never a poet" (ibid., 3).

While the symposium would go on to qualify, nuance, and temper some of Harris's opening remarks, neither Macdonald nor Mailer would challenge his general depiction of mass and popular culture. Macdonald, who would publish his famous essay "Masscult and Midcult" in the *Partisan Review* a year later, lamented the lack of a "cultivated class" in the United States that he saw in England and answered that "the serious writer has to . . . write for his peers" and not for a larger or more general audience (7–8). Calling mass culture "a dreadful thing"—and speaking forty-five years before he would guest star on a 2004 episode of WB's *Gilmore Girls* titled "Norman Mailer, I'm Pregnant"—Mailer proceeded to lend the symposium a rhetorically inflated but otherwise characteristically modernist misogynist depiction of mass culture by saying, "I consider it a war, I consider the mass media really as if I were living with a cancerous wife and each day I have to see her all the time and she gives me a bit of her cancer. That is about the way I feel about the mass media" (14–15). Only Ellison argued for a more sophisticated position. "A democracy," he cautioned, "is not just a mass, it is a collectivity of individuals. And when it comes to taste, when it comes to art, each and every one of these people must have the right, the opportunity, to develop his taste and must face the same type of uncertainty which all of us face on this platform" (16).

In the symposium's transcript, however, Engle is silent on these matters. From one perspective his silence is completely understandable; his job as moderator was to introduce the speakers, referee the question-and-answer periods that followed, and specifically not inject his own feelings on the subject. From another perspective, however, his silence is more provocative. For Engle—the man who had been elevating the profile of the Workshop for seventeen years, who had brought John Berryman, Robert Lowell, and Kurt Vonnegut to Iowa City to teach, who would mentor writers like Robert Bly, Philip Levine, Donald Justice, William Stafford, Charles Wright, and Flannery O'Connor, and who would go on for almost another decade to shape the Workshop into the gold standard for creative writing programs—was not only writing for publications such as *Better Homes and Gardens*, *Good Housekeeping*, *Ladies' Home Journal*, and *Reader's Digest*, but he was writing poems for Hallmark greeting cards as well.

I begin this book's final chapter with Engle and the University of Iowa Writers' Workshop in part because they symbolize a shift that began taking place in how "serious" literature would come to be produced and funded in the United States after World War II, when poets, for the first time in history, started to regularly find training as students and paychecks as teachers within the walls of higher education. Of the more than seven hundred graduate and undergraduate creative writing programs currently being administered in the United States—many imitating the model of the Workshop—not one existed before 1936, when Iowa founded its program and Ezra Pound and Edgar Guest were both over fifty years old.[5] Until the Cold War and the advent of what Mark McGurl has recently called the program era, creative writing training and careers teaching in higher education were comparatively unavailable to aspiring and accomplished poets—there wasn't the thriving market in creative writing classes that there is now, nor were universities' admissions processes as inclusive as they currently are—or else a college degree and teaching position were held to be unnecessary, even suspect, credentials when it came to the writing of poetry.[6] Edgar Guest, for example, started work as a newspaper copy boy and worked his entire career for the *Free Press*, publishing over twenty books and a reported eleven thousand poems, and receiving an honorary degree from the University of Michigan without ever earning a college credit, and many other poets of his generation—especially iconoclastic modernist or avant-garde writers—regarded colleges and universities as conservative institutions that stifled, rather than inspired, poetic innovation and creativity.[7] Robert Frost, who dropped out of Dartmouth and Harvard and became a chicken farmer, for example, would call the college teacher's approach to poetry "the worst system of teaching that ever endangered a nation's literature."[8] When he was appointed Poet in Residence at the University of Michigan in 1921—the second such designated position in the United States and what Frank Lentricchia has called "an industry inaugurating moment"[9]—it was on the condition that he wouldn't have to do any classroom teaching and could instead practice what he would come to call "education by presence."[10]

The rapid change in writers' attitudes toward colleges, universities, and teaching that occurred in the years leading up to and following the establishment of the Iowa Writers' Workshop is partly the subject of McGurl's study, *The Program Era: Postwar Fiction and the Rise of Creative Writing*, which examines how the institutionalization of creative writing has affected American fiction. For McGurl this shift is one of the most important developments in literary production and patronage in the history of Western literature.[11] "The gradual conjoining of the activities of literary production and teaching over the course of the postwar period is," he writes, "in the sheer scale of the institutional program building upon which it has depended, and in the striking reversal of attitudes that it suggests, about as close to a genuine historical novelty as one could hope to see."[12] There is no doubt that Engle and the Writers' Workshop drove this era and its new patronage and professionalization of writing in unparalleled ways, including how poetry would be imagined to interface with (or, more commonly, be insulated from) mass and popular culture.[13] That said, given their historical significance—as well as the Workshop's history of self-promotion and its promotion or publication of graduates' work through agents, presses, and contest judging—surprisingly little scholarship has emerged about Engle, the Workshop, or the impact they had on postwar America's sense of poetry as an art form and as a presence in the larger culture.[14]

The only recent study of note is Loren Glass's "Paul Engle and the Iowa Writers' Workshop," which argues, by way of Fredric Jameson's description of the "vanishing mediator," that Engle's charismatic leadership helped to routinize the once-unconventional idea of an MFA program in terms of a campus bohemia that would not stifle a writer's creativity but, instead, "would insulate the writer from mass culture and ensure the maintenance of a literary elite for the rest of the century and beyond."[15] So effectively did Engle serve as oracle and bureaucrat for this vision, Glass argues, that people have more or less forgotten there might be some other way of justifying or administering university-based creative writing programs and have thus forgotten Engle himself as an initial bearer of change.[16] I don't disagree with Glass's assessment of how Engle helped to sell the hospitality of the college campus to writers, but in this chapter I want to expand the view of Engle beyond his bureaucratic accomplishments and consider him as an aspiring, if ultimately unsuccessful, *aesthetic* mediator as well—someone who, as we can see in his relationship to Hallmark and elsewhere, not only had a foot in both popular and elite literary cultures but also tried to sustain, participate in, and even legitimize connections between both rather than, as the 1958 and 1959 symposia participants encouraged, advocate for one at the expense or exclusion of the other.

If Engle's vision of a poet who bridged popular and elite poetry cultures was not successfully routinized as part of Iowa's trend-setting ethos, that was due not just to the program era's general and ongoing impatience with mass culture but to a corresponding shift in the culture of popular poetry during the 1950s and 1960s as well. The subject of popular poetry's claims to cultural legitimacy—once taken for granted or debated with vigor because of its wide availability in the press, on radio, and elsewhere—would begin to disappear almost entirely from many poetry debates during the Cold War, as the terms of those conversations narrowed in focus, shifting, for example, from the broad high-versus-low binary to a more particular "raw"-versus-"cooked" one.[17] The disappearance of the popular from academic and artistic discourses is paralleled by, and perhaps even partly responsible for, a significant decrease in the amount of poetry published by newspapers and magazines— the *New York Times* phased out poetry from its Op-Ed pages in the 1950s, for instance—which contributed to a steep decline in poetry scrapbooking and related networks of poetry (re)circulation. Likewise, if poetry wasn't eliminated entirely from advertising campaigns as in the case of Burma-Shave, those campaigns incorporated fewer and shorter poems than before. The daily radio poetry shows of the 1920s, 1930s, and 1940s also began to drop off the air, no doubt run out in part by television comedians like Ernie Kovacs, who portrayed the tipsy, effeminate, bug-eyed poet Percy Dovetonsils in the 1950s and 1960s, and Henry Gibson, famous for his flower-holding poet on *Rowan and Martin's Laugh-In* in the late 1960s and early 1970s, who did television a favor by outing radio poets as shams, queers, or fops hiding behind the invisibility of their medium.[18] In short the culture of popular poetry in the late 1950s and 1960s looked and functioned very differently than it did just two or three decades earlier when Engle—who was raised in the earlier era of newspaper, magazine, radio, and advertising poetry—first joined the English Department at Iowa and soon after began leading the Workshop.

This doesn't mean that popular poetry ceased to exist; just as the world of "serious" poetry moved from bohemia onto college and university campuses, so the culture of popular poetry was reconfigured in relation to a range of different media and patronage systems. Its metered, rhyming, market-friendly lyrics found new application, for example, in the robust and expanding popular music industry, which transformed the energy of poetry scrapbooks into fanzines and (eventually) mix tapes, which reimagined write-in poetry programs as call-in music shows, and which created an authorial category of its own in the figure of the singer-songwriter; it is not unusual, in fact, to hear Bob Dylan described as the "people's poet"—the same term used to describe Edgar Guest during the first half of the century. Also during this time Hallmark Cards—which for decades had been marketing poetry via a wide range of consumer-oriented products and media (including record and radio) and not just on greeting cards—identified a growing vacuum at the center of popular poetry's print life and sought to fill that void by printing well-selling, reader-friendly anthologies like *Poetry for Pleasure: The Hallmark Book of Poetry*, by sponsoring poetry contests, by televising Shakespeare, and by creating new expectations for its greeting card verse. Hallmark's intervention in this market was so successful that, as a result, in many spheres today, the term "Hallmark poetry" is synonymous with "popular poetry."

That Engle, leading advocate for the new MFA system that was promising to save writers from the pressures of mass culture and the consumer marketplace, and Hallmark, a newly invigorated player in the production and distribution of poetry for that marketplace, should find each other in "the decade during which [the Workshop] consolidated its national reputation" is thus remarkable.[19] That such a partnership might have been part of Engle's larger vision for how an MFA program could operate is equally remarkable and challenges what we typically imagine to have been the aesthetic and historical impulses driving creative writing in the program era. That Engle's endeavors along these lines have by and large been ignored, forgotten, preemptively disparaged, or abandoned by scholars and historians of postwar poetry and the program era—not to mention by the beneficiaries of the very industry that Engle helped to create—seems less remarkable, though it is one reason, perhaps, why MFA programs have been accused of killing off a once publicly available poetry that, from the perspective of many readers outside the walls of higher education, may have been changing faces and sponsors during this time but never in fact died out.[20]

Straight From the Heartland

Engle was born on October 12, 1908, in Cedar Rapids—Iowa's second largest city, located twenty-five miles north of Iowa City, and home at the time to American regionalist painter Grant Wood. Engle came from a farming family of German descent. His parents, Thomas and Evelyn, ran a horse business, buying, selling, training, and renting race horses, work horses, and saddle horses; for a time they operated the Engles Riding Academy ("Learn the Thrill of Riding Horseback," one of the business's documents reads). Both of his grandfathers were Civil War veterans—a significant enough distinction for Engle to include it on his résumé. That same résumé reports that Paul helped with the family business, sold newspapers, and worked at a drug store and as a chauffeur and gardener while still in school. He attended McKinley Junior High School in Cedar Rapids, where his art teacher was Grant Wood; then he attended Washington High School (which was not only Wood's alma mater but also Carl Van Vechten's) where he served as class poet, penning among other things "Dedication Poem Read at the Planting of the Cedar by the Class of 1927," a verse, he explained on his résumé, that was "buried in a bottle under a new-planted class tree in schoolyard."[21] His early writing mentor was Jay G. Sigmund, a Cedar Rapids insurance executive and midwestern regionalist author who wrote over twelve hundred poems, who loaned Engle books (by Baudelaire, Longfellow, Edgar Lee Masters, Arthur Rimbaud, Carl Sandburg, and William Carlos Williams, among others), and who was friends or acquaintances with Sandburg, Sherwood Anderson, Sinclair Lewis, Robinson Jeffers, and Gertrude Stein. Engle would posthumously edit Sigmund's work and would contribute a poem ("For Jay G. Sigmund") to the Cedar Rapids *Gazette* on the occasion of Sigmund's death in 1937.[22] This literary world—where there were no inherent contradictions between reading Baudelaire, writing occasional verse for local newspapers, corresponding with Stein, and discussing poetry with insurance executives— would inform the rest of Engle's career.[23]

Engle graduated from Coe College in Cedar Rapids in 1931, preached for a time at Stumptown church "on edge of town," and might have entered the ministry were it not for the fact, included on his résumé, that he "heard no call." Nevertheless he would return to overtly religious themes throughout his career in poems like "Easter," which ran in *Better Homes and Gardens* in April 1960. That poem begins:

> From the dead winter comes
> Live season of rebirth,
> The old, gray rain now falls
> To green the turning earth.
>
> Christ once in that dim time
> Brought life and light to men,
> Hold of their hope: to die
> Once, and be born again.[24]

Given Engle's literary background and the points I want to press later in this chapter about his facility with popular verse formats, this poem is worth considering at some length before I move on.

Like much of Engle's popular writing, "Easter" routes a craftsman's skill through the conventions of popular poetry. From the perspective of what Macdonald called a "serious writer," the chief offense of "Easter" is probably the earnest and unqualified didacticism that spells out the metaphorical relationship between the current "season of rebirth" and Christ's resurrection "in that dim time" and thus (like a lot of popular and occasional verse) directly establishes or spotlights the importance of the subject rather than leaving it implicit or to be discovered; in the parlance of the creative writing workshop, "Easter" is a failure partly because it tells rather than shows. At the same time, however, Engle is hardly inattentive to language; in the pairing of alliterative and near-rhyming words within individual lines (gray/rain, dim/time, life/ light, hold/hope), "Easter" produces a rich sonic experience through the repetition of particular sounds—a repetition that arguably tropes the seasonally recurring resurrection that is Engle's subject and that also encourages readers to listen for the semantic relationships between those sets of words: from a Christian viewpoint in particular, there are thematic as well as phonemic relations between "life" and "light," "gray" and "rain," and "hold" and "hope." This is especially the case with the phrase "dim time," which not only echoes with the "Him" of Christ's person (line 21) and even the "hymn" of religious celebration, but potentially reads *backward* as well, figuring—in the legibility of "mid" and "emit" ("dim" and "time" in reverse)—Christ's own reversal of death and subsequent springtime rebirth in the *Mid*west, as well as the reversal of dimness through the "life and light" that Christ the "living fire" (line 19) is imagined to "emit." Prompted by the sense of these sounds, and also by the poem's self-reflexive claim that the "Shape of His Word is made / Out of our living breath" (lines 25–26), to read both forward and backward, it is difficult not to also hear or see the thematically relevant "son" in "season" and the "gain" in "again," not to mention the humble first-person speaker subordinated to the greater drama but nonetheless present in the "I've" and "I'm" of "live," "dim," "time," and "life"—all sounds that embed the lyric self and religious subject in the seasonal and acoustic renewals that preacher-turned-poet Engle finds in Easter.

The subject of immanence—of the resurrection in every spring, of the sacred in the natural, of the past in the present, of "God-in-man" (line 23), of one word (or Word) in the sounds or shapes of another—introduced and performed by the poem is further developed not just by the rest of "Easter" but also by the layout it later was given by Hallmark, which printed a shortened version of the verse in the shape of a cross inside a greeting card titled "A Message at Easter" (see figures 5.1 and 5.2).[25] In asking the reader to read and hear "Easter" in relation to the "shape of His Word," Engle and Hallmark likely take George Herbert's 1633 poem "Easter Wings" as a model, not just in terms of the religious subject matter and concrete format they share, but also for how Herbert's poem develops its own theme of immanence in nearly the exact same acoustic way that Engle's does; the word and phoneme "in"

FIGURE 5.1. "A Message at Easter," Hallmark greeting card, circa 1960. Courtesy of the Hallmark Archives, Hallmark Cards, Inc.

EASTER
By Paul Engle

From the dead winter comes
Live season of rebirth,
Now the old, gray rain falls
To green the turning earth.

Christ once in that dark time   Christ on that hand-hewn wood
Brought life and light to men,   Proved death could not avail,
Hold of their hope: to die   Proved it by hands that bore
Once, and be born again.   The hand-hewn, beaten nail.

Earth like a stone rolls back
Before the cave we seek
To show the God-in-man
And make our voices speak:

Shape of His Word is made
Out of our living breath,
Shape of our life is made
Out of His living death.

May your Easter

be blessed

with peace and joy

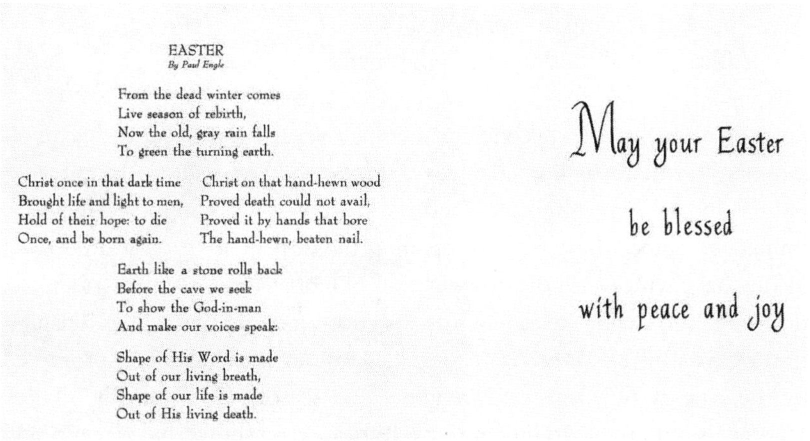

FIGURE 5.2. Interior of "A Message at Easter," featuring the poem "Easter" by Paul Engle. Courtesy of the Hallmark Archives, Hallmark Cards, Inc.

(present in the first, last, and two middle or hinge lines of Herbert's poem) structures the acoustic economy of "Easter Wings" and echoes throughout in the words "beginne," "sinne," "combine," "thine," and even "wing" itself:

> Lord, who createdst man in wealth and store,
>   Though foolishly he lost the same,
>   Decaying more and more,
>   Till he became
>   Most poore:
>   With thee
>   O let me rise
>   As larks, harmoniously,
>   And sing this day thy victories:
> Then shall the fall further the flight in me.

> My tender age in sorrow did beginne
>   And still with sicknesses and shame.
>   Thou didst so punish sinne,
>   That I became
>   Most thinne.
>   With thee
>   Let me combine,
>   And feel thy victorie:
>   For, if I imp my wing on thine,
> Affliction shall advance the flight in me.

In its own appearance as a concrete poem, however, Engle's "Easter" acquires a dimension that was unavailable to Herbert in the seventeenth century— publication as a greeting card—and that further develops Engle's focus on immanence, since the activity of opening the card itself is an act of looking inside that rhymes with the investigation of Christ's tomb in lines 13 and 14, not to mention with the acts of introspection (looking inward) and inspira- tion ("Shape of His Word is made / Out of our living breath") prompted by the synergy of poem, card, religion, and season. Unexpectedly, Engle's "Easter" is not just an argument that tells more than shows, but it makes and develops its argument about Christ's immanence as a self-consciously literary poem would do, taking advantage of, and mixing, the many resources at its disposal: the precedent of literary tradition, the acoustic and semantic thickness of language, material layout and typography, popular convention, and the additional medium of the greeting card.

Partly out of a commitment to the region and literary culture in which "Easter" would have been an acceptable poem, and unlike many midwestern-born poets who went or would go East, Engle stayed in the Midwest for graduate school, completing an MA at Iowa in 1932 and submitting a collection of poems (*One Slim Feather*) that would become his first book, *Worn Earth*, to fulfill the thesis requirement. That year Stephen Vincent Benét selected *Worn Earth* as the winner of the Yale Series of Younger Poets prize—he gave the same award to socially inclined poets James Agee and Muriel Rukeyser in 1934 and 1935, respectively. Engle then spent 1933 to 1936 in Oxford, England, as a Rhodes Scholar, where, in addition to playing wicket keeper on the Merton College cricket team and rowing well enough in the college eights to compete in the International Regattas at Marlowe and Henley on the Thames, he also published in the explicitly leftist *New Masses* ("Maxim Gorky" appeared December 29, 1936). Neither his extracurricular activities nor his *New Masses* publication earned him much favor; W. H. Auden, C. Day Lewis, and Stephen Spender expressed "disapproval" at the diversions the former offered,[26] and years later the Marxist sentiments expressed in "Maxim Gorky" and elsewhere got Engle pegged "as a possible member of the Communist front,"[27] though he never faced the sort of scrutiny from the House Un-American Activities Committee that other writers did; in fact, during the 1960s he would work closely with the U.S. government in the funding and operation of the International Writing Program at Iowa.

Upon his return to the United States in 1937, Engle was invited to join Iowa's English Department faculty as a poetry lecturer, and he was appointed acting director of the Writers' Workshop in 1942, when Workshop founder and then director Wilbur Schramm left for Washington, D.C., to participate in the war effort. At the time the Workshop was still part of the English Department. Today, in a separation that is emblematic of a divide between creative writers and scholar-critics at the university level, the Workshop has its own faculty, occupies its own building, and offers its own courses open (with a few exceptions) only to Workshop students and taught only by creative writing faculty.[28] In the mid-1960s personality conflicts and an administrative rift that Stephen Wilbers calls "the upheaval of 1964–66"—an upheaval that Glass argues is the inevitable product of a clash between the institutional authority of literary studies and the anti-institutional, charismatic authority of bohemian-leaning creative writing—precipitated this split at Iowa and eventually led to Engle's resignation as director, an event that Wilbers positions as central to the Workshop's maturation, calling the years that followed (1966–1980) a "postscript."[29]

After Engle left the Workshop—and working with his second wife, the Chinese-born novelist Hualing Engle—he founded the International Writing Program (IWP), which is headquartered today across the street from the Workshop on the northeast corner of the campus and serves in large part as a literary arm of the U.S. State Department. Engle was instrumental in getting start-up money from the United States Information Agency, which sponsored the Fulbright scholarship program and Voice of America broadcasts, and he reportedly raised over two million dollars to fund the program. For building the IWP, which has since brought over a thousand writers from 120 countries to Iowa City, Paul and Hualing were nominated for the 1976 Nobel Prize. Engle retired in 1977, and there is not much information on how he spent the following years; he died in O'Hare Airport in March of 1991 while traveling to Poland to accept that government's Order of Merit. He has been described as "charming, difficult, cantankerous, demanding, generous, cold and reserved, warm and open, a man of so many contradictions it would be presumptuous . . . to resolve them."[30] Joseph Wilson's short biography of Engle in *American Poets, 1880–1945* claims that Engle's "impact has been felt in three areas [poetry writing, the Writers' Workshop, and the IWP], any one of which would have been an entire career for someone less determined and energetic."[31] Engle is a major historical reason behind the University of Iowa's ability to brand itself, as it now does, as "the Writing University," and the programs he shepherded are some of the primary reasons why UNESCO designated Iowa City a "World City of Literature" in 2008. All indicators would suggest, as Vince Clemente has written, "there is no escaping Paul Engle."[32]

A Popular Angle

And yet, as Glass has observed, "few Workshop graduates know anything about him, and none read his poetry."[33] Indeed, despite the effects of Engle's lifework, today it is not hard to escape him almost entirely; in fact, to escape him—to have him vanish as the symbol of change he was—is now virtually a precondition of the Workshop's prestige as the world's oldest and most proven writing program. From the artistic values the Workshop has come to represent, to the institutional and pedagogical practices it models and the purposes of creative writing in American culture it promotes, it is difficult to imagine, much less establish, a creative writing workshop philosophy structured any other way, even though the Iowa program is just over seventy-five years old. I was in my fourth or fifth year of graduate study in Iowa's English Department before I happened upon a poem by Engle— a sonnet titled "American Child: 3" that Engle published and republished in the 1940s and 1950s. "American Child: 3" first appeared in the January 1945 issue of *Ladies' Home Journal* and was part of a sonnet sequence Engle developed between 1944 and 1956. Published as *American Child: A Sonnet Sequence* by Random House in 1945, then reprinted in 1956 by the Dial Press with an additional thirty-six poems as *American Child: Sonnets for My Daughters*, the sequence had a public life beyond these volumes as well. Eleven of its poems were printed locally in an edition of three hundred copies at Carroll Coleman's Prairie Press of Muscatine, Iowa, in 1944 (just before the press would move to the University of Iowa, where Coleman would teach in the School of Journalism and later serve as the university's director of publications), and others appeared individually in an eclectic mix of little magazines and mass-circulation periodicals, including the *Kenyon Review*, *Poetry*, *Life*, and *Mademoiselle*.

I didn't come across "American Child: 3" in any of these places, however. Instead I found it in the poetry scrapbook that I showcased at the end of chapter 1—the anthology assembled by Joyce Fitzgerald, who collected the verse in the "Authorized Edition" of her *Shirley Temple Scrap Book* in the early 1940s, mixing it with poetry by Edna St. Vincent Millay, Louis Untermeyer, Christina Rossetti, Emily Dickinson, Carolyn Kizer, and Ogden Nash as well as with childhood rhymes, genteel and sentimental poetry, and poems about the war in Europe, including religious verse about pacifist responses to American military intervention. I bring up Fitzgerald's anthology here in part to read Engle's poetics alongside the antipopulist rhetoric of "The Writer in a Mass Culture." For while Harris, Macdonald, and Mailer might have had a difficult time taking seriously the aesthetic or intellectual project of Fitzgerald's scrapbook, I think it would have made perfect sense to Engle and Ellison, both of whom understood, as Ellison explained, that "when it comes to taste, when it comes to art, each and every one of these people must have the right, the opportunity, to develop his taste and must face the same type of uncertainty which all of us face on this platform." Engle, who could hire Lowell and Berryman to teach at the Workshop while simultaneously drumming up ideas for Hallmark cards, believed in and understood the importance and artistic challenges of a range of poetries engaging U.S. culture and opted for a model of the author's involvement in everyday life rather than the firm and steadfast separation from the "mindless society" that the symposium's participants were advocating. In an essay or lecture he drafted in the late 1950s (then titled "The Need for Poetry"), he writes, "In our age of mass communication, it is poetry which steadily asserts the need for individual communication. Of all the arts, it is poetry which most exactly deals with the life of the self in its dailiest daily ways."[34] Nor was this an idea he would abandon. His drafts for "Why Read Poetry?"—which are undated but appear to be from the mid-1960s—also call for the poet's engagement with his or her culture. "If poetry, as I have said earlier," he writes, referencing political poetry by John Milton and Percy Shelley, "is a whole life experience put intensely into words, then the poet must be a whole person, and it is for that reason that he cannot be an aloof individual cutting himself off from the rest of the world."[35]

Here is "American Child: 3" as it appeared in *Ladies' Home Journal* in 1945, four months before the end of World War II in Europe and eight months before the Allied victory in the Pacific:

Lucky the living child born in a land
Bordered by rivers of enormous flow:
Missouri running through its throat of sand,
Mississippi growling under snow;
A country confident that day or night,
Planting, plowing or at evening rest
It has a trust like childhood, free of fright,
Having such powers to hold it east and west.
Water edged with willow gray or green
Edges the hours and meadows where she plays.
Where the black earth and the bright time are piled,
She lives between those rivers as between
Her birth and death, and is in these bold days
A water-watched and river-radiant child.[36]

Employing a diction strikingly similar to that of "Easter"—the words "born," "land," "green," "time," "gray," "living," "earth," "hold," and "death" appear in both poems and suggest that Engle was consciously using a vocabulary that had particular resonance in the popular tradition—"American Child: 3" is, by most modernist and workshop criteria, an unsuccessful poem. It is filled with what Pound called the "painted adjectives" characteristic of popular verse ("living child," "bright time," "bold days," "enormous flow"), it hardly goes in fear of abstractions (birth, death, childhood, trust, fright), and it offends the "show don't tell" mantra of institutionally taught writing. Its inverted syntax ("with willow gray or green") and apparently sentimental celebration of national or regional innocence in which the land is represented by a child—these and other aspects damage the poem's literary credibility and no doubt helped to fuel critical assessments of Engle's poetry as "painstakingly derivative" and even "pompous."[37] In fact, in a judgment that Mark Harris would echo in his dismissal of Edgar Guest at the 1959 symposium, Malcolm Cowley once described Engle as an "orator" and "not a poet at all."[38]

Yet, like "Easter," "American Child: 3" is more complicated than these assessments suggest. In employing the poeticisms of popular verse that would make it unsuccessful from a workshop standpoint—that is, in engaging the discourse of popular poetry in ways that other writers could not or would not—Engle purchases a voice in a public discussion about the nature of American privilege and moral righteousness during wartime. "American Child: 3" is nothing if not a wartime poem; like Robert Frost's "The Gift Outright," which was published in the *Virginia Quarterly Review* three years earlier, Engle's poem is a rhetorically inflated sonnet celebrating the power and plenty of the "land" and "country" that is protected by "such powers" in the "bold days" of the 1940s. For all of that rhetoric, however, "American Child: 3" ends up troubling assumptions common to the patriotic or sentimental poem genre more generally. Its first line ("Lucky the living child born in a land"), for example, relies on an otherwise unnecessary word, the adjective "living," in order to alliterate with, and thus acoustically highlight, the circumstantial nature of national identity and national privilege posited in the poem's first word, "lucky"; as with "Easter" "American Child: 3" uses the sounds of the language to help direct the poem's sense. At a time when claims to American moral superiority were at a fever pitch in the United States, Engle's opening "lucky" reminds his readers that the relationship between the individual and the United States is a product of chance, not destiny, and thus not a marker or determining factor of moral goodness. The American child, his poem argues, is not inherently more righteous than other people around the world by virtue of having been born American, just luckier; lucky, too, is the land and nation the child represents, edged and protected by the Atlantic and Pacific just as the child "lives between" the Mississippi and Missouri rivers, but not morally one thing or another because of that fact. Compared to "The Gift Outright"—which also emphasizes the word "land" (using it six times), which also genders that land as female, and which even pairs "land" with "living" (line 10) as Engle does, but which otherwise focuses on the relationship between nationality and manifest destiny rather than nationality and luck—"American Child: 3" uses the conventions of patriotic poetry in order to enter but then recalibrate a discussion of national identity and its privileges.

Written at a time of mass human displacement and migration, Engle's first line further presses the subject of American circumstance by adding—again via alliteration (with the words "lucky" and "living" alliterating with "land")—that the poem's child is lucky for having been "born in [that] land." In casting native birth as the product of good fortune and not entitlement or reward, Engle not only challenges the moral superiority of nativist rhetoric but indirectly asks his reader to consider the experiences of individuals who have *not* been born in the United States and what American responsibilities to those people might be. In fact, all of the "painted adjectives" in "Lucky the living child born in that land" (and throughout the poem) ask the reader to consider their alternatives: the unlucky child, the dead child, the child not born in that land, a childhood that is not free of fright, and so on. As someone who grew up "doing odd jobs for families in the local Jewish community" and who "lit fires on Sabbath as a 'Shabas goy,'" it is possible that Engle responded particularly acutely to the forced displacement of Jews and other groups during World War II and the lack of privilege that brought them to, and in some cases got them turned away from, the security his archetypal child enjoys by virtue of her American birth. In engaging discourses of nationality on the level of myth rather than the specifics of history—Engle does not, for example, address how some Americans are more privileged than others despite their common birthplace—"American Child: 3" certainly plays to depictions of the nation as innocent and thus works to sustain the untroubled moral position of the U.S. war effort. Yet the depiction of that position is not an evangelical one, as it encourages or gives readers the opportunity (Ellison's word) to examine the sources of their American privilege rather than simply capitulate to a rhetoric of patriotism based on appeals to manifest destiny or divine mandate.

As with every close reading it is difficult to tell if these aspects of "American Child: 3" actually resonated with its readers. That is, did *Ladies' Home Journal* audiences actually triangulate the sonic and semantic aspects of "lucky," "living," and "land" as the poem encourages them to? Fitzgerald's *Shirley Temple Scrap Book* suggests that, yes, some readers—or at least one young woman— keyed into the subject of Engle's poem and used it as a way of thinking through the issues as they pertained to her life. As I explain in chapter 1, Fitzgerald's scrapbook has many themes; her editorial rubric includes poems about new shoes and housework as well as poems about soldiers leaving for war and the status of conscientious objectors; "The Death of the G-A-R (a rhyme for Memorial Day)," for example, is immediately followed by the nature poem "Dune Flowers"; "Air Burial" is preceded by "The Girl I Prize." Throughout the album, though, Fitzgerald regularly includes poems about the war and especially the subject of immigration as it intersects with American nationality and the moral obligations therein. Take, for example, Jan Struther's "The American Way of Life." Struther's narrator encounters an "old man" spouting "His own particular / Hymn of Hate," in which he decries "Helping the Russians / And helping the Jews" and lobbies, instead, for preserving "Our own, / Known, / Sure, / Secure, / Great American Way of Life." The narrator begins her rebuttal by appealing precisely to her own comparatively insecure experience as a recent immigrant. "I'm only a guest / From across the sea," she explains, "And I've only been here / Two years or three." It is exactly this status as a nonnative U.S. speaker that enables Struther's speaker to recognize, think about, and promote an American tradition of extending help to those in need rather than simply preserving or resting sure and secure in one's own privileged way of life. "And, though they ached / From their own day's labors," the speaker concludes, referencing "The men who founded / And built this land" and thus engaging the debate in terms of the national mythology (as Engle does) as well as her own life experience, "They were never too tired / To help their neighbors."

Many of the poems that follow "The American Way of Life" in Fitzgerald's scrapbook also investigate the extent to which U.S. foreign policy is a function of, or morally contingent upon, the nation's immigrant past. In "Stars

Through the Perilous Night," for example, Kizer argues that "by our deeds shall liberty / be manifest" and concludes the poem's second section with a partial catalog of liberty's agents:

> By Gutzon Borglum's presidents in Black Hills,
> by Carl Sandburg and the People,
> yes, always by the people,
> shall liberty be known. By John Curry's
> murals of John Brown,
> by Albert Einstein playing the violin at Princeton,
> by our sad-faced refugees, learning
> to smile again.

Five pages after Kizer's "sad-faced refugees," the anonymous poem "This Is Worth Fighting For" concludes, "We must not fail the world now. / We must not fail to share our freedom with it—afterwards." Engle's "American Child: 3" follows two pages later, its thematic place in the sequence secured three pages on by Struthers Burt's "My People Came to This Country," also cut out of *Ladies' Home Journal*, which recognizes the pattern of wartime displacement and notes that "the ghosts of countless countrymen / Are on the march again." I think it is fair to say from this context that Fitzgerald is responding to Engle's poem not because it simply celebrates the innocence of the American childhood but because of the moral obligations that Engle indirectly suggests that the luck of "being born in [that] land" entails. Judging from the poems about pacifism that she includes, Fitzgerald appears to have been conflicted on the morality of U.S. involvement in the war, even at its late stage. What matters for the purposes of this chapter is not whether she made up her mind—or even whether Engle's poem helped her make up her mind—but rather that "American Child: 3" provided her with an opportunity to think through the subject of American privilege and moral accountability during wartime. I would submit that Engle's grasp of the painted adjective, poetic abstraction, and other conventions of popular verse appreciated by popular audiences but typically avoided by workshop-era writers is what probably secured "American Child: 3" its readership and relevance. I also suspect that Engle knew the aesthetic balances and challenges that such writing entailed and envisioned it as something the creative writing student at Iowa might legitimately be trained to do.

Hallmarks of Achievement

The press release for "The Writer in a Mass Culture" identifies Engle as a professor but goes to significant lengths to highlight his connections with the popular press—so much so that his reputation in more literary venues is not only syntactically subordinated but also evoked, it seems, only for the purpose of paying it lip service. In addition to running the Workshop, the release explains, "Professor Engle has written widely also for nationally circulated popular magazines, as well as for literary publications. He is author of articles in the July issue of *Reader's Digest* and the magazine *Holiday*."[39] Curiously, the press release then proceeds to track the history and provenance of the *Reader's Digest* piece, establishing its value by connection to—not separation from—its mass-cultural contexts: "The *Reader's Digest* feature, 'That Old-Time Fourth of July,' is sub-titled, 'A lament for the vanished day that wasn't "safe and sane" but *was* gloriously exciting.' It gives a nostalgic description of the Fourth of his boyhood. The article appeared originally in the July, 1958, issue of *Better Homes and Gardens*."[40] Engle would go on to do further work for *Reader's Digest*, authoring among other things the major part of *Country Ways: A Celebration of Rural Life* (1988), but the press release's description of his writing life is nonetheless an odd one, especially considering how it leaves unnoted the facts that, by the time of the symposium in 1959, he had published ten books and had judged the O. Henry Awards for five years in a row.[41]

Whether or not Engle had a hand in crafting the release—and I suspect he did—it is evident that a certain amount of his credibility as writer and administrator hinged not only on his position at the Workshop but on his work's broader appeal. No doubt this was part of his strategy for publicizing the Workshop; when Engle himself wrote about his ongoing public relations efforts, it was also in relation to the "newspapers and magazines" of mass culture. "Publicity and fund-raising are not peculiar gifts given some people and not others," he has said:

> Without proper and dignified publicity, with facts to back it up, no program can survive or even keep the reputation it once had. It took years of failure, years of finding the right approaches, to persuade newspapers and magazines to recognize the uniqueness and productivity of the Writers' Workshop. The same with money—it took years of failing, of refusing to accept NO as a suitable answer, before I learned

about fund-raising. Self-taught, since no one in this University could give me practical advice (I speak of the humanities, since the sciences are a special case), I learned the hard and obstinate way, and not for self-aggrandizement, but for the Workshop.[42]

Engle secured corporate sponsorship of the Workshop from Iowa-based companies Quaker Oats and Amana Refrigeration, and certainly this was one incentive for also partnering with Hallmark. When he judged the Hallmark-sponsored Kansas City Poetry Contests in 1967, for example, he teamed with fellow judges William Stafford (an Iowa graduate) and Donald Hall to award four of the contest's six top one-hundred-dollar Hallmark Honor Prizes to Workshop students (Jon Anderson, Michael Dennis Browne, Peter Klappert, and Steven Orlen), all of whom would go on to careers teaching at the university level.[43] And when he assembled the 470-page anthology *Poetry for Pleasure: The Hallmark Book of Poetry* in 1960, he did so with the aid of a paid Iowa student assistant, poet Lewis Turco, and opened the book with a "New Voices" section of thirty-three poems, at least eight of which were by Iowa students or graduates.[44]

And yet Engle's partnership with Hallmark—which included writing greeting cards throughout the 1950s and a libretto for the Hallmark Hall of Fame television feature *Golden Child: A Christmas Opera* (1960)—is not entirely explained by the impulse to publicize or raise money for the Workshop or to promote its students' careers. In the introduction to his 1961 Random House anthology of Workshop literature *Midland: Twenty-five Years of Fiction and Poetry, Selected from the Writing Workshops of the State University of Iowa*, Engle explains that his vision for Iowa resulted from his belief that "there must be an alternative between Hollywood and New York, between these places psychically as well as geographically."[45] Engle did not think small. In what Donald Justice has described as "a kind of pyramid scheme," Engle set up a system by which Workshop students would graduate from Iowa and start similar programs at other universities, channeling more students to Iowa and providing more job opportunities for Iowa graduates while institutionalizing the campus bohemia as the midwestern alternative he envisioned.[46] Similarly, when he set up the IWP it was to bring writers from around the world to Iowa (not to send Iowans around the world) and to thus establish Iowa as an alternative international literary hub. I think that Engle saw a similar opportunity in partnering with Hallmark, which not only had in place a well-oiled machine for producing and distributing poetry to popular audiences but also had its own charismatic leader in the person of company founder Joyce C. Hall, seventeen years Engle's senior, who, like Engle, came from a midwestern farming background (Nebraska) and who had committed to keeping his business in the Midwest (Kansas City). Hall's grandfathers, like Engle's, had fought in the Civil War. Like Engle, Hall had relationships with national and international dignitaries—he once exhibited Winston Churchill's paintings in Kansas City—yet he rooted his vision for Hallmark in the culture of midwestern popular poetry that had propelled Ted Malone (from Missouri) and Tony Wons (from Wisconsin) to stardom on radio, that had underwritten the success of the Burma-Vita Company (headquartered in Minnesota), and that Engle had experienced growing up in Cedar Rapids.[47] With a partnership with Hallmark in place Engle could have achieved a perfect literary trifecta, rerouting not only elite American and international writing circuits through Iowa City but the circuits of popular poetry as well.

What made the prospects of such a partnership especially possible was Hallmark's decision to hitch its marketing strategy in the 1950s and 1960s to the rhetoric and promotion of good taste, offering a wide range of products that appealed to people's individual preferences while also committing itself to public programming aimed at improving the public's taste more collectively.[48] ("Good Taste Is Good Business," reads a subheading in Hall's 1979 autobiography, *When You Care Enough*,[49] a sentiment echoed in the book's foreword by Chairman of the Board Dr. Franklin D. Murphy, who explains that "there are two characteristics that have been central to [Hall's] remarkable achievements—great but disciplined imagination and a deep commitment to the concept of good taste."[50]) This commitment led to a Hallmark Editions imprint that published and sold millions of copies of gift books featuring poetry by Shakespeare, Ralph Waldo Emerson, Elizabeth Barrett Browning, Walt Whitman, Emily Dickinson, and others. It led to sponsorship of the Kansas City Poetry Contests, judged in the 1960s and 1970s by Conrad Aiken, Karl Shapiro, Louis Untermeyer, Robert Penn Warren, Carolyn Kizer, John Hollander, James Dickey, Kenneth Rexroth, May Swenson, Engle, and others. And it led to what is now the second-longest-running program in the history of television, the Hallmark Hall of Fame series that produced the first nationally televised performance of Shakespeare (a two-hour version of *Hamlet* starring Maurice Evans in 1953) and to which Engle would later contribute by writing the libretto for *A Golden Child*. "The [broadcasts] established the concept of the TV special," Hall explains in *When You Care Enough*. "But perhaps the most important first was that *Hamlet* was seen that April Sunday by more people than had seen it in the 350 years since it had been written."[51] Hall isn't exaggerating. A year after the *Hamlet* broadcast— and five years before Dwight MacDonald would tell symposium audiences at Iowa that for the "serious writer . . . an ideal size public is about 5,000" (Symposium transcript, "The Writer in a Mass Culture," box 4)—the Hallmark-sponsored production of *The Tempest* had over forty million viewers.

This commitment to elevating tastes affected the poetry printed in Hallmark greeting cards as well. While regularly citing Edgar Guest's "A Friend's Greeting"

> I'd like to be the sort of friend that you have been to me.
> I'd like to be the help that you are always glad to be,
> I'd like to mean as much to you each minute of the day
> As you have meant, Good Friend of Mine, to me along the way.
> And this is just to wish somehow that I could but repay
> A portion of the gladness that you've strewn along my way,
> For could I have one wish today, this only would it be,
> I'd like to be the sort of friend that you have been to me.

as the best-selling verse in Hallmark history, Hall repeatedly wrote about changes in the public's taste since 1916 when Guest's verse was first used. In "Taste and Times," Hall's introduction to *Poetry for Pleasure*, for example, Hall praises how records, magazines, and television have made opportunities to experience art more widely available than ever before, improving the public's taste in the process—its taste in greeting card poetry included. "Taste is becoming more refined," he explains:

> Our ability to appreciate the finer things in life has increased in every respect. Personally, I have seen these gradual changes in taste during a half century of watching the American public improve its taste from year to year in the selection of greeting cards. I am amazed when I look back ten years at the cards people preferred then; and when I look back twenty years, I am shocked. . . . I just don't agree with the talk I sometimes hear about the American public having the mind of a twelve-year-

old. . . . We've published several great poets of the past on Hallmark
Cards (Wordsworth, Shakespeare, Tennyson, FitzGerald) as well as a
number of fine contemporary poets (Pasternak, MacLeish, Engle, and
Williams). They sell.[52]

Likewise, in *When You Care Enough* Hall uses high circulation figures of greet-
ing cards featuring respected poets (Shakespeare, Elizabeth Barrett Brown-
ing, John Keats, Dickinson, Whitman, Archibald MacLeish, Boris Pasternak,
Phyllis McGinley, and Ogden Nash) as a barometer of both Hallmark's and
the public's taste for poetry. "Our writers," he explains, "see their work pub-
lished on millions of greeting cards that reach many more millions of people
since each card is shared by at least two individuals—and usually more."[53] The
"tough work" and pressure of writing for so many readers, Hall implies, actu-
ally brings out the best in Hallmark's "talented and prolific" writers.[54]

No wonder, then, that Engle would have been attracted to a relationship
with Hallmark. Linking the Workshop to Hallmark's publication machine
would have been a remarkable scheme from an otherwise remarkable schemer
aiming to establish the Midwest as a primary center of literary production,
but that long-term partnership ultimately didn't happen—perhaps because
of the "upheaval of 1964–66," which led to Engle's departure from the Work-
shop—even though, over the years, Hallmark has regularly hired poets (some
of them educated at Iowa, no doubt) to visit Kansas City and lead workshops
with staff writers (some of whom may have been educated at Iowa as well).
Other than *Poetry for Pleasure* and *A Golden Child*, the only remaining trace of
Engle's relationship with Hallmark (outside of Hallmark company archives)
is a slim file folder labeled "Poems for Hallmark" that is stored in box 12 of
the Paul Engle papers at the University of Iowa Libraries Special Collections
and contains a number of greeting card verses Engle had been working on
between 1952 and 1957. Some of the poems are marked as successful; others
are not, perhaps indicating that they did not get picked up for Hallmark pub-
lication or that they needed more work. Many have handwritten comments
on them, and their Edgar Guest–like titles are not surprising: "A Little Boy
Means," "Friendship," "For A Birthday," and so on.[55] There is even a copy of
Guest's "A Friend's Greeting," perhaps supplied by Hallmark, that presum-
ably served as a reference point for Engle's writing.[56]

When I found it, the "Poems for Hallmark" folder opened with a fin-
ished Hallmark greeting: a Christmas card with a green cover showing

three wise men embossed in gold (see figures 5.3 and 5.4). Inside, the right-hand panel reads, "May your Christmas be filled with true joy," and the left-hand panel—which we are accustomed to seeing left blank so that users can gloss the industrially printed greetings with messages of their own—contains "The Wise Men" with Engle's byline centered immediately below the title:

> Seeing that star,
> The Wise Men, swift
> To bow to the Boy,
> Gave Him their gift.
>
> Their gift was gold,
> And the bent knee,
> Hard metal and
> Humility.
>
> Now He, the Son
> Of Joseph's wife,
> Gives them His gift:
> Immortal life.
>
> This is the hope
> Of a world gone wild:
> When proud men kneel
> To a little Child.[57]

As with "Easter" and "American Child: 3," there is much to dislike about this verse from the perspective of a creative writing workshop: the beginner-level rhymes (swift/gift, wife/life, wild/child); the simplified, preachy narrative; the didactic impulse that tells rather than shows and results in a clichéd moral ("This is the hope / Of a world gone wild"). Not coincidentally, though, Engle uses some of the same strategies he used in "American Child: 3" and "Easter," including heavy alliteration (seeing/star, bow/boy, gave/gift, gift/gold) and a vocabulary (hope, gift, child, life) that was particularly common and freighted with special importance in discourses of sentimental and schoolroom poetries.[58]

FIGURE 5.3. "The Wise Men," Hallmark greeting card, circa 1960. Courtesy of the Hallmark Archives, Hallmark Cards Inc.

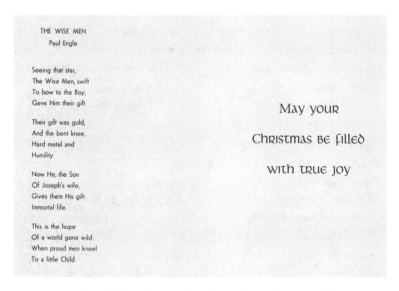

THE WISE MEN
Paul Engle

Seeing that star,
The Wise Men, swift
To bow to the Boy,
Gave Him their gift.

Their gift was gold,
And the bent knee,
Hard metal and
Humility.

Now He, the Son
Of Joseph's wife,
Gives them His gift.
Immortal life.

This is the hope
Of a world gone wild
When proud men kneel
To a little Child

May your

Christmas be filled

with true joy

FIGURE 5.4. Interior of "The Wise Men," featuring Paul Engle's poem of the same title. Courtesy of the Hallmark Archives, Hallmark Cards Inc.

Characteristically, though, and perhaps in sync with Hallmark's desire to up the reputation of its poetry, Engle's poem uses but then stretches the conventions of greeting card verse. "The Wise Men" does not, for example, pursue a more conventional expression of sentiment couched in abstractions like Guest's "A Friend's Greeting," nor does it work with a clear, familiar, and manageable metaphor like the one linking spring and the Resurrection in "Easter." Rather, it uses a narrative, which requires not only that the writer meet an additional set of demands (a reasonable retelling of the biblical story) within the already demanding meter and rhyme of the abbreviated ballad stanza and the limited space of the card's left panel, but that the reader then relate the present-day Christmas season and conventional Hallmark greeting ("May your Christmas be filled with true joy") to the example of gift-giving in "The Wise Men." For what should be understandable reasons, most seasonal greeting card poems don't risk alienating consumers by directing them to think about the activity of giving as Engle's does; rather than offering an external or historical interpretive framework by which to understand the implications of the card's possible market or gift transactions, they typically offer readymade sentiments that consumers can distribute in whatever manner they see fit. Engle's didactic impulse challenges this dynamic, not just by offering a narrative about gift giving but also by switching, at the word "now" in the poem's third stanza, from past to present tense, a move that goes beyond merely presenting a story to actively soliciting readers' involvement in that story and asking them to read its lesson about "humility"—a key word that attracts attention not only because it stands on its own line but also because, like "immortal," it is longer than any other word in the poem—in relation to a present-day gift-giving holiday and a contemporary "world gone wild." Given this set of unconventional generic aspirations, "The Wise Men" could not have been an easy poem to write. Given that Engle did so in fifty-eight words may in fact make it a little masterpiece.

Ultimately, these pressures result in some awkward moments. Referring to Jesus as "the Son / Of Joseph's wife," for example, is perhaps an inventive way of finding a story-appropriate rhyme for "life" in line 12, but its introduction of two characters (Joseph and Mary) who have only secondary relevance to the central drama of the magi is distracting if not difficult to parse: Why doesn't Engle refer to Mary by her first name? Why shift focus from the magi to the nature of Jesus' parentage? Why come up with a new way of referring to the Son of man at this particular moment? Be that as it may, I think the most awkward, and ultimately most problematic, aspect of "The Wise Men" is not due to any particular flaw in the execution of "the poem itself" (as New Critics would put it) but to its uncertain relationship with the commercial market of gift giving of which Hallmark is part. Unlike with "Easter"—which, as I explained earlier, produces a rich poetic experience that synchronizes with the card's material format to further elaborate the themes of immanence and introspection—Engle is ultimately unable to bend Hallmark's material packaging to the purposes of "The Wise Men," largely because the poem's religiously oriented gift logic does not align with the commercially oriented gift logic of the Hallmark card. In the biblical story the magi's gifts of gold and humility are symbols of earthly power (the wise men surrender capital and social status to Jesus), and in return, Jesus gives them a gift of even greater value—immortal life; this exchange is partly what makes the wise men so wise and Jesus so generous. Because of the tense shift from the magi who "*gave* Him their gift" to the Son who "*gives* them His gift," the poem prompts the consumer to emulate or even reenact this exchange in the present day. But whereas Engle's poem links this reenactment to an act of biblical humility, Hallmark's card links it to a more immediate and available act—the purchasing and gifting of a material good—thereby suggesting that buying and giving a greeting card is as much a cure for "a world gone wild" as Engle's religious virtue of humility.

Hallmark is able to link its commercial activity to the biblical story through the exchange of gold in "The Wise Men," which does not make the market transaction between Hallmark and the consumer anathema to the nativity story but parallels or even sacralizes the exchange of currency within it, obscuring the fact that the Jesus whom the poem celebrates was a religious figure who might have overturned Hallmark's table in the marketplace. Linking the values of immortal life and capital in this way benefits Hallmark, but it confuses the religious or gift logic at play in Engle's poem. Given the economic transaction framing the purchase and use of the greeting card, one begins to wonder what, exactly, is the exchange being commemorated in Engle's story of the magi—the exchange of gold for eternal life, or the exchange of humility for eternal life? And is this really a gift exchange, or is it a commercial contract between the wise men and Jesus that parallels the relationship between the consumer (who offers a version of the magi's gold) and Hallmark (who promises something of more lasting value—a gift that keeps on giving)? If the card buyer is encouraged to occupy the role of the gift-giving magi in Engle's poem, then into what messianic role does that cast the card's recipient—or Hallmark for that matter? And if humility is "the hope / of a world gone wild" in Engle's verse, does its appearance in Hallmark's card suggest that the buying and sending of a commercial good, and the economic structure of which that exchange is part, is just as reasonable a solution to the problems of "a world gone wild"?

These questions are difficult if not impossible to answer, in part because the logic is unclear except for the role that capital (gold or money) plays as a central and motivating aspect of the biblical event and its present day seasonal celebration. By escaping scrutiny or deflecting it to other parts of the exchange, the logic of capital's centrality not only pays off financially for Hallmark but works to naturalize the relationship between capital and Christianity, between capital and Christmas, and paradoxically, between capitalist and gift economies. Read in relation to "Easter" and "American Childhood: 3," the example of "The Wise Men" is thus instructive for a number of reasons, chief among them being how Engle was not always able to anticipate some of the effects mass culture would have on his poetry, not because, as Harris claimed during the 1959 symposium, "art and mass distribution are simply incompatible" (Symposium transcript, "The Writer in a Mass Culture," box 4), but because sometimes they can be much more compatible than we think.[59]

The Engle of History

In the first four chapters of *Everyday Reading* I have focused my attention on the complicated and diverse culture of popular poetry from the first half of the twentieth century—on ordinary readers and their poetry scrapbooks, on old-time radio poetry shows that helped to establish the feedback loop common to mass media, on the unexpected innovation of Burma-Shave advertising poetry, and on the popular reading practices that formed one foundation for William Carlos Williams's poetry. Another possible way to describe this sequence is to say that, in examining the impact of popular poetry on American culture, I have examined its influence on the individual reader, a medium, a genre, and a canonical poet. In this chapter I have tried to extend that sequence to include Engle and the Iowa Writers' Workshop in order to help account for how the culture of popular poetry brokered—and, but for a variety of forces frustrating Engle's vision, might have gone on to broker more prominently—an unanticipated relationship between two institutions of significant literary influence in Cold War America: the university-based creative writing workshop and Hallmark Inc. Admittedly, I chose this relationship for the drama that the combination of Iowa and Hallmark produces, but also because I think that the very source of that drama is emblematic of the way that the nonrelationship between university writing programs and mass culture has been imagined more generally. While the culture of popular poetry looks much different in the program era than it did a century ago, I suspect that, as was the case between high and low or modernist and popular poetries in the first half of the century, there has in fact been a far greater exchange between workshops and mass and popular cultures in postwar America than many people would believe. As with the relationship between modernist and popular writing, those exchanges have more or less been excluded from histories of U.S. literature and the operating logic of creative writing programs themselves; they have been allowed, or made, to vanish in much the same way that Engle has been made to vanish.

There is not space in this book to fully track the culture of popular poetry in today's America—its intersection with and incorporation into movies, television, popular music, and the Internet, as well as surviving traditional formats—or even, more narrowly, the exchanges that have taken place between popular culture and creative writing programs. It is worthwhile thinking about the fact that only a small fraction of the people who attend, temporarily teach in, and graduate from degree-granting creative writing programs actually go on to become college or university creative writing professors. Where do the rest of these programs' graduates—nearly twenty thousand poets per decade according to one figure—take their talents and training? As writers they contribute to many spheres of public and corporate activity, no doubt bringing their interests to that work. As readers, writers, and bureaucrats they start and sustain many of the small presses and publications that have proliferated outside the university since the 1960s and 1970s. As parents they value poetry of many sorts and share it with their children. They use it at weddings and funerals. As audiences they respond to the knowing winks—perhaps embedded by fellow graduates of MFA programs— offered by poetry citations in television programs like *Breaking Bad*, *Heroes*, *Firefly*, *Mad Men*, *The Office*, *Rescue Me*, *Twin Peaks*, and *The West Wing* and in commercials for Chrysler, Levis, and Nike, which have in recent years referenced Walt Whitman, Charles Bukowski, Maya Angelou, and Edgar Guest. These audiences are certainly not the only, the largest, or even the most important force in today's culture of popular poetry, which remains ancillary to the university, even though the two spheres regularly intersect. Nevertheless, despite the fact that their educations train them in separation from mass and popular cultures, they take that training into the larger world, where it does not remain dormant, but where they in fact become the readers and writers that Engle imagined were possible. These people are usually not spoken of in the same breath as other MFA graduates. But I believe that a full study of the program era—as with a full study of poetry in modern America—will reveal the practitioners and institutions of literary poetry to have been in more regular conversation with, and have had more influence on, the culture of popular poetry and its various manifestations than we might anticipate. In fact, it might even be argued that the greatest legacy of Engle and Iowa may not be the laurelled writers, administrators, and workshop teachers shaped by the program era but the many other poets who, like their peers in other disciplines, have taken their training into the rest of American life.

That said, it is clear that while the culture of popular poetry has changed significantly since the modern period and even since the end of the Cold War, it is still as complicated, diffuse, and difficult to track as it would have been in the late nineteenth and early twentieth centuries. There are moments—as with the outpouring of poetry in public and private in the wake of the September 11 attacks—when this culture becomes momentarily visible in a way that reminds us it is still there, somehow always just beyond our ken. Future studies will undoubtedly show massive amounts of poetry being read and exchanged online within the commercialized do-it-yourself and Web 2.0 frameworks of blogs, Internet businesses, a range of social media, and the broader World Wide Web: my recent "poetry" search on eBay netted over 105,000 results (over 464,000 when I checked the "include description" box); my search on Google produced 142 million results; Poetry Daily receives a million hits per month; and David Alpaugh estimates that one hundred thousand poems are published in print and online literary magazines each year. The culture of popular poetry will not be book based, and it will rarely (with the exception of a Jim Morrison, Jimmy Carter, Allie Sheedy, or Jewel) make the best-seller list. But then again, most popular poetry in the first half of the twentieth century was not book based and thus was never entirely measurable by that marketplace rubric, even though it was regularly pressed into—and regularly taken out of—the service of the market.

Ed Folsom, now the University of Iowa's Roy J. Carver Professor of English and a leading Whitman scholar, has told me he remembers hearing Engle recite a poem to Folsom's six-year-old son at a party in 1982 celebrating a visit to Iowa by W. S. Merwin. When asked the verse's source, Engle—in the company of a poetry critic and one of the era's most celebrated poets—unapologetically said it was from a greeting card he wrote for Hallmark in the late 1950s. As with this example, poetry will go on to have many expected and unexpected uses, audiences, distributors, participants, viewers, and effects, only some of which I have been able to touch on in this book. My hope is that other people will find it compelling enough to help teach us about the rest.

Epilogue

In Memoriam

Sophia "Danny" Salvatore was born Sophia Juliana Danca on August 29, 1911, a year before Harriet Monroe founded *Poetry* magazine, two years before the New York Armory show that introduced Americans to modern art by the likes of Marcel Duchamp and Pablo Picasso, and eight months after December, 1910, when, as Virginia Woolf would famously declare in her 1924 essay, "human character changed."[1] Danny's father Andrew was, in good Longfellowian fashion, the village blacksmith for Fremont, Ohio, a town of about ten thousand people located forty miles southeast of Toledo on the Sandusky River. An undocumented family story has Andrew fleeing military conscription in his native Romania or Hungary under an assumed name and passport before immigrating to the United States. He was followed a few years later by his sister Maria; according to her the rest of the Danca family—both parents and eleven siblings—had all died of diptheria in Europe. Andrew married Bertha Paraschiva, and as their family grew he purchased thirty-six acres of land in Ballville Township on the outskirts of town, where Danny, the oldest of eight brothers and sisters, grew up. Something of a new woman, she eventually moved eighty-five miles away to Cleveland, where she completed a two-year degree at a women's business school and where she met James ("Jimmy") Salvatore, an Italian machinist, painter, and trumpet player whom she married in 1936, one year before Paul Engle joined the faculty of the English Department at the State University of Iowa (see figure 6.1).

FIGURE 6.1. Sophia (Danny) and James (Jimmy) Salvatore, 1944.

In 1943, during Engle's second semester of directing the Writers' Workshop and six months before Jimmy was drafted for naval combat in World War II, Jimmy and Danny had their first child, Ann Carol, my mother, whom they nicknamed "Snooks." As with many other working families, Danny and Jimmy did not have an easy time during World War II; their brothers and sisters were serving around the world in Europe, Africa, and Asia, and the Dancas had no choice but to sell the family farm, since no one was left to work it and times, hard since the Depression, were still tight. Eventually, Danny would leave 79th Street in Cleveland and move with my mother to Detroit, where they would live with Danny's mother and three sisters in order to work and make ends meet until the war ended and a return to Ohio was possible. There was always a lot of news for Danny to relay to Jimmy, who had been stationed in the South Pacific, and she kept him up to date and in her mind by typing single-space letters to him almost daily. On Christmas in 1944 she poetically described the day's "beautiful snowfall which shines like a million diamonds in the moonlight."[2] "Oh, it's so beautiful and so forlorn," she explained. "Perhaps a feeling because of this war with its misery, sufferings and heart-aches. One just can't enjoy anything knowing of the dear ones far away being lonely and suffering. How can I enjoy anything without you?"[3]

Danny's letter three days later, on December 28, was not much different; she comments on the newspaper headlines and the war's indeterminate progress in her first paragraph only to conclude, "Oh, I suppose I sound very pessimistic but these are the obstacles that stand between you and me."[4] Away from her small library—which included the worn *Walker's Rhyming Dictionary* that now sits on my desk; a copy of Edna St. Vincent Millay's propaganda poem *The Murder of Lidice*, which Millay had written at the bequest of the Writers' War Board in 1942; and the collections by Carl Sandburg and Robert Service that introduced me to poetry—Danny nevertheless found the third stanza of "The Brookside" by Richard Monckton Milnes (Lord Houghton) and used that excerpt to conclude her day's letter:

He came not—no he came not;
The night came on alone;
And as it grew still longer,
I did not feel afraid;
For I listened for a footfall,

I listened for a word;
But the beating of my own heart
Was all the sound I heard.[5]

Although it was written in the mid-nineteenth century (circa 1850), "The Brookside" enjoyed a fairly wide circulation in twentieth-century America, as its appearance in Danny's letter might suggest. It was available not only in print via Edmund Clarence Stedman's popular anthologies of Victorian poetry, but out loud and possibly over the air as well, as its lines were eventually put to music, and it was the sort of poem that would have made an appealing broadcast on *Between the Bookends* or *R Yuh Listenin'*? My beat-up copy of Bartlett's *Familiar Quotations*—which may have also come to me by way of Danny's bookshelves—contains an excerpt from "The Brookside" as well, included in the 1951 edition just a year after Randall Jarrell told audiences at Harvard University's Defense of Poetry conference that, on the whole, American readers were "unused to any poetry"[6] at all, "even of the simplest kind."[7]

In her letter my grandmother treats "The Brookside" as the sort of public resource that a lot of popular poetry appears to have been, using it to help meet the situation at hand without bothering to cite Houghton as the poem's author and reading instead for the poem's relevance to her life, treating it according to a "principle of utility" that, in *The World's Body*, from 1938, critic and new Kenyon College professor John Crowe Ransom said poems should never serve.[8] And yet for all of the ways that Danny reads "The Brookside"— in contexts one might unfairly call sentimental, without bibliographic attribution, and for the purposes of utility it might serve—Danny doesn't appear "unused" to poetry at all, nor is she incapable of reading it for its subtleties. In fact, the stanza she quotes is the only part of the poem that would have worked for her purposes in 1944, as it is the single moment in the verse when the repeated "footfall" that the speaker awaits is actually attributed to a "he" of unspecified origin: "He came not—no he came not." Nowhere else is the figure gendered; nowhere else, as Danny most certainly recognized in her own study of Houghton's verse, could the poem have figured her experience of waiting for Jimmy to come home as it does at this exact moment.

Danny would keep writing to Jimmy, and he would return from the war bringing all of her letters with him. They would move back to Cleveland, have another child, and live in a close suburb for almost fifty years, until

Jimmy died of a heart attack and she—her Parkinson's disease eventually making it impossible for her to live alone—moved in with my mother and father; I was in college when this happened and still there when she died in 1993. My memories of her are thin. She collected hatpins and miniature shoes. She canned tomatoes and beans from the garden. She kept plastic runners on the carpet and stairs and covered the living-room coffee table with a protective oilcloth. She always had a plastic bag of circus peanut candies in the kitchen drawer that she would bring out and share when we visited. She liked flea markets. I knew her as a grandson knows his grandmother, but she never mentioned that she knew or read any poetry, and it never crossed my mind that she would have. How amazing it is that I had to discover this fact in her letters, which she kept private until her death. How amazing, and yet how everyday.

Introduction: Poetry and Popular Culture

1. *Modern Highway*, "St. Paul Picked Poet As Mayor," 10.

2. *Time*, "The Press: Eddie Guest's Rival," para. 6.

3. Lewis, *Babbitt*, 111.

4. See, for example, Marquis, *Archy and Mehitabel*, *Archy's Life of Mehitabel*, *Archy Does His Part*, and *The Lives and Times of Archy and Mehitabel*. See also Marquis, *The Annotated Archy and Mehitabel*.

5. Van Wienen, *Partisans and Poets*, 2.

6. Suckow, "Iowa," 44.

7. Rubin, *Songs of Ourselves*, 4.

8. Walt Mason, "A Kansas Poet's Income," 341–42.

9. Burt, "When Poets Ruled the School," 508. One of many variations on the sentiment Burt expresses includes Adam Kirsch's statement—made in a 2007 review of Rubin's *Songs of Ourselves* and intended as words of consolation for those mourning the passing of poetry's mythical golden age—that "American poetry was certainly better in the 1920s than in the 1870s even if far fewer people were reading it" (para. 9).

10. Newcomb, *Would Poetry Disappear?* 231.

11. Jackson, "Who Reads Poetry?" 182.

12. Nelson, *Repression and Recovery*, 4.

13. Readers may find *Songs of Ourselves* to be the recent study that is most similar to *Everyday Reading*, because both books focus on roughly the same time period and are concerned with practices of poetry consumption, not just poetry production, among uncredentialed or ordinary readers. Rubin's study certainly adds to the picture of the poetry-saturated culture that Van Wienen, Suckow, Mason, and I have described, and its archival orientation makes a valuable contribution to reconstructing the lived poetic landscape of modern America. Rubin's study is not a work of literary or cultural criticism, however; it is a history and thus stops short of analyzing or interpreting poetic texts themselves as literary or cultural phenomena. It does not venture to speculate on what relationship poetry and poetry readers had to broader contexts, including the culture industries, the development of consumer capitalism, and the functional dynamics of popular culture. Nor does it consider, alongside the poetry of social uplift that readers were encountering in school and at church, the highly commercialized uses of poetry (such as advertising) that also marked poetry usage in modern America. Thus, while I am indebted to *Songs of Ourselves* for helping both to justify a study of the ordinary poetry reader and to identify new archives for study, *Everyday Reading* as a work of literary and cultural criticism does not have as much in common with it as might initially appear.

14. See Damon and Livingston, *Poetry and Cultural Studies*; and Bean and Chasar, *Poetry After Cultural Studies*.

15. Keillor, *Good Poems for Hard Times*, 85–87.

16. Eliot, *Selected Essays*, 13. In extending my attention to the activities of mass cultural audiences, consumers, and users, I am extending the work of cultural studies theorists and scholars such as Walter Benjamin, Pierre Bourdieu, Michel de Certeau, John Fiske, Dick Hebdige, Henry Jenkins, Constance Penley, Janice Radway, Paul Willis, and many others. While this is not a common mode of inquiry in poetry studies, it is regular practice in cultural studies. Rubin also extends her attention to the activities of readers, but by and large she does so via the discipline of book studies (also known as the history of the book), which intersects with cultural studies but can tend, as the name suggests, to privilege print culture over other media, the historical or descriptive over the critical, and the material over the textual. In addition to *Songs of Ourselves* a good example of poetry-related book studies is Darnton's *Poetry and the Police*, which traces the circulation histories of French antiroyalist poems from the eighteenth century but rarely examines the poems themselves, and rarely speculates on the implications of their circulation for how we understand the cultural significance of poetry more broadly.

17. For leading studies of literary regionalism, neither of which address the subject of poetry in any substantial way, see Brodhead's *Cultures of Letters* and Fetterley and Pryse's *Writing Out of Place*. A good example of the regionalist conflict I describe is Frank Capra's 1936 film *Mr. Deeds Goes to Town*, which pits the values of small-town

poet Longfellow Deeds (played by Gary Cooper) against those of modern New York City writers.

18. Huyssen, *After the Great Divide*, 46.

19. Pound, "A Retrospect," 12.

20. Eliot, *Selected Essays*, 247.

21. Harrington, *Poetry and the Public*, 7.

22. Rubin, *Songs of Ourselves*, 147.

23. Jarrell, "The Obscurity of the Poet," 4, 22.

24. Symposium transcript, "The Writer in a Mass Culture," 1954 (papers of Paul Engle, box 11), 3.

25. Gioia, preface to *Can Poetry Matter?* xvii.

26. Kirsch, "The Old World of American Readers," para. 2.

27. Hall, "Notes on Deconstructing 'the Popular,'" 232.

28. Pound, "A Retrospect," 12.

29. Jarrell, "The Obscurity of the Poet," 20.

30. Pound, "A Retrospect," 12. In a current era that studies a wide range of mass cultural texts—movies, music, periodicals, advertisements, television shows, etc.—as sophisticated or knowing productions that produce complex cultural phenomena, it is curious that no such sophistication or complexity is attributed to mass-produced poetry, which is widely perceived to be too watered down, small, or inconsequential to be of interest or cultural import. That is, while scholars will study such things as conduct manuals, tour guides, fanzines, Oprah's book club, *The Daily Show,* and *Buffy the Vampire Slayer*, they rarely consider something like the poetry of greeting cards to merit the same sort of critical attention.

31. Adorno, "Lyric Poetry and Society," 71.

32. Symposium transcript, "The Writer in a Mass Culture," 1954 (papers of Paul Engle, box 11), 4.

33. Sleigh, "The Ordinary Reader," para. 6.

34. Jameson, "Reification and Utopia in Mass Culture," 133.

35. It is telling, for example, that no study with a twentieth-century focus is comparable to David Reynolds's *Beneath the American Renaissance*, a voluminous 640-page examination of how nineteenth-century literature was founded on, and absorbed, much of the popular literature of its day.

36. Nelson, *Repression and Recovery*, 25.

37. Hall, "Notes on Deconstructing 'the Popular,'" 235, 239.

38. Berlant, *The Queen of America Goes to Washington City*, 12–13.

39. It is worth mentioning here that studies of the mass cultural artifact, the silly object, or the mass-produced commodity item take many different forms and employ many different perspectives. In seeking to explore the relationship between the artifact and the consumer, rather than the object itself or the act of consumption itself,

I by and large approach the popular text as Stuart Hall does. Theorizing that they "cannot get by without preserving some of [their] roots in a real vernacular," Hall explains that popular texts are dialectical in makeup. "Alongside the false appeals, the foreshortenings, the trivialisation and shortcircuits," he writes, "there are also elements of recognition and identification, something approaching a recreation of recognisable experiences and attitudes, to which people are responding" (233). This is similar to the approach that Fredric Jameson takes in "Reification and Utopia in Mass Culture." Jameson argues that every mass cultural text introduces or gives voice to a utopian impulse only to then repress and thus further obscure that impulse in relation to the dominant ideology. For Jameson as for Hall, the critic has a responsibility to untangle the utopian from the ideological. I follow their leads in this study and also want to show that ordinary readers, not just trained critics, are capable of such disentanglement.

40. Brown, *Readies for Bob Brown's Machine*, 168.

41. Radway and Frank, "Verse and Popular Poetry."

42. De Certeau, *The Practice of Everyday Life*, xxi.

43. Ibid., 165.

44. *Time*, "Press: Scrapbookman," para. 4.

45. Ibid., para. 1.

46. Ong, *Orality and Literacy*, 106.

47. Burma-Vita, *Minutes of Directors' Meeting of the Board of Directors of Burma-Vita Company*, April 10, 1952.

48. Pinsky, introduction to *William Carlos Williams: Selected Poems*, xxiv.

49. Austin, "Regionalism in American Fiction," 140.

50. Williams, "Money," 43.

51. Suckow, "Iowa," 44.

52. Van Wienen, *Partisans and Poets*, 2.

53. Suckow, "Iowa," 44.

1. Saving Poetry

1. Pound, "A Retrospect," 12.

2. Pound, *How to Read*, 10.

3. Ngai, "Our Aesthetic Categories." For Ngai the aesthetic and literary-critical category of the "interesting" is marked by the "serial, recursive aesthetic of informational relays and communicative exchange" (948–49) — an "informational and discursive aesthetic" that is evident in, if not performed by, the compilation that is Ashley's scrapbook (ibid.). "Cute" describes the "surprisingly wide spectrum of feelings, ranging from tenderness to aggression, that we harbor toward ostensibly subordinate

and unthreatening commodities" and often in relation to domestic objects and spaces gendered female—objects and spaces such as a young woman's poetry album (949). For more on the relationship between the interesting and cute, consumer aesthetics, and modernist poetry, see Ngai, "Merely Interesting," and "The Cuteness of the Avant-Garde."

4. Moss, *Printed Commonplace-Books and the Structuring of Renaissance Thought*, 1.

5. While the study of scrapbooking has grown in recent years, very little attention has been paid to the poetry that was part of—and sometimes imagined to be the height of—the practice. See Garvey, *The Adman in the Parlor*, "Scissoring and Scrapbooks," and "Imitation Is the Sincerest Form of Appropriation"; Helfand, *Scrapbooks*; Scandura, *Down in the Dumps*; and Tucker, Ott, and Buckler, *The Scrapbook in American Life*. For scholarship that has begun to worry the poetry-scrapbook intersection in various ways, see Brinkman, "Scrapping Modernism"; Chasar, "Material Concerns"; and sections of Virginia Jackson, *Dickinson's Misery*; Nelson, *Revolutionary Memory*; and Rubin, *Songs of Ourselves*.

6. Volosinov, *Marxism and the Philosophy of Language*, 22. Volosinov argues that this "animal cry, the pure response to pain in the organism, is bereft of accent; it is a purely natural phenomenon. For such a cry, the social atmosphere is irrelevant, and therefore it does not contain even the germ of sign formation" (22). What Braley's poem reveals, however, is that the social atmosphere of such a response is not irrelevant, for while the mothers' wailing does not acquire the characteristics of a linguistic sign, it nonetheless signifies quite clearly in relation to the court's decision.

7. John Stuart Mill, "Thoughts on Poetry and Its Varieties." Mill famously wrote, in 1833, that "the peculiarity of poetry appears to us to lie in the poet's utter unconsciousness of a listener. Poetry is feeling confessing itself to itself, in moments of solitude" (348). American scrapbookers regularly scrapbooked in groups, and—as Eckert's album also shows—read with other readers in mind. Thus, poetry scrapbooking was not necessarily private, did not necessarily happen in solitude, and was used to confess feeling to others as much as to oneself. For more on the connection between Mill and "lyric reading," see Virginia Jackson, *Dickinson's Misery*, especially pages 129–33.

8. Ted Nelson, "Computer Lit / Dream Machines," 330.

9. Ibid., 310.

10. Pound, *How to Read*, 19. I am not the first to argue for a link between commonplace books, scrapbooks, and digital technologies. Garvey argues that "web bookmarks or favorite web pages echo earlier scrapbook forms and uses, in creating coherence from broadly miscellaneous materials and materials without attribution, even if the coherence or associations are clear only to the creator" ("Scissoring and Scrapbooks," 222). More recently, Steven Johnson has constructed a schematic family tree linking the "reflexive thought" processes of notebook and commonplace book keeping to the development and operation of the World Wide Web (*Where Good Ideas*

Come From, 85). (All proceed by what World Wide Web inventor Tim Berners-Lee calls "a process of accretion, not the linear solving of one problem after another" [quoted in ibid., 90].) Interestingly, in the genealogy he traces from the commonplace book to the Web, Johnson skips from the mid-nineteenth century to the 1960s with little speculation about what media technology served as a bridge between the two periods. The century or so over which he glosses was the great age of the American scrapbook.

11. Baldick, *The Modern Movement*, 109.

12. At this point I see poetry scrapbooks informing a number of fields and subfields, including but not limited to the history of reading (see Cavallo and Chartier, *A History of Reading in the West*), which includes "uncritical" reading (Warner, "Uncritical Reading"), "distant" reading (Moretti, "Conjectures on World Literature," and *Graphs, Maps, Trees*), and "uncreative writing" (Goldsmith, *Uncreative Writing*); studies of authorial and literary economies building on Leon Jackson (*The Business of Letters*) and Brodhead (*Cultures of Letters*); a history and practice of American reprinting, appropriation, and copyright after the antebellum period McGill studies (*American Literature and the Culture of Reprinting*), as well as the development of twentieth- and twenty-first-century participatory cultures (Jenkins, *Textual Poachers*, and *Confronting the Challenges of Participatory Culture*); studies of "lyric obscurity" within vernacular culture (Tiffany, *Infidel Poetics*), the history and practice of "lyric reading," and the "new lyric studies" (Prins, *Victorian Sappho*; and Virginia Jackson, *Dickinson's Misery*, and "Who Reads Poetry?"); the history of life writing; women's history and women's writing; theories of literary regionalism (Fetterley and Pryse, *Writing Out of Place*); theories and practices of memory, collecting, and archiving in digital and nondigital formats; the history of book design; and the intersection of chirographic, print, and typewriter cultures that comprised the turn-of-the-century United States.

13. Walt Whitman, Samuel Clemens, Willa Cather, Lillian Hellman, F. Scott Fitzgerald, Vachel Lindsay, Gertrude Stein, H. D., Marianne Moore, E. E. Cummings, Amy Lowell, Carl Sandburg, Sylvia Plath, and Anne Sexton all kept scrapbooks, sometimes filled entirely with articles about themselves. An avid scrapbooker, Clemens reserved Sunday as his designated time for the activity and eventually hired a personal assistant to do his scrapbooking for him (Twain, *Mark Twain's Autobiography*, 139). Whitman's disciple Horace Traubel remembers being with Whitman in 1889 and "looking over his famous old scrap book today. It lay open on the round table" (Traubel, *With Walt Whitman in Camden*, 116). Emily Dickinson "scissored out images and texts from journals and mailed them to friends" who likely kept scrapbooks (Tucker, Ott, and Buckler, *The Scrapbook in American Life*, 19). Pound used his grandfather's scrapbook as source material for the *Cantos* (Marsh, "Thaddeus Coleman Pound's 'Newspaper Scrapbook'"). Scrapbooking probably provided a cognitive model for William

Carlos Williams, who relied on "old newspaper files" in composing *Paterson* (Williams, *Paterson*, 98) and who admired Moore as an author who "clips her work into certain shapes" (Williams, *The Collected Poems of William Carlos Williams*, 1:230). Like Doris Ashley, Lorine Niedecker pasted pieces of handwritten verse directly on top of the pages of a pocket calendar to create "Next Year or I Fly My Rounds, Tempestuous." Perhaps recognizing that such items were often gifted from one person to another (as with the album Myrtle made for Fred), Jenny Penberthy has described Niedecker's creation as a "gift-book palimpsest" (Penberthy, introduction, 5). Possibly the most recent high-profile example of how the scrapbook continues to inform contemporary art writing is Anne Carson's *Nox*, a boxed, accordion foldout book that collages letters, photographs, drawings, and poems, which Megan O'Rourke has called a "mashup of old and new" giving the impression of being a "handmade original" (O'Rourke, "The Unfolding").

14. Gernes, "Recasting the Culture of Ephemera," 116.

15. Anonymous, *New York Sun*, 1903, quoted in Gernes, "Recasting the Culture of Ephemera," 119.

16. Agee and Evans, *Let Us Now Praise Famous Men*, 177–78.

17. Gernes, "Recasting the Culture of Ephemera," 116.

18. Goldman, *Living My Life,* 212.

19. Katriel and Farrell, "Scrapbooks as Cultural Texts," 2–3.

20. In nineteenth- and twentieth-century America people literalized the term "anthology" by keeping herbaria—books or portfolios of flowers and plant specimens—sometimes linking that practice and poem collecting by pairing "cuttings" of verse and preserved flowers in their portfolios, albums, autograph books, and letters. (Scrapbooks would extend this practice by collaging die cuts and other pictures of flowers with poems.) This is the tradition to which William Carlos Williams refers in "Asphodel, That Greeny Flower" when he writes:

When I was a boy
        I kept a book
                  to which, from time
to time,
        I added pressed flowers
                until, after a time,
I had a good collection.

21. Moss, "Commonplace Rhetoric and Thought-Patterns in Early Modern Culture," 56.

22. Stabile, *Memory's Daughters*, 14.

23. Parker, "The Importance of the Commonplace Book," 31.

24. Stabile, *Memory's Daughters*, 5.

25. Marotti, *Manuscript, Print, and the English Renaissance Lyric*, 210.

26. Ibid., 61.

27. Gernes, "Recasting the Culture of Ephemera," 116.

28. Fiske, "Popular Discrimination," 111.

29. Louisa May Alcott, quoted in Garvey, "Scissoring and Scrapbooks," 224.

30. Garvey, *The Adman in the Parlor*, 24.

31. Andy Warhol's *Campbell's Soup Cans* was produced in 1962.

32. First distributed by Roycroft after Hubbard's death in 1915, *Elbert Hubbard's Scrapbook* sold well—it was perhaps the best-selling celebrity-endorsed scrapbook item since *Mark Twain's Adhesive Scrap Book*—and would stay in print for a long time, with editions in 1923, 1927, 1928, 1949, 1950, 1951, 1952, and 1955. It was most recently republished by Hesperides Press in 2007.

33. Dawson, *The Scrap Book as an Educator*, 7–8.

34. Walt Mason, "A Kansas Poet's Income," 341–42.

35. Howells, *A Hazard of New Fortunes*, 26–27.

36. Cather, *My Ántonia*, 204.

37. Lewis, *Babbitt*, 78.

38. Miriam Garrison to Ted Malone, October 14, 1935, Arthur B. Church Papers, 16.48.

39. The most famous of these collectors were diarist Samuel Pepys, legal scholar John Selden, shoemaker-turned-antiquarian John Bagford, and first Earl of Oxford Robert Harley. Harley's collection, known as the Roxburgh collection and assembled with Bagford's assistance, contains over 1,300 ballads and is now part of the British Library. Pepys began his collection by purchasing a set of ballads from Selden. Over the next two decades Pepys "cut and pasted [broadsheets] with abandon" in order to fit them to the page dimensions of the albums he was using to preserve and order them (Fumerton, "Recollecting Samuel Pepys"). By the time of his death in 1703 Pepys had collected 1,857 ballads, which are now part of the Pepys Library at Magdalen College, Cambridge University. See the *English Broadside Ballad Archive* for more on these artifacts and their collectors.

40. For more on the subject of scrapbooking and developing filing systems, see Garvey, "Scissoring and Scrapbooks."

41. The second (1918) edition of *Granger's* would swell to fifty thousand entries, and the third (1940), subtitled *A Practical Reference Book for Librarians, Teachers, Booksellers, Elocutionists, Radio Artists, Etc.*, would cover seventy-five thousand entries. Now electronic, *The Columbia Granger's Index to Poetry* is in its thirteenth edition and offers subscribers access to two hundred fifty thousand full-text poems and four hundred fifty thousand citations organized under six thousand subject headings.

42. Fiske, *Understanding Popular Culture*, 25.

43. De Certeau, *The Practice of Everyday Life*, 174. I am not the first to find de Certeau's metaphor inadequate or less than appropriate in describing phenomena like poetry scrapbooks. Ellen Gruber Garvey, for example, prefers the term "gleaning" in her discussion of scrapbooks ("Scissoring and Scrapbooks," 207–8), and Henry Jenkins (*Textual Poachers*, 24–28) redefines the word to emphasize how social bonds are created between members of popular or "nonauthorized" communities that are neither transitory nor "despoiling" anything.

44. McGill, *American Literature and the Culture of Reprinting*, 4–5.

45. Harrington, *Poetry and the Public*, 24.

46. The impact of poetry's special status—as a consumer good both exempted from, and representing alternatives to, prevailing economic or legislative logic—is visible within both popular and commercial culture as well as in discourses of literary modernism. This status helps us see, for example, why many people believe that poetry has little value in a market economy while at the same time accounting for its complex and not always consistent symbolic value within that market. As a representation of noncapitalized value, poetry poses an implicit threat to a capitalist order, and thus the culture industries either disparage it—conducting a sort of smear campaign that impugns poetry as frivolous, impractical, emotion-driven, feminine, dreamy, or romantic—or else attempt to reroute the alternative value economies it represents back into a capitalist frame of meaning (by printing poems on commercial gift items, for example, and thus encouraging people to make the functioning of gift economies dependent on the consumer marketplace).

Modernist and avant-garde writers also believed that poetry's social power lies in its perceived lack of use value and sought to extricate that power from larger commercial discourses depicting it (and thus the alternate economies it represents) as trivial. ("For poetry makes nothing happen," W. H. Auden famously wrote; "it survives / in the valley of its own making where executives / would never want to tamper.") In doing so, however, these writers also rejected some of the very values that led to poetry's economic freedom in the first place, replicating aspects of the culture industries' logic by disparaging popular poetry (as feminine, for example) and thus missing its appeals to aspects of human experience unaccounted for by capitalism. For more on this aspect of the relationship between modernism and mass culture, especially modernism's gendering of mass culture (and thus mass cultural poetry) as feminine, see Huyssen's *After the Great Divide*.

While the period of popular poetry under investigation in this book has more or less disappeared—in part the discursive split between high and low sent "high" poetry into the university system and "low" poetry into the world of popular music—the logic pertaining to poetry's values is still somewhat evident. The music industry, for example, has had such a difficult time enforcing and getting people to buy into musical and lyrical copyright in part because popular music is rooted in (and is even a version of) the way people conceived of poetry's exceptional status in the age of foundational copyright legislation. Similarly, many of the arguments that emerged after Ruth Lilly's $100 million bequest to *Poetry* magazine in 2002 centered largely on whether poetry's value could be measured in dollars. Had Lilly spent $100 million on fine art—a form readily measured in dollars and cents even though the criteria for appraisal and pricing are obscure to all but the most informed insiders—there wouldn't have been nearly the controversy; however, because Lilly made her bequest to a poetry-centered operation, many people responded with pain and anguish, feeling the values of the capitalist economy her donation represented (especially with its connection to the pharmaceutical industry) clashing with, if not buying out, the non- or extracapitalist values of poetry. More on the conflict between these value systems can be found in chapter 2.

47. Emaline Knoop to Ted Malone, December 29, 1935, Arthur B. Church Papers, 16.52.

48. Helen Glass to Ted Malone. November 12, 1935, Arthur B. Church Papers, 16.47.

49. A bum at the beginning of Kerouac's *Dharma Bums* carries a prayer to St. Theresa that he "[cut out] of a reading-room magazine in Los Angeles" (5); an elderly African American couple evicted from their apartment in Ellison's *Invisible Man* have newspaper clippings among their belongings (271–72); Ma Joad from Steinbeck's *The Grapes of Wrath* burns her collection of clippings before leaving the farm in Oklahoma (108); Sophie in Algren's *The Man with the Golden Arm* assuages her fear of having "no true place of her own at all" by "reaching for an outsized album labeled . . . *My Scrapbook of Fatal Accidence*" (236, 34); institutionalized for attempting suicide, Esther from Plath's *The Bell Jar* is given a pile of clippings reporting on her act (197–99); an immigrant Bajan woman from Marshall's *Brown Girl, Brownstones* carries "in her pocketbook" a clipping of the house she hopes to one day own (36); living in a shelter so basic that it is "more like an idea of a house than a real one," Edwin Boomer keeps a beach free of paper scraps in Bishop's "The Sea and Its Shore" (*The Collected Prose*, 171); and in Cisneros's *The House on Mango Street*, Minerva, who "is always sad like a house on fire," writes poems "on little pieces of paper that she folds over and over and holds in her hands a long time" (84).

50. De Certeau, *The Practice of Everyday Life*, xix.

51. Bishop, "The Sea and Its Shore," in *The Collected Prose*, 171.

52. Gramsci, *Selections from the Prison Notebooks of Antonio Gramsci*, ed. and trans. by Hoare and Smith, 419.

53. Berlant, *The Queen of America Goes to Washington City*, 12.

54. Baldwin, "Down on Bugger Run," 236.

55. Williams, *The Long Revolution*, 48.

56. Rittenhouse, *The Little Book of Modern Verse*, and *The Second Book of Modern Verse*, 57. *The Little Book of Modern Verse* included 160 poems by seventy poets; *The Second Book of Modern Verse* increased those numbers to 200 and ninety-two, respectively.

57. *Time*, "Education: Trouble at Trinity."

58. Untermeyer, *Modern American Poetry*. I use the word "rival" in this context because Rittenhouse and Untermeyer were using their anthologies to identify and define distinctly different versions of modern poetry—"modern" being a vague category that was in a constant state of flux during these years. Even the two Rittenhouse anthologies differ significantly, as the 1919 collection includes only twenty-eight of the seventy poets featured in 1917; Willa Cather, Percy MacKaye, Edwin Markham, William Vaughn Moody, James Whitcomb Riley, and George Santayana are among the authors Rittenhouse drops; she also excludes Clinton Scollard, whom she'd marry in 1924. Of the eighty poets Untermeyer includes, only thirty-two appeared in *The Little Book of Modern Verse*, and thirty-eight in *The Second Book of Modern Verse*. To put it another way, out of the 160 poets that the three anthologies present at one point or another during a span of only three years, only *sixteen* authors make appearances in all three books, and they are a somewhat surprising group at that: Anna Hempstead Branch, Witter Bynner, Orrick Johns, Thomas S. Jones, Joyce Kilmer, Vachel Lindsay, Amy Lowell, Edna St. Vincent Millay, Josephine Preston Peabody, Edwin Arlington Robinson, George Sterling, Sara Teasdale, Ridgley Torrence, Louis Untermeyer, and John Hall Wheelock. Of the 117 individual poems representing these sixteen poets, only nine get reprinted in more than one anthology, and none in all three. Shepard's scrapbook fits this state of critical uncertainty perfectly. Of the sixteen poets who appear in all three of the Rittenhouse and Untermeyer collections, for example, nine show up in Shepard's (Branch, Bynner, Kilmer, Lindsay, Millay, Sterling, Teasdale, Untermeyer, and Wheelock). And of Shepard's 150 total authors, forty-eight appear in at least one of the Rittenhouse or Untermeyer books.

59. Poet laureates in Shepard's scrapbook include Joseph Auslander (the first person appointed Consultant in Poetry to the Library of Congress [1937–1941]), Conrad Aiken (1950–1952), Robert Frost (1958–1959), Louis Untermeyer (1961–1963), and British poet laureate John Masefield (1930–1967). Pulitzer winners include Sara Teasdale (1918), Margaret Widdemer (1919), Edna St. Vincent Millay (1923), Frost (1924, 31, 37, 43), Stephen Vincent Benet (1929), Aiken (1930), Robert Hillyer (1934), John Gould Fletcher (1939), and William Rose Benet (1942).

60. While not meaning "flower collection," the term "magazine" nevertheless refers to methods of storage or collection, originally meaning "a place where goods are kept in store" or "a portable receptacle (usually for articles of value)." The martial connotations of the word (i.e., "a store for large quantities of explosives") were first used in relation to rhetorical skill in the mid-seventeenth century ("a store or repertoire [of

resources, ideas, rhetorical weapons, etc.]"), setting the conceptual stage for the term's later meaning as a media format, as in *"Poetry* magazine" (*Oxford English Dictionary,* s.v. "magazine.").

61. Anderson, *Imagined Communities,* 7.

62. I suspect—based on the presence of poems by Carolyn Kizer (Washington), Ethel Romig Fuller (Oregon), Carl Sumner Knopf (Oregon), Struthers Burt (Wyoming), and Phyllis McGinley (Oregon, Colorado, and Utah)—that Fitzgerald might have lived in the Pacific Northwest. However, since a good number of the poems in the collection appear to have been sourced from the nationally available *Ladies' Home Journal,* this may be an incorrect judgment on my part; in fact other poems (such as an advertisement for the Maine Highway Safety Campaign) suggest she might have lived in New England. As is the case with other scrapbookers—including Shepard, Eckert, and Ashley—Fitzgerald cut off bibliographical information about the poems themselves, and so it is difficult to assess where they came from, to say nothing of determining whether she was reading magazines like the *Journal* herself or receiving clippings from other readers. See Rooney, "Freighted with Memory," for more on the aesthetically eclectic mix of poetry published by the *Journal* between 1948 and 1962—when, under the poetry editorship of Elizabeth McFarland, the magazine paid ten dollars per line and thus attracted verse by Sylvia Plath, Marianne Moore, W. H. Auden, and other prominent writers.

63. Pulitzer winners include Edna St. Vincent Millay (1923), Robert P. Tristram Coffin (1936), Phyllis McGinley (1961), and Carolyn Kizer (1985). Fitzgerald also included poetry by Laura Benét, elder sister of Stephen Vincent Benét (who won the Pulitzer in 1929 and 1944) and William Rose Benét (who won the Pulitzer in 1942). Other noteworthy poets include future U.S. poet laureate Louis Untermeyer (appointed in 1961) and longtime director of the University of Iowa Writers' Workshop, Paul Engle.

64. Whether or not Helene Mullins's (1899–1991) "Satire on a Satirist," pasted at the bottom of this page, is of dubious merit, there is no mistake about Mullins's literary pretensions. After being educated at convent boarding schools she moved to Greenwich Village in the 1920s. Thornton Wilder introduced Mullins to his publisher, after which she published a number of books, including a novel, *Convent Girl* (1929), *Earthbound and Other Poems* (1929), *Balm in Gilead* (1930), and *Streams from the Source* (1938). In 1935 Mullins attracted national attention when she survived a near-fatal car accident after lying unconscious for several weeks. Her writing also appeared in the *New York Times,* the *New Yorker, Scribner's,* the *American Mercury,* and the *Saturday Review.*

65. Susan Miller, *Assuming the Positions,* 29.

66. Ibid., 10.

67. Not all of the women poets Fitzgerald included are familiar to readers today, but many were accomplished and familiar to readers of Fitzgerald's America. Laura

Benet (1884–1979) published over ten books, including biographies of Edgar Allan Poe, Washington Irving, Samuel Taylor Coleridge, and Emily Dickinson. Elizabeth Coatsworth (1893–1986) published over seventy books of mainly children's fiction, including *The Cat Who Went to Heaven*, which won the 1931 Newbery Medal. Catherine Cate Coblentz (1897–1951) published over ten books and was runner up for the 1950 Newbery Medal. Frances Frost (1905–1959), mother to Paul Blackburn, won the 1929 Yale Younger Poets Award. Ethel Romig Fuller (1883–1965) was poetry editor of the *Oregonian* for over twenty-five years, served as Oregon's state poet laureate from 1957 to 1965, and published three books of poetry. Sara Henderson Hay (1906–1987) published six books of poetry. In addition to winning the 1961 Pulitzer Prize for Poetry, Phyllis McGinley (1905–1978) wrote for the *New Yorker*, was poetry editor of *Town and Country*, published over twenty books, and received nearly a dozen honorary degrees. Margaret Sangster (1838–1912) published over ten books. Nancy Byrd Turner (1880–1971) published fifteen books, including eight books of poetry.

68. A biblical scholar and Assyriologist, Carl Sumner Knopf (1889–1942) became president of Willamette University in 1941 but was fired by the university's board of directors when, as a Quaker, he publicly took a stance as a conscientious objector after the bombing of Pearl Harbor. He died, shortly after his firing, of what his medical records describe as a heart attack, but which local legend suggests was suicide. I believe that this George Stewart (1892–1972) was son-in-law to Arnold Klebs, whose rare book collection formed part of the basis for the Medical Historical Library at Yale; Stewart, who received BA, PhD, and DD degrees from Yale, gave the "Blessing Over the Books" at the library's formal dedication on June 15, 1941, and also wrote the lines that were carved over the library's fireplace.

69. Katriel and Farrell, "Scrapbooks as Cultural Texts," 2.

70. Ibid., 5.

71. Ibid., 7.

72. Kizer, interview by Richard Zahler.

73. Kizer, "Pro Femina," in *Cool, Calm and Collected*, 115.

74. Kizer, "Thrall," in *Cool, Calm and Collected*, 238.

75. Overlapping poets include Joseph Auslander, Robert Tristram Coffin, Emily Dickinson, Paul Engle, Frances Frost, Ethel Romig Fuller, Sara Henderson Hay, Phyllis McGinley, Edna St. Vincent Millay ("God's World," included in both Shepard's and Fitzgerald's collections), Ogden Nash, Dorothy Parker, Christina Rossetti, Margaret Sangster, and Nancy Byrd Turner. Other familiar poets, perhaps befitting a schoolteacher's album, include Robert and Elizabeth Barrett Browning, Rudyard Kipling, Edgar Lee Masters, Carl Sandburg, Sara Teasdale, Walt Whitman, Margaret Widdemer, and William Wordsworth.

2. Invisible Audiences

1. Transcript of "Between the Bookends," February 14, 1940, in Gibson Jr., "Notes on the Broadcast Interpretation of Ted Malone," 203. Gibson's dissertation contains two transcripts of "Between the Bookends," two transcripts of the "Ted Malone Show," and five transcripts of "Pilgrimage of Poetry," which featured reports from Malone's visits to the homes of noted American poets.

2. Gibson Jr., "Notes on the Broadcast Interpretation of Ted Malone," 197–201.

3. According to the Favorite Poem Project Web site, "During the one-year open call for submissions, 18,000 Americans wrote to the project volunteering to share their favorite poems—Americans from ages 5 to 97, from every state, of diverse occupations, kinds of education and backgrounds" (Favorite Poem Project). Housed at Boston University's Mugar Library, the Favorite Poem Project's archives also include nearly 25,000 letters sent in by readers.

4. Harrington, *Poetry and the Public*, 21–55. For Harrington the "row between popular and elite literary cultures" that produced the poetry wars of the 1930s was such an "established institution" by 1936 that Frank Capra relied on it to write the character of Longfellow Deeds, the small-town poet and hero of *Mr. Deeds Goes to Town* (46).

5. Bourdieu, *The Field of Cultural Production*, 115.

6. Moretti, *Graphs, Maps, Trees*, 1. See also "Conjectures on World Literature," in which Moretti writes that distant reading "allows you to focus on units that are much smaller or much larger than the text: devices, themes, tropes—or genres and systems" (57).

7. Hilmes, *Radio Voices*, 7. For more on what Hilmes calls "our dominant mythology of 'consensus' broadcast history"—in which the development of a regulatory structure most favorable to a few national networks is made to seem logical and natural, and in which historical disagreements about the cultural meaning, use, funding, and ownership of U.S. radio are subordinated—see Smulyan, *Selling Radio*.

8. *News-Week*, "Poetry: A Tear-Jerking Cupid Seeks to Make Good in Big City," 25.

9. Voils, "Ted Malone, Radio's Poetaster," 87.

10. Armstrong, "Radiopinions."

11. Gibson Jr., "Notes on the Broadcast Interpretation of Ted Malone," 201–3.

12. As far as I can tell from online searches, "I Wish You . . ." was written by Louise W. Sumlin for her daughter and reads:

> I wish you Happiness . . .
> > Not just the kind that bubbles up,
> But Happiness that is a quiet peace
> > Within your heart.

I wish you Faith . . . Faith that faces the blackest sky,
> And says, "I trust."
I wish you Understanding . . .
> So that your dreams will not be shattered,
Because you do not see the other side.
> I do not wish you Fame, or Power, or Gold . . .
But I think what share of these that come your way
> Will be the brighter, and the dearer, and still more sweet,
Because these things belong to you.

See Ann Gray's post at http://www.authorsden.com/visit/viewPoetry.asp?id=268825.

13. Presentation book, "Between the Bookends," 13, Arthur B. Church Papers, 45.30.

14. In lobbying for a regulatory structure most favorable to a few national networks rather than a necklace of independent stations, corporate radio promised to devote a certain portion of its air time to public service, rather than for-profit, programming. The unsponsored *Bookends* is one example of how that compromise worked. Unfortunately, I have found no record of what specific programming surrounded *Bookends*, nor what the sponsors for those shows were.

15. For Jameson "even the most degraded type of mass culture" contains a dimension that "remains implicitly, and no matter how faintly, negative and critical of the social order from which, as a product and a commodity, it springs" ("Reification and Utopia in Mass Culture," 144). The project mass cultural texts take on in order to be both popular and ideologically effective, then, is the faint expression of this utopian dimension followed by its repression. See Jameson for more on this dynamic.

16. Monroe, "The Radio and the Poets," 32–35.

17. Jarrell, "The Obscurity of the Poet," 20. In actuality, poetry radio programs presented a wide variety of verse, some with the express intent of bringing culture to the masses, and others in keeping with the method of Malone and *Bookends*. Examples include A. M. Sullivan's *New Poetry Hour* on WOR (New York), which strove for "no pandering whatever to the sentimentality of the moron, who will respond to the third rate poetry of the cheap ballad type" (Kaplan, *Radio and Poetry*, 212–13); Eve Merriam's *Out of the Ivory Tower* on WQXR (New York), which featured interviews with leftist poets such as Genevieve Taggard, Muriel Rukeyser, and Kenneth Fearing; David Ross, who, as early as 1926, broadcasted Christopher Marlowe, William Blake, Samuel Taylor Coleridge, Emily Dickinson, Matthew Arnold, and Robert Frost (ibid., 212); George Ward, whose *Melody and Rhyme* aired on WNYC; Harvey Hays's *Words and Music* on KDKA (Pittsburgh) and NBC; and Edgar Guest, who had a weekly

NBC appearance. Malone tried broadcasting poets ranging from Shakespeare to John Keats, William Butler Yeats, and even T. S. Eliot; Kaplan reports that while Malone gave "The Love Song of J. Alfred Prufrock" a try, he "never used it again because he discovered that the audience was indifferent" (208). In addition to these shows individual poets would embrace radio poetry and experiment with verse drama; Edna St. Vincent Millay's wartime propaganda poem *The Murder of Lidice*—which was translated into different languages and broadcast internationally in 1942—was perhaps the most widely-distributed but far from the only example.

18. For recent inquiries into recorded poetry or poetry on the radio, see Wheeler, *Voicing American Poetry* and Furr *Recorded Poetry and Poetic Reception*.

19. Hayles, *How We Became Posthuman*, 202.

20. Williams, "A Sort of Song," in vol. 2 of *The Collected Poems of William Carlos Williams*, 55.

21. Nelson, "Only Death Can Part Us," 26.

22. Adorno, "Lyric Poetry and Society," 58.

23. NBC, the first broadcast network, was formed in 1926; CBS was formed in 1929.

24. Davis, introduction to *Jim and Bob's Victory Album of Poems as Performed on KMA*, 1.

25. Hayles, *How We Became Posthuman*, 17–32. "Skeuomorphs," Hayles writes, "[act] as threshold devices, smoothing the transition between one conceptual constellation and another" by couching new technologies explicitly in terms of older, more familiar ones. "It calls into play a psychodynamic," she continues, "that finds the new more acceptable when it recalls the old that it is in the process of displacing and finds the traditional more comfortable when it is presented in a context that reminds us we can escape from it into the new" (17). The concept of the skeuomorph helps Hayles articulate how new media are predicated on previous media forms—a theoretical orientation that recalls Marshall McLuhan's earlier and more famous claim that "the effect of the medium is made strong and intense just because it is given another medium as 'content'" (*Understanding Media*, 32).

26. Douglas, *Listening In*, 55, 63.

27. Ibid., 26. Douglas also finds that "listeners inhabited multiple personas as they tuned in" (145), and the sudden transitioning from subject to subject that radio required "also fostered people's tendency to feel fragmented into many selves, which were called forth in rapid succession, or sometimes all at the same time" (11). McLuhan describes this experience as a sort of "mental breakdown" caused by "uprooting and inundation with new information and endless new patterns of information" (*Understanding Media*, 31).

28. When fans of *Bookends* wrote to Malone, they often did so in reference to their own scrapbooks and the scrapbooks they imagined he kept. Mrs. A. S. Mayo of

Hammond, Louisiana, explains, "I am sending you a few more poems I copied from the scrapbook that I have that belonged to my aunt. It is over sixty years old. Also there are several little poems that my baby June, age 9, asked me to copy and send you" (Arthur B. Church Papers, 16.55). Mrs. Fred J. Barrett of Texarkana, Arkansas, writes, "I operate a rental library and keep on hand a scrape-book [*sic*] of all kinds of lovely poems. Wish I could make some arrangement with you, whereby I could get a copy of all of your poems weekly or monthly" (16.42). Mrs. Cecil Cole of San Francisco apologizes for never sending any poems by saying "some day I'll make it up by going through my scrapbook and enclosing some poems" (16.43). Rose Cross of Oakland says, "I wish I could have every poem you gave this morning for my scrap book" (ibid.). Ann Churchill writes, "I'll send you some verses out of my scrap-book. Would you like one or two I wrote myself?" (ibid.). Miss Hazel Fuller of Montgomery, Alabama, offers, "Speaking of poems, I might add that I have quite a collection myself and if I might ask I'd like to have two or three of yours that I particularly like" (16.47).

29. Appeals to the print practice of scrapbooking—which also resulted in the application of the words "album" and "clipping" to describe acoustic phenomena like the "record album" or "sound clip"—were part of a more comprehensive set of strategies that early radio found to ease audiences' transition from print to the new medium; I focus on the language of scrapbooking here not to suggest it was the only transitional logic, but to suggest the types of frameworks in which listeners were asked to think about poetry and the corporatization of poetry on the radio, as opposed to radio in its entirety. That said, by 1933 the word "scrapbook" had acquired such a wireless affiliation that the *Oxford English Dictionary* now lists the second meaning for "scrapbook" as "A loosely-constructed documentary review programme, normally covering a particular year or period, presented on the radio by the B.B.C." I have no doubt that the scrapbook—which, as I show in chapter 1, was one way of managing a potentially fragmented modern self—also helped to resolve, or at least to treat, some of the feelings of fragmentation that Douglas and McLuhan describe (see note 27).

30. Hilmes, *Radio Voices*, 62.

31. Ong, *Orality and Literacy*, 101; hereafter cited in text.

32. For Ong the industrial/electronic and "closed" system of secondary orality is "based permanently on the use of writing and print, which are essential for the manufacture and operation of the equipment and for its use as well" (ibid., 136). By contrast "the word in its natural, oral habitat is part of a real existential present. Spoken utterance is addressed by a real, living person to another real, living person or real, living persons, at a specific time in a real setting which includes always much more than mere words. Spoken words are always modifications of a total situation which is more than verbal. They never occur alone, in a context simply of words" (101). Therefore, "learning or knowing means achieving close, empathetic, communal identification with the known" (45).

33. In addition to posing acoustic challenges radio also worried first-generation audiences because it severed the mutually informative relationship between the visual and acoustic that they were used to in daily life; on radio, a white person could sound like a black person or—worse—a black person could cross acoustic Jim Crow lines and sound like a white person. In "The Radio Announcer" Edgar Guest addresses a similar source of listener skepticism:

> The radio announcer is a man I never see
> But a friendlier sort of person I am sure that he must be
> And I sometimes sit and wonder as his voice I recognize
> If he wears the sort of garments he is paid to advertise.

34. Ong, *Orality and Literacy*, 137.

35. "For fifteen minutes," *Time* wrote of that initial broadcast, Russell "half-moaned, half-groaned William Cullen Bryant's 'Thanatopsis'" ("Pilgrim").

36. Dunning, *On the Air*, 82.

37. Voils, "Ted Malone, Radio's Poetaster," 87.

38. Rubin, *The Making of Middlebrow Culture*, 317.

39. Ibid., 316.

40. As Ong reminds us, "Reading aloud to family and other small groups was still common in the early twentieth century, until electronic culture mobilized such groups around radio and television sets rather than around a present group member" (157).

41. Gibson Jr., "Notes on the Broadcast Interpretation of Ted Malone," 205–6.

42. Flint, "Ted Malone, 81; Was Radio Pioneer with Talk Programs."

43. *Time*, "Pilgrim," 54.

44. Huyssen, *After the Great Divide*, 46.

45. *Time*, "Pilgrim," 54.

46. Canfield, "Ladies And Gentlemen—Ted Malone."

47. *News-Week*, "Poetry," 25.

48. Ibid.

49. Pound, "A Few Don'ts by an Imagiste."

50. McLuhan, *Understanding Media*, 36. For more on McLuhan's distinction between "hot" and "cool" media—the former requires less participation on the part of the user than the latter and tends to be linear and logical—see the first part of *Understanding Media*. Given that McLuhan describes radio as a "hot" medium, the popular poetry on *Bookends*, as well as Malone's own crafted abstractions, might be seen to considerably cool the media experience for listeners.

51. Guest's poem reads:

Somebody said that it couldn't be done
     But he with a chuckle replied
That "maybe it couldn't," but he would be one
     Who wouldn't say so till he'd tried.
So he buckled right in with the trace of a grin
     On his face. If he worried he hid it.
He started to sing as he tackled the thing
     That couldn't be done, and he did it!

Somebody scoffed: "Oh, you'll never do that;
     At least no one ever has done it;"
But he took off his coat and he took off his hat
     And the first thing we knew he'd begun it.
With a lift of his chin and a bit of a grin,
     Without any doubting or quiddit,
He started to sing as he tackled the thing
     That couldn't be done, and he did it.

There are thousands to tell you it cannot be done,
     There are thousands to prophesy failure,
There are thousands to point out to you one by one,
     The dangers that wait to assail you.
But just buckle in with a bit of a grin,
     Just take off your coat and go to it;
Just start in to sing as you tackle the thing
     That "cannot be done," and you'll do it.

52. Examples of how individual readers applied such poems to different sets of life circumstances can be hard to come by. However, the case of William Ernest Henley's "Invictus" offers a provocative, if miniature, example, as both Republican senator John McCain and civil rights leader Al Sharpton have cited it as a particularly inspiring and empowering piece of verse in their lives. In a speech he delivered after winning the South Carolina Presidential primary in 2008, McCain alluded to the poem, saying "But nothing is inevitable in our country. We are the captains of our fate." In a follow-up *New York Times* article about McCain's "neo-Victorian" value system, William Kristol reported that McCain memorized "Invictus" in school and "actually recited snatches of the poem in our cellphone conversation" (Kristol, "Thoroughly Unmodern McCain"). In 2011 David M. Halbfinger reported for the *New York Times* that Sharpton, a 2004 presidential candidate who recites two poems every day for

inspiration, reads "Invictus" regularly for the same message: "I'm the captain of my fate, the master of my destiny" (Halbfinger, "'The Wake-Up Is a Victory'"). It is only the abstraction of Henley's poem that allows two politicians, who otherwise have little in common with each other, and who often seem to be pursuing very different agendas, to find the same poem to be equally relevant to, and empowering in, their lives.

53. For a variety of reasons, it is difficult to find biographical information on Malone's listeners. I have found Afton Elaine Clegg, however. She was born July 31, 1917, died January 28, 2001, and married Ward M. Hicken on October 20, 1941, though I can't say if Hicken is the "dearest friend" Clegg mentions in her letter to Malone. According to her obituary in the January 30, 2001, issue of the *Deseret News*, she interviewed and wrote biographies of fifty Mormon Relief Society sisters, gave book reviews in schools and clubs, and wrote over two hundred poems that "are an inspiration to all who have read them" ("Obituary").

54. Afton Clegg to Ted Malone, November 4, 1935, Arthur B. Church Papers, 16.43.

55. Ibid.

56. Some of Malone's listeners didn't wait to write but responded vocally during the broadcasts themselves. Westena Avera writes, for example, "I always, say Hello, back, when you say (Hello There) and I say, yes, Ted, you may come in, And I always talk back to you" (Arthur B. Church Papers, 16.40); Evelyn Byrd Gillery writes, "In fact, every [*sic*] since I first heard them [Malone's programs] I have simply worshipped the time when I could hear you say, 'Hello there'. You know Mr. Malone, when I hear you say that in your wonderful soothing voice, I smile (although it very hard [*sic*] to do these days) and answer you back" (ibid., 16.47)

57. Ong, *Orality and Literacy*, 45.

58. Ibid., 106.

59. Glasselle Adams to Ted Malone, November 28, 1935, Arthur B. Church Papers, 16.40.

60. Ruby Benson to Ted Malone, November 1935, Arthur B. Church Papers, 16.42.

61. John Allen Jr. to Ted Malone, November 9, 1935, Arthur B. Church Papers, 16.40.

62. Westena Avera to Ted Malone, n.d. [late 1935?], Arthur B. Church Papers, 16.40.

63. I take Cary Nelson's recent work on wartime postcards as my immediate model for reading Malone's fan letters this way ("Only Death Can Part Us"). In reading across an archive of ten thousand postcard messages, Nelson finds a "textual microhistory" wherein otherwise discontinuous individual messages "begin to cluster and reinforce one another." In the process, he explains, "the popular voice of poetry—and remnants of the voices of readers and users of poetry, their fears and aspirations and mechanisms for coping—when gathered together like this gain a certain collective, generational, and circumstantial coherence, something a single card from a single correspondent could rarely have. The result is a kind of chorus of the ordinary, variously

rhymed and semi-literate, as popular poetry and fragmentary personal writing interact and gain collective force in a process of historical recovery" (26).

I'm aware that the construction of such a microhistory is an imprecise endeavor. The narrative I tease out of the correspondence Malone received in 1935 is not the only nor even the most clear narrative to be found. For example, one might read this archive in terms of the access to publication and national audiences that Malone and *Bookends* gave aspiring poets who sent in original poems that he later read on air. I can't trace every one of these microhistories in the present book, however. So for the purposes of providing at least one alternative to the dominant image of a uniformly "beguiled" and "helpless" listener perpetuated by the press and high-cultural spokespeople like Monroe and Jarrell, I forward the particular narrative I do.

64. Pound, "A Retrospect," 12.

65. Ruth Carroll to Ted Malone, October 13, 1935, Arthur B. Church Papers, 16.43.

66. Other fans also made it clear that the purpose of their writing was not of an amatory nature. Mrs. Edwin E. Ballard of Portland, Oregon, writes, for example, "I am extremely fond of poetry. . . . I want to assure you that my interest in this program is poetry and nothing else. I am much too highly educated and sensible for the cheap thrills as radio or movie idols afford some women" (Arthur B. Church Papers, 16.42). Another (and I am sorry to have not recorded in my notes the exact folder location of this or the next letter in the Church Papers) writes, "I am *not* just a silly dame who fell in love with a voice"; yet another, "Do not think I'm a flapper."

67. Carroll wasn't the only reader using the host-listener relationship as a model by which to trigger more expansive emotional activity. Using a rhetoric similar to Carroll's, Margaret Campbell of Hollywood, California, described this emotional interpolation in a four-line poem she sent to Malone on November 6, 1935:

NEW LIFE
(Dedicated to Ted Malone)

Before high noon I heard your voice
And I'm in love again—this time
With Life itself, impersonal, sublime.
And I rejoice!

68. T. E. Kalas to Ted Malone, September 29, 1935, Arthur B. Church Papers, 16.52.

69. Earle E. Liederman to Ted Malone, October 11, 1935, Arthur B. Church Papers, 16.53.

70. Mrs. Francis Golemon to Ted Malone, November 15, 1935, Arthur B. Church Papers, 16.48.

71. For the most influential use of the term "the poem itself," see the Cleanth Brooks and Robert Penn Warren textbook *Understanding Poetry: An Anthology for College Students*, first published in 1938 and issued in three subsequent editions (1950, 1960, 1976).

72. Taussig, *The Devil and Commodity Fetishism in South America*, 37.

73. Miriam Garrison to Ted Malone, October 14, 1935, Arthur B. Church Papers, 16.48.

74. Whitman's poem concludes:

When I sitting heard the astronomer where he lectured with much applause in
   the lecture-room,
How soon unaccountable I became tired and sick,
Till rising and gliding out I wander'd off by myself,
In the mystical moist night-air, and from time to time,
Look'd up in perfect silence at the stars.

Staging escapes from institutional sites of learning (Whitman's lecture room, Garrison's college), both texts find treatment for their speakers' illnesses (Whitman's fatigue, Garrison's sleeplessness) in the heavens.

75. Hyde, *The Gift*, 75.

76. William J. Hodges to Ted Malone, October 26, 1935, Arthur B. Church Papers, 16.49.

77. The classic study of gift economies is "Essay sur le don" (in *The Gift*), in which Marcel Mauss observes that gift exchanges are marked by several related obligations—the obligation to give, the obligation to accept, and the obligation to reciprocate—and that they occur in a total cultural context of understanding that includes economic, moral, aesthetic, religious, and mythological aspects. As a result gift economies tend to be locally specific and various in kind and function, and their rules and assumptions about giving, accepting, and reciprocating frequently go unarticulated; we are members of a gift-giving group precisely because we feel or understand, and don't need to be told, how gifts circulate and signify. In affirming an entire range of cultural assumptions, gifts thus create and maintain community coherence, while, in Hyde's words, "the conversion of gifts to commodities [whose values are separate from social relationships] can fragment or destroy such a group" (80).

78. Lucille D. Angell to Ted Malone, n.d. [late 1935?], Arthur B. Church Papers, 16.40.

79. Hyde, *The Gift*, 24.

80. Helen Glass to Ted Malone, November 12, 1935, Arthur B. Church Papers, 16.47.

81. Emaline Knoop to Ted Malone, December 29, 1935, Arthur B. Church Papers, 16.52.

82. Vivian Barritt to Ted Malone, October 24, 1935, Arthur B. Church Papers, 16.41.

83. Myrtle Braaten to Ted Malone, November 12, 1935, Arthur B. Church Papers, 16.41.

3. The Business of Rhyming

1. Will Shortz, The New York Times Crossword. This particular puzzle was designed by Jerry E. Rosman and edited by Will Shortz. Readers can find a completed version of the puzzle online at http://www.xwordinfo.com/Crossword?date=4/30/2003&g=45&d=D. For good histories of outdoor advertising, including its regulation, see Gudis, *Buyways*, and Fraser, *The American Billboard*. I am deeply grateful to Clinton Odell, who graciously allowed me access to his family's collection of Burma-Vita materials and company archives for the writing of this chapter. Burma-Shave is a registered trademark of Eveready Battery Company, Inc.

2. Zinsser, "Goodbye Burma-Shave," 65.

3. The word "Burma" in "Burma-Vita" and "Burma-Shave" refers to the national origin of the company's secret formula. Burma-Vita founder Clinton M. Odell claimed an old sea captain gave him the recipe (Rowsome Jr., *The Verse by the Side of the Road*, 12).

4. Dunphy, "A Lament for the Passing of the Highway Poets."

5. *Ventura County Star*, "Rhyme on the Highway," D8.

6. Bell, "Do You Know."

7. In calling out the often explicit commercial orientation of popular verse forms, I don't want to suggest that other verse forms—particularly those most associated with modernist poetry—were in some way exempted from commercial networks. As Lawrence Rainey, Claire Badaracco, and others have shown, modernist literary economies often imitated and cultivated aspects of consumer culture in less overt but not less substantial (or less profitable) ways. Just as lines between elite and popular become increasingly difficult or even impossible to draw when one investigates the actual circulation histories of individual poems, so the distinctions between for-profit and not-for-profit verse are much more nebulous than they initially appear. Pound, for example, lobbied hard for William Butler Yeats's "The Grey Rock" (and against Vachel Lindsay's "General William Booth Enters Into Heaven") to win *Poetry* magazine's first (1913) Guarantor's award of $250, an amount that, accounting for inflation, would be worth approximately $5,500 today; in my mind, it is impossible to read "The Grey Rock" as commercially unrelated, even though Yeats didn't necessarily write it with financial gain foremost in his mind. Given the large amounts of money at stake in the distribution of grants and awards in our current time, plus royalties and permissions fees entailed in textbook printings, plus the economics of tenure-track jobs, graduate

assistantships, and poetry reading circuits in and out of creative writing programs around the country, I would have to say that today's literary scene is certainly a highly monetized, if not commercial, one as well. That said, even as distinctions between commercial and noncommercial poetries blur, it is worth keeping the discourse of those distinctions in mind, because modernist poetry purchased a good deal of its cultural credibility and prestige via its claims to noncommercial activity, and because a lot of for-profit verse has been ignored or disparaged by literary critics because of its origin in the consumer marketplace.

8. *Time*, "The Press: Eddie Guest's Rival."

9. *Time*, "Press: Scrapbookman."

10. Rooney, "Freighted with Memory."

11. Auden, *Collected Poems*, 246.

12. Draper reads poetry (Frank O'Hara's "Mayakovsky," from *Meditations in an Emergency* [1957]) and is portrayed as a poet in his brooding temperament, his sudden sources of inspiration, and the often lyrical, heavily condensed language of the ads he develops.

13. Adorno, "Lyric Poetry and Society," 71.

14. Perloff, *Radical Artifice*, 105.

15. Upon resigning from his job at Madison Avenue's James Walter Thompson Advertising agency in 1923, Crane wrote to Charles Harris, "I got so I simply gagged everytime I sat before my desk to write an ad" (Crane, Papers). Gilman designed a number of trade cards for Soapine and possibly for Welcome Soap and Pearline Soap, among others. Harte wrote jingles for Sapolio's Spotless Town campaign. Hubbard worked for Larkin Soap before founding Roycroft Press. Moore was associated with Ford in 1955, famously proposing names (such as the Utopian Turtletop and the Mongoose Civique) for the car that would eventually be called the Edsel; David Wallace, a manager of marketing research at Ford, explained his rationale for approaching Moore by saying, "Who better to understand the nature of words than a poet?" Additionally, Lord Byron was said to have written shoe-blacking ads, James Dickey wrote for Coca-Cola, and Dana Gioia, a recent head of the National Endowment for the Arts, more recently marketed Jell-O for General Foods. As of 2011 yours truly has also tried his hand at—and gotten paid for—writing advertising verse for Stuckey & Co., insurance wholesalers of Lake St. Louis, Missouri.

16. Pound, "A Few Don'ts by an Imagiste," 203. Pound wasn't the only person to contrast poetry and soap advertising. Ironically, Webster Schott would pursue the same strategy nearly fifty years later when introducing the 1960 Hallmark anthology *Poetry for Pleasure: The Hallmark Book of Poetry*. "Shakespeare's sonnets," he wrote, "are not simple-minded jingles waiting to be set to soap" (33).

17. For more on the history of advertising poetry during this period—especially the history of patent medicine and soap advertisements (two ubiquitous products

that served as proving grounds for new and different advertising strategies in emerging consumer culture as well as a major impetus for the regulation of the advertising industry more generally)—see Nelson and Chasar, "American Advertising."

18. Lewis, *Arrowsmith*, 133.

19. Josephson, "The Great American Billposter," 309.

20. See Badaracco, *Trading Words*, on Pound and Harriet Monroe; Bryant, "Plath, Domesticity, and the Art of Advertising," on Sylvia Plath; Mason, "Building Brand Byron," and "'The Quack Has Become God,'" on romantic-era advertising; Moretti, *Signs Taken for Wonders*, on T. S. Eliot; and Rainey, *Institutions of Modernism*, on Pound, Eliot, and Joyce. For what is perhaps the best study of advertising poetry and its relationship to literary writing in any period, see Strachan, *Advertising and Satirical Culture in the Romantic Period*. My blog, *Poetry & Popular Culture*, regularly addresses the subject of advertising poetry as well; for various considerations of poems designed to plug a range of products—bird food, Blatz Beer, Breethem's breath neutralizers, the Calvert Savings & Loan Association, the City Cab Company of Hays, Kansas, Corn Flakes, Duke of Durham tobacco, Ex-Lax, Gosh's Burr Oaks Cabins, the Great Diagraphic Corset, Hallmark, Nike sneakers, the Salem Brewery Association, the Trovillion Tavern, various soaps, and more—see www.mikechasar.blogspot.com.

21. Excellent cultural histories of advertising include Laird, *Advertising Progress*; Lears, *Fables of Abundance*; and Marchand, *Advertising the American Dream*.

22. McGann, *Black Riders*, 113. It is important to note that this discussion of complicity and oppositionality is a rhetorical feature of a specifically avant-garde-based critical discourse. Recent scholars of the American Left have shown that leftist poets regularly tried to harness or highjack mass cultural forms and technologies in order to more widely distribute oppositional political messages; for them, and for their comrades in postrevolutionary Russia, using the tools of mass culture (like advertising and radio) didn't necessarily translate to complicity with capitalist ideology. Scholars such as Badaracco, Corn, and Rainey have chronicled how some modernist artists were also willing to imitate the formal or marketing techniques of mass culture. Such historical attitudes and practices suggest a critical vocabulary founded on binaries like Perloff's is incomplete and based on a very small sample group of writers.

23. Burma-Vita, *Minutes of Directors' Meeting of the Board of Directors of Burma-Vita Company*, April 10, 1952.

24. Fraser, *The American Billboard*, 44.

25. Burma-Vita, *Advertising Copy Manual for "Burma-Shave" Road Signs*, 4. King C. Gillette patented the first safety razor in 1904, and it became a permanent part of men's lives during World War I, when the U.S. government distributed Gillette's product to all men in the military.

26. Jacob Schick patented the first electric razor in 1928, and the technology first hit the market in the 1930s. Neither Odell nor company records suggest that electric

shaving contributed to Burma-Vita's decreasing market share, perhaps because the company designed a shaving lotion for use with electric razors, Burma-Shave Electric Pre-Shave Lotion, which "removes oil and perspiration from your face and thus sets up your whiskers for a faster, easier, more comfortable shave" (see figure 3.10). The challenges of television advertising—which started in the 1940s—combined with billboard regulations and changing traffic patterns to pose a much greater hurdle for the company (see note 28).

27. The American Safety Razor Company resurrected the brand in the late 1990s. But while Burma-Shave now occupies space on drugstore shelves, the television spot created for the revival, which showed a middle-aged couple driving a classic Corvette past a series of signs, did not last long either.

28. As significant, the Cold War development of the interstate highway system eclipsed the slower-moving system of two-lane highways on which the Burma-Shave poems depended for careful readers. Burma-Vita experimented with larger signs, but increasing regulation and taxation of roadside advertising cleared landscapes of visual clutter and helped to end wide-scale billboard advertising. The company resisted such regulation for years, criticizing the "sinister forces" ("Forty-Three Legislatures to Convene Next Year") and aesthetic fanatics ("City Extremists Plan Drive Against Roadside Property") of antibillboard lobbies and urging farmers, via the *Burma-Shavings* newsletter, to stand up for their property rights. "Of course, Burma-Vita Company is willing to pay a reasonable tax," explains a prophetic *Burma-Shavings* from 1931. "But there is a danger in any tax. Once the law goes into effect, it is a comparatively simple matter to raise the tax until signs are taxed completely out of existence" ("New Jersey Taxes Road Signs").

29. Rowsome Jr., *The Verse by the Side of the Road*, 78.

30. *Drug Trade News*, "Road Signs in Series, Presenting Jingles, Put Over Burma Shave," 14; *Advertising Age*, "Jingle Copy to Carry On for Burma-Shave," 19; *Time*, "Rhymes on the Road," 99; Dugas, "The Jingle Man of Burma Shave"; ibid.

31. Scherman, "Speaking of Pictures . . ." Unfortunately, I have not been able to discover which big-name poets Odell initially contacted.

32. Burma-Vita Company, *Minutes of Directors' Meeting of the Board of Directors of Burma-Vita Company*, June 14, 1951; Fleming, "Perk Up, Jack / The Rhymes Are Back," 143; Corbett, "Too Late I Read," 82.

33. Fleming, "Perk Up, Jack / The Rhymes Are Back," 144; Scherman, "Speaking of Pictures . . ." 14.

34. Rubin, *Songs of Ourselves*, 147.

35. Van Wienen, *Partisans and Poets*, 10.

36. This isn't to say that advertising poetry was immune from aesthetic criticism before modernism, but the nature of that criticism hinged less on advertising's lowbrow status and more on how advertising and poetry could actually work together to

benefit the market, poets, and readers alike. Consider, for example, the July 1900 issue of *Munsey's Magazine*, which—probably in reference to Sapolio's "Spotless Town" street car jingles—wondered, "Why is it that the rhymed advertisements which assault our eyes in the surface and elevated cars are generally so atrocious and so pointless? . . . If a thing is worth rhyming at all, it's worth rhyming well. So come, ye dealers in dress goods, ye soap sellers and pickle purveyors, and employ our rising young Longfellows and Lowells and Alfred Austins, and the course of trade and literature will alike be benefited" ("The Advertising Poet").

37. Harrington, *Poetry and the Public*, 7.

38. Ibid., 46.

39. Odell, "No Salesmen—No Reason-Why Copy—Sales Increase."

40. Burma-Vita, "Burma-Shave Signs Along the Pacific Highway"; Odell, "President's Corner," April 1930, 1.

41. Burma Vita, "1930 Road Sign Copy."

42. Odell, "President's Corner," November 1935, 1.

43. Vossler, *Burma-Shave*, 85.

44. Nelson, *Repression and Recovery*, 25.

45. Perloff, *Radical Artifice,* 93.

46. Ibid., 100.

47. Brown, *Readies for Bob Brown's Machine*, 174, 168.

48. McGann, *Black Riders*, 93.

49. De Certeau, *The Practice of Everyday Life*, 174.

50. Vossler, *Burma-Shave*, 52.

51. Fiske, "Popular Discrimination," 109.

52. For more on the distinctions between hot and cool media, which I also reference in chapter 2, see McLuhan, *Understanding Media*. While McLuhan uses television and comics as the primary examples of participatory "cool" media, it is clear that the line breaks in poetry—made especially visible by the Burma-Shave poems—make it a cool medium as well.

53. Andrews, *Paradise and Method*, 54–55.

54. Vossler, *Burma-Shave*, 85.

55. Ibid., 90.

56. Spahr, *Everybody's Autonomy*, 60.

57. Brown, *Readies for Bob Brown's Machine*, 186.

58. Rasula, *The American Poetry Wax Museum*, 319.

59. Rowsome Jr., *The Verse by the Side of the Road*, 119.

60. Burma-Vita, "No Rubbing."

61. Hejinian, "The Rejection of Closure," 621.

62. Corbett, "Too Late I Read," 82–84.

63. Vossler, *Burma-Shave*, 127.

64. Easthope, *Poetry as Discourse*, 92; hereafter cited in text.

65. Rowsome Jr., *The Verse by the Side of the Road*, 92.

66. Vossler, *Burma-Shave*, 82–83.

67. For a good introduction to nineteenth-century literary competitions, see chapter 5 ("Literary Competitions and the Culture of Emulation") in Leon Jackson, *The Business of Letters*.

68. Bers, "Sing, O Sing of Billboards." Bers, who designed seventy-one crossword puzzles for the Sunday *New York Times* (the sixth most prolific Sunday designer in the newspaper's history), is credited with inventing the "internal-clue" crossword, in which the puzzle's theme emerges as clues are solved—the model, in fact, for the "Burma-Shave" crossword that begins this chapter.

69. Burma-Vita, "1957 Burma-Shave Contest."

70. Burma-Vita, *Advertising Copy Manual for "Burma-Shave" Road Signs*, 12.

71. Bers, "Sing, O Sing of Billboards," 23.

72. Rowsome Jr., *The Verse by the Side of the Road*, 101.

73. Ibid., 77.

74. Burma-Vita, *Burma Shave Jingle Book*, no. 1, 5.

75. Burma-Vita, *The Burma-Shave Signs—A National Institution*, 22.

76. Ibid., 12.

77. Emma P. Jensen, letter to the editor, *Burma-Shavings*, March 1935, 2.

78. Rowsome Jr., *The Verse by the Side of the Road*, 84.

79. Ibid., 57–58.

80. Bart, "Advertising: Road Signs Will Stay."

81. Fleming, "Perk Up, Jack / The Rhymes Are Back," 143; *Minneapolis Star*, "Signs of Spring / Make Poets Rave, / Writing Signs / —(For Burma-Shave!)"; *Forbes*, "We Still Pine for Those Rhyme Signs," 24; *Yakima Herald-Republic*, "For Ad Nostalgia / There Is No Lack; / Burma-Shave Signs / Are on Way Back."

82. *The Chuckle Corner*, "Burmashave."

83. Rowsome Jr., *The Verse by the Side of the Road*, 114.

84. Burma-Vita, *Minutes of Directors' Meeting of the Board of Directors of Burma-Vita Company*, June 14, 1951.

85. Burma-Vita, *Minutes of Directors' Meeting of the Board of Directors of Burma-Vita Company*, April 10, 1952.

86. Burma-Vita, *Minutes of Directors' Meeting of the Board of Directors of Burma-Vita Company*, June 12, 1952.

87. *News*, "Could It Be Verse?" clipping from Odell family scrapbook with no page number noted.

88. Burma-Vita, *Minutes of Directors' Meeting of the Board of Directors of Burma-Vita Company*, February 8, 1962.

89. Rowsome Jr., *The Verse by the Side of the Road*, 107.

4. The Spin Doctor

1. Crane, "Air Freshener Responsible for Teen's Pricey Ticket." According to news reports Illinois law states, "No person shall drive any motor vehicle with any object or material hung from the inside rear-view mirror" (para. 9).

2. Car Freshner Company, "About Car-Freshner."

3. Perloff, *Radical Artifice*, 93.

4. Creeley, *For Love*, 38.

5. Bishop, *The Complete Poems*, 128.

6. Stewart, *Reading Voices*, 9; hereafter cited in text.

7. Stewart presents these examples not as a prelude to a deeper discussion of commercial language uses but as a springboard into a study of such linguistic phenomena as they appear in literary works by writers ranging from Geoffrey Chaucer to James Joyce.

8. Politically conservative family values lobbyists have linked religion and the automobile in other ways, arguing, for example, that government automobile regulations encouraging the use of smaller, fuel-efficient cars make it increasingly difficult for large families to travel in the same vehicle together and thus discourage procreation.

9. Austin, "Regionalism in American Fiction," 140.

10. Churchill, "William Carlos Williams and the Poetics of Ending Others," 34.

11. Williams, *The Collected Poems of William Carlos Williams*, 2:260; hereafter cited in text.

12. Williams, *The Great American Novel*, 2.

13. Ibid., 9.

14. Between the time of writing and time of publication of *Everyday Reading*, Bartholomew Brinkman has very convincingly argued that Moore did in fact use scrapbooking as a compositional model.

15. Williams, *Paterson*, 98; hereafter cited in text.

16. De Certeau, *The Practice of Everyday Life*, xix.

17. Venturi, Brown, and Izenour, *Learning from Las Vegas*, 10.

18. Drucker, *Figuring the Word*, 90.

19. Perloff, *Radical Artifice*, 111.

20. Ibid., 121.

21. Venturi, Brown, and Izenour, *Learning from Las Vegas*, 36.

22. Ibid., 10.

23. Lefebvre, *Everyday Life in the Modern World*, 62.

24. For additional material on the legislation and control of billboards and public signage other than that presented in this chapter, see also Belin, Bilotto, and Carhart, *A Legal Handbook for Billboard Control*; Brown, *The Mechanics of Sign Control*; and Duerksen and Goebel, *Aesthetics, Community Character, and the Law*.

25. Catherine Gudis, *Buyways*, 9–10; hereafter cited in text.

26. Brennen, "Billboards of the Dream," 27.

27. Venturi, Brown, and Izenour, *Learning from Las Vegas*, 10.

28. President's Research Committee on Social Trends, *Recent Social Trends in the United States*, 172.

29. Opdycke, *The Language of Advertising*, 198.

30. Ibid., 244.

31. Ibid., 225–26. In "combination," Opdycke writes, "Syllables or words [such as Neverbreak, Everwear, Auto-lite, Safetea, and Autocar] are combined with or without hyphen"; for "curtailment," "Syllables or letters may be taken from names and reunited so as to form a euphonious word: Socony (*S*tandard *O*il *Co*mpany of *N*ew *Y*ork) . . . [and] Crudol (*Cru*de *O*il)"; in "derivation," "A Word may be so derived as to define the commodity it stands for: Resinol (resin and oil), vinol (wine and oil)" (ibid.).

32. Venturi, Brown, and Izenour, *Learning from Las Vegas*, 57.

33. Ibid., 44.

34. Trachtenberg, foreword, xiii.

35. Schivelbusch, *The Railway Journey*, 53.

36. Ibid., 57.

37. Ibid., 64.

38. President's Research Committee on Social Trends, *Recent Social Trends in the United States*, 177.

39. Ibid., 190.

40. O'Brien, "Machinery and English Style," 464.

41. Ibid., 467–68.

42. Ibid., 468–69.

43. Mariani, *William Carlos Williams*, 196.

44. Williams, *The Autobiography of William Carlos Williams*, 279.

45. Mariani, *William Carlos Williams*, 23.

46. Corn, *The Great American Thing*.

47. Pound, "A Few Don'ts by an Imagiste," 203.

48. Josephson, "The Great American Billposter," 304.

49. Ibid., 309.

50. Eiseman, *Charles Demuth*, 77. For an excellent discussion of Demuth and other visual artists' appropriation of commercial subject matter and form, see Corn, *In the American Grain*, and *The Great American Thing*.

51. Pinsky, introduction, xxiv.

52. Corn, *In the American Grain*, 234–35.

53. As in chapter 3, I am borrowing the term "wild reading" from Andrews, *Paradise and Method*. For Andrews this is a practice of reading that challenges the "paradigms of sense" set up by conventional or normative, often school-based ways of reading.

"The job," he writes, "is to go beyond these norms and limits, to *read them backward*, to offer up a different refraction of the circumstance" (emphasis in original, 54–55).

54. Williams, "Measure," 149.

55. Williams, *Selected Essays of William Carlos Williams*, 302.

56. Williams, *The Great American Novel*, 9.

57. *New York Herald Tribune*, "Doctor-Author Calls Writing Balance Wheel," 11.

58. Williams, *January*, 16.

59. Mariani, *William Carlos Williams*, 682.

60. Williams, "Money," 43.

61. Mariani, *William Carlos Williams*, 100.

62. For a good introduction to the way scholars approach this aspect of Williams's work, I would recommend the essays by Churchill, Broughn, Holsapple, Layng, and Gorey in *William Carlos Williams and the Language of Poetry*, edited by Hatlen and Tryphonopoulos. Churchill writes of Williams's "new effort to isolate the edges of words" (9), Broughn of "each word and its movement to the next word" (26), Holsapple of "centrifugal" language use with a "zigzag, elliptical sense of progress" (97), Layng of a "sharp disruption of the oral by the visual" (183), and Gorey of tropes that "interlace" (20). As these critics use words like torsion, tension, edges, restlessness, unsettlement, disruption, interlacing, dissolution, and rebuilding to write about Williams's poetry, they might just as easily be describing Stewart's interlexical effects or, for that matter, the experience of reading in the billboard landscape of the early twentieth century.

63. Morris, *How to Live / What to Do*, 57, 58.

64. Ibid., 58.

65. Williams, *Selected Letters*, 102. For other work exploring the intersection of modernist poetry (including and especially that of Williams) and technology, see Barnstone, *The Poetics of the Machine Age*; Kenner, *The Mechanic Muse*; Steinman, *Made in America* (especially chapter 4, "William Carlos Williams: There's More Than Just One Kind of Grace" [78–112]); and Tichi, *Shifting Gears* (especially chapter 5, "Machines Made of Words" [1987, 230–288]), not all of whose arguments are entirely consonant with my own.

66. These compound words also recall John Dos Passos's use of language in *Manhattan Transfer* (1925) and *U.S.A.* (1930–1936). Tichi writes, "He [Dos Passos] also underscores the rapid-transit age with the technique of jamming words together to suggest rapid-fire speech and instantaneous perception. . . . To participate in twentieth-century life is to see, hear, speak, read, and write fast" (198).

67. Given the special relationship between Pound and soap advertising on which I elaborated in chapter 3, it is worth noting that this issue of *Contact* brings them together again—via the ad for Babbitt's Soap, another lubricant that headlines the cover and that, like Nujol and other patent medicines, promoted itself with positive

health claims; for Pound, soap and oil form a sort of core to the slippery business of American capitalism.

68. Fraser, *The American Billboard*, 44.

69. Williams, *The Great American Novel*, 8.

70. Williams, *The Autobiography of William Carlos Williams*, 237.

71. Here the subject of Andrews's call to "*read . . . backward*" (*Paradise and Method*, 54) is even more suggestive for a discussion of Williams's poetry. Not only does Williams claim in *The Great American Novel* that "words are the reverse motion" (9), but reading (or listening) backward is also consistent with Stewart's conception of the backward/forward exchange of phonemic material in the transegmental drift as well. Stewart grounds his understanding of "reverse motion" in chapter 14 of Coleridge's *Biographia Literaria*, which he uses as one of the book's epigraphs: "The reader should be carried forward, not merely or chiefly by the mechanical impulse of curiosity, or by a restless desire to arrive at the final solution; but . . . like the path of sound through the air; at every step he pauses and half recedes, and from the retrogressive movement collects the force which carries him onward" (*Reading Voices*, 1).

72. Stewart, *Reading Voices*, 55.

73. See Morris, *How to Live / What to Do*, 19–55.

74. Williams, *January*, 18.

75. Mariani, *William Carlos Williams*, 206.

76. See, in Williams, *The Collected Poems of William Carlos Williams*, for example, "Choral: The Pink Church" (2:177–80), "Brief Lief" (2:25), and "May 1st Tomorrow" (2:189).

77. Mariani, *William Carlos Williams*, 518.

5. Popular Poetry and the Program Era

1. Stephen Wilbers writes, "More than 1,500 students, writers, critics, teachers, and professors from all over the country attended the symposium," including editors from the *Des Moines Register*, *Chicago Daily News*, the *Chicago Sun-Times*, the Meredith Publishing Company, and the Dial Press. *Newsweek*, *Reader's Digest*, and *Esquire* also reported on the event (*The Iowa Writers' Workshop*, 103).

2. Press release, "The Writer in a Mass Culture," 1959, Papers of Paul Engle, box 11.

3. Iowa-affiliated Pulitzer Prize–winning poets include Robert Lowell (1947), Robert Penn Warren (1958 and 1980), W. D. Snodgrass (1960), John Berryman (1965), Anthony Hecht (1968), Donald Justice (1980), James Tate (1992), Philip Levine (1995), Charles Wright (1998), and Mark Strand (1999)—all of whom were students or faculty at Iowa during Engle's tenure as director—as well as Carolyn Kizer (1985), Rita Dove (1987), Mona Van Duyn (1991), Louise Gluck (1993), Jorie Graham (1996),

Robert Hass (2008), and Philip Schultz (also 2008). Iowa poets have won many other major awards, but the Pulitzer-Workshop link has been a special point of pride over the years. When the Workshop staged its 75th Anniversary Reunion in June, 2011, for example, its Web site explained, "The centerpiece of the reunion will be our panel discussions: we have invited fifty writers (eight of them Pulitzer Prize winners) to address a variety of topics."

4. Symposium transcript, "The Writer in a Mass Culture," 1959, Papers of Paul Engle, box 11, 3; hereafter cited in text.

5. For a statistical account of the growth of creative writing programs in the U.S., see Fenza's "About AWP." According to Fenza's figures, the growth of creative writing programs was sudden and exponential, increasing from fifteen MFA and five PhD programs in 1975 to 184 MFA and 36 PhD programs in 2010.

6. In addition to McGurl's history of the program era, see also Myers, *The Elephants Teach*.

7. Examples are not hard to come by. After spending two years at the University of Pennsylvania, for instance, Pound managed a degree from Hamilton College and declared that higher education was not the place for the "unusual young man" (Moody, *Ezra Pound*, 16). Pound did find his first job teaching French and Spanish at Wabash College in Indiana, but, after less than a year, was dismissed for having a woman in his room after hours. Edna St. Vincent Millay broke rule after rule at Vassar College and was expelled on the eve of her graduation; were it not for a petition from her fellow students, for whom she had written a commencement hymn, she might not have graduated at all. Vachel Lindsay dropped out of Hiram College after two years. With some exceptions—including the circle around George Santayana at Harvard and, later, the Fugitive poet-critics like Donald Davidson (Vanderbilt), John Crowe Ransom (Vanderbilt and Kenyon), Allen Tate (Kenyon), and Robert Penn Warren (Louisiana State)—poets did not find university life hospitable, so they opted to live in bohemia, wrote for newspapers and magazines, or got day jobs doing something other than poetry. Thus, William Carlos Williams was a doctor, Wallace Stevens and Edgar Lee Masters were lawyers, and Louis Untermeyer dropped out of high school and worked for his father's jewelry company.

8. Frost, *Selected Letters of Robert Frost*, 146.

9. Lentricchia, *Modernist Quartet*, 106.

10. Mabie, "Robert Frost Interprets His Teaching Method," 67. The first writer-in-residence position went to Percy MacKaye (1875–1956), who served at Miami University in Ohio from 1920–1924. MacKaye would go on to use his experience to advocate for such appointments more generally, writing in "University Fellowships in Creative Art," for example, "If it be worth while for a university to provide opportunity to study a living author's work, may it not be equally worth while to provide opportunity for the author to create it?" MacKaye was joined and even encouraged in his advocacy

by Miami president Raymond Hughes, who spoke before the National Association of State Universities in 1920 and suggested providing fellowships to creative artists. The precedent set by Hughes and MacKaye led directly to Frost's appointment at the University of Michigan. For more on MacKaye, Hughes, and their efforts and communications with other institutions, see the Percy MacKaye Collection in the Walter Havinghurst Special Collections at the Miami University Libraries.

11. McGurl and Myers ascribe this transformation to many things, including changing attitudes about writing and teaching at primary and secondary educational levels that filtered up to the university level, changes in the discipline and profession of English itself, the postwar expansion of the university system fueled by the G.I. Bill, and the movement of New Criticism into the mainstream.

12. McGurl, *The Program Era*, 21.

13. McGurl focuses on fiction to the almost complete exclusion of poetry, even when the emergence of the program era is in fact most clearly visible via poetry. The first writers in residence (MacKaye at Miami University in Ohio and Frost at the University of Michigan) were poets. Engle was a poet. Crucial program era textbooks were written about poetry and edited by poets, especially *Understanding Poetry*, the 1938 Cleanth Brooks and Robert Penn Warren guide that, six years later, spawned *Understanding Fiction*, which McGurl does highlight for its historical significance. Even the low-residency creative writing program came into existence thanks to a poet, Ellen Bryant Voigt, who founded the Warren Wilson MFA program at Goddard College in 1976.

14. A statement now common in many poetry contest guidelines prohibiting judges from selecting the work of friends or former students is informally known as the "Jorie Graham rule," partly because of Graham's history of selecting her Iowa students and former students as winners. The only history of the Workshop to date is Stephen Wilbers's *The Iowa Writers' Workshop*, published by the University of Iowa Press and now over thirty years old; minus notes, photographs, and chapter divisions, it is only 100 pages long and ends in the mid 1960s. It is my sense that in subtitling the book *Origins, Emergence, and Growth*, Wilbers was inviting a second volume, which has yet to be written. For other Workshop-related histories and studies, mostly recollections contributed by Workshop participants, see Dana, *A Community of Writers*.

15. Glass, "Middle Man," 257.

16. Jameson uses the term "vanishing mediator" to describe that person or force that "serves as a bearer of change and social transformation, only to be forgotten once that change has ratified the reality of institutions" ("The Vanishing Mediator," 26).

17. For more on the nature of the postwar period's canon and anthology wars, see Golding, *From Outlaw to Classic*; Rasula, *The American Poetry Wax Museum*; and Filreis, *Counter-Revolution of the Word*.

18. Kovacs claimed that he modeled the character of Percy Dovetonsils on Ted Malone, host of *Between the Bookends*.

19. Wilbers, *The Iowa Writers' Workshop*, 93.

20. The most famous such accusation came in Dana Gioia's 1991 *Atlantic* essay "Can Poetry Matter?" Given the high profile of the resulting debate, I think it is unnecessary and—more to the point—unhelpful to trace it here. Instead I will point out that while Gioia has held MFA programs responsible for the marginalization of poetry in contemporary America, he himself has described popular culture in much the same way that the 1959 symposium's participants did, cartooning popular audiences as "the incurious mass audience of the popular media" (*Can Poetry Matter?* xviii) even while claiming to write for a "general readership" (ibid., 2). Gioia's views would have had more in common with the symposium's participants than with Engle's or mine.

21. Many poets who would go on to make marks for themselves in the publishing world were elected or designated class poets in grade school, high school, or college. Robert Frost served as his high school class poet in 1892. Edna St. Vincent Millay ran for class poet in high school but her peers, thinking her an intellectual snob, denied her the position. This was, she would later write, "The first big disappointment of my life" (quoted in Milford *Savage Beauty*, 42). Melvin Tolson was class poet in 1911. Langston Hughes was elected class poet in grade school and later thought it was because his fellow students suspected he, as an African American, had a greater sense of rhythm than his white classmates. Arthur Davison Ficke, Conrad Aiken, and e.e. cummings were class poets at Harvard. Stephen Vincent Benét was class poet at Yale. Archibald MacLeish was elected class poet in high school as well as at Yale. William Meredith was class poet at Princeton, where his class poem caught the eye of Allen Tate, who recommended Meredith to MacLeish for the Yale Series of Younger Poets. A study has yet to be done on how these and other such awards and distinctions given to poets early in their careers—often coming from the public school system and often entailing the composition of occasional verse like Engle's dedication poem—affected their career trajectories.

22. For more on the relationship between Engle and Sigmund, who helped to anchor a dynamic Iowan literary community before the Workshop was even a glimmer in the University of Iowa's eye, see Jack ("America's Forgotten Regionalist, Jay G. Sigmund").

23. Describing Iowa's literary climate in 1926, novelist Ruth Suckow wrote in the *American Mercury* that "it is snatched at by everybody—farmer boys, dentists, telegraph editors in small towns, students, undertakers, insurance agents and nobodies. All have a try at it" (43).

24. Engle, "Easter," 35.

25. Hallmark's version of "Easter" cuts stanzas 4 and 5 from the *Better Homes and Gardens* version, changes the placement of "now" in line 3, and capitalizes "Word" in the first line of the final stanza. Stanzas 4 and 5 of the *Better Homes* version read:

> He hung there, owning no
> Money, or thing, or land,
> With one thief on His left,
> And one on His right hand.
>
> Friends brought Him to a dark
> Cave, where He would not stay,
> But rose in living fire.
> Now in our green today . . .

26. Wilson, "Paul Engle," 161.

27. Ibid., 164.

28. Glass attributes the creative-scholastic tension in English departments around the United States to the different economies of prestige and institutional allegiance that Engle's charismatic leadership of the Workshop brought into being and conflict. Glass explains, "Literary studies, for all its political, methodological, and demographic transformations over the past decades, remains a creature of its institutional habits, comfortable with the protocols and credentialing procedures sustaining English departments at the curricular center of the liberal arts education. Creative writing, on the other hand, maintains a firmer allegiance to the anti-institutional ethos of both the bohemian and the monastic lifestyles, and therefore, in the vast majority of academic configurations, it remains ancillary to the larger department on whose resources it continues to depend" ("Middle Man," 266).

29. Wilbers, *The Iowa Writers' Workshop*, 93.

30. John Engels, quoted in Stephen Wilbers, *The Iowa Writers' Workshop*, 78.

31. Wilson, "Paul Engle," 160.

32. Clemente, "Paul Engle's Long Reach," 186.

33. Glass, "Middle Man," 266. Glass writes, "The only event dedicated to Engle's memory in Iowa City is the International Writing Program's Paul Engle Memorial Reading, which has been held on his birthday every year since 2000, when then Iowa Governor Tom Vilsack established the date as 'Paul Engle Day'. . . Otherwise, it is hard to find evidence in Iowa City of Paul Engle's time here. There is no street, building, chair, or scholarship named for him. Few Workshop graduates know anything about him, and none read his poetry" (ibid.). More recently, it was proposed that a new elementary school in Iowa City should be named for Engle, but that suggestion

was turned down on the basis, one local journalist has told me, that people felt Engle "never did anything for children, and his poetry wasn't much good anyhow."

34. Engle, "The Need for Poetry," Papers of Paul Engle, box 14, folder 2.

35. Engle, "Why Read Poetry?" Papers of Paul Engle, box 15, folder 6.

36. Paul Engle, "American Child: 3," 89.

37. Quoted in Wilson, "Paul Engle," 161.

38. Malcolm Cowley, quoted in Wilson, "Paul Engle, "162.

39. Press release, "The Writer in a Mass Culture," 1959, Papers of Paul Engle, box 11. *Holiday* was a travel magazine that once had a circulation of over one million and was owned by the Curtis Publishing Company, which also published *Ladies' Home Journal* and the *Saturday Evening Post*.

40. Ibid.

41. I have been unable to find a list of symposium sponsors, but it is possible that Engle or Gingrich secured sponsorship from *Reader's Digest*, which would have been ironic given the symposium's expressions of antipathy toward mass culture, but which could explain the press release's focus on Engle's *Digest* article as well as the *Digest*'s presence at the event.

42. Paul Engle, quoted in Wilbers, *The Iowa Writers' Workshop*, 93.

43. According to Hallmark records eleven hundred poems were submitted to the contest in 1965 (judged by Conrad Aiken, Karl Shapiro, Winfield Townley Scott, and Louis Untermeyer), and two thousand five hundred poems were submitted in 1966 (judged by Carolyn Kizer, John Frederick Nims, and Robert Penn Warren). There are no records as to how many poems were submitted in other years.

44. A prolific writer of poetry, prose, criticism, and poetry handbooks and textbooks, Turco also went on to a career in teaching, first working at Fenn College in Cleveland (now Cleveland State University), where he founded the Cleveland Poetry Center, and then at the State University of New York at Oswego, where he founded that school's Program in Writing Arts.

45. Engle, introduction to *Midland*, xxv.

46. Donald Justice, quoted in Myers, *The Elephants Teach*, 164.

47. Hall was credited with reconciling Presidents Truman and Eisenhower after an eight-year feud and later attended their private funerals. He knew Churchill and printed Churchill's paintings on greeting cards, and he was named an Honorary Commander of the Order of the British Empire by Queen Elizabeth II.

48. I am grateful to Melissa Girard for introducing me to this chapter of Hallmark's history.

49. Hall, *When You Care Enough*, 163.

50. Franklin D. Murphy, foreword to Hall, *When You Care Enough*, xi.

51. Hall, *When You Care Enough*, 177.

52. Hall, "Taste and Times," 21–22.

53. Hall, *When You Care Enough*, 155.

54. Ibid.

55. Hallmark's company archivists were able to furnish me with copies of seventeen different Christmas, Easter, Valentine's Day, and anniversary cards from 1960–1966 containing eleven different poems identified as Engle's: "The Wise Men," "The Holly," "The Name of Love," "By Day or Night," "The Shepherds," "The Angel," "The Animals," "Easter," "The Hand of God," "The Child," and "The Nativity."

56. Engle wasn't the only poet involved in making greeting cards. For nearly thirty years (from 1935 to 1962, at least) Robert Frost and printer Joseph Blumenthal partnered to produce limited edition, fine-press cards featuring Frost's poetry.

57. According to William Carlos Williams's editor, Christopher MacGowan, Hallmark used Williams's 1956 poem "The Gift"—also a poem about the magi—in a 1962 card to accompany a reproduction of Giotto's *Adoration of the Magi*. MacGowan says that Giotto's painting is not the subject of Williams's poem and "WCW was not involved in the decision to pair his work with the Giotto" (*The Collected Poems of William Carlos Williams*, 2:514). One wonders whether Engle knew the Williams poem, which begins, "As the wise men of old brought gifts / guided by a star," as the two poems share a fair amount of vocabulary in common. Both use "gift," "wise men," "star," "gold," and "child"; Williams uses "humble," "kneeled," and "bowed"; Engle uses "humility," "kneel," and "bow." All told, one-seventh of the fifty-eight words in Engle's poem overlap with Williams's "The Gift."

58. Engle's pedagogical impulse and use of children in "The Wise Men" and "American Child: 3" root the two poems in a history of American schoolroom verse that, Angela Sorby has argued, resulted in the "infantilization of American poetry: poets framed as children, children seen as poets, children posited as readers, children recruited as performers, and adults wishing themselves back into childhood" (*Schoolroom Poets*, xvii).

59. A privately owned company, Hallmark typically does not release sales figures for its products, and the one handwritten record of figures for Engle's cards that was made available to me is difficult even for current Hallmark archivists to parse. That said, it appears that one set of four Christmas cards featuring Engle's poems from 1960 (including another version of "The Wise Men") was estimated to have sold around thirty thousand copies.

Epilogue: In Memoriam

1. Woolf, "Mr. Bennett and Mrs. Brown," 194.

2. Sophia Juliana Danca to James Salvatore, December 25, 1944, private collection.

3. Ibid.

4. Sophia Juliana Danca to James Salvatore, December 28, 1944, private collection.

5. Richard Monckton Milnes, quoted in Sophia Juliana Danca to James Salvatore, December 28, 1944, private collection.

6. Jarrell, "The Obscurity of the Poet," 4.

7. Ibid., 22.

8. John Crowe Ransom, *The World's Body*, 29.

Adorno, Theodor. "Lyric Poetry and Society." *Telos: A Quarterly Journal of Radical Social Theory* 20 (Summer 1974): 56–71.

Advertising Age. "Jingle Copy to Carry On for Burma-Shave," September 29, 1934.

Agee, James, and Walker Evans. *Let Us Now Praise Famous Men, A Death in the Family, and Shorter Fiction*. New York: Library of America, 2005.

Algren, Nelson. *The Man with the Golden Arm*. 1949. New York: Seven Stories Press, 1999.

Alpaugh, David. "The New Math of Poetry." *Chronicle of Higher Education,* February 21, 2010. http://chronicle.com/article/The-New-Math-of-Poetry/64249/.

Anderson, Benedict. *Imagined Communities: Reflections on the Origin and Spread of Nationalism*. New York: Verso, 1993.

Andrews, Bruce. *Paradise and Method: Poetics and Praxis*. Evanston: Northwestern Univeristy Press, 1996.

Armstrong, Dale. "Radiopinions." *Los Angeles Times*, March 15, 1936.

Auden, W. H. *Collected Poems*. Edited by Edward Mendelson. New York: Modern Library, 2007.

Austin, Mary. "Regionalism in American Fiction." In *Beyond Borders: The Selected Essays of Mary Austin*, edited by Reuben J. Ellis. Carbondale: Southern Illinois University Press, 1996.

Badaracco, Claire Hoertz. *Trading Words: Poetry, Typography, and Illustrated Books in the Modern Literary Economy*. Baltimore: Johns Hopkins University Press, 1995.

Baldick, Chris. *The Modern Movement, 1910–1940*. Oxford: Oxford University Press, 2004.

Baldwin, Lois Karen. "Down on Bugger Run: Family Group and the Social Base of Folklore." PhD diss., University of Pennsylvania, 1975.

Barnstone, Anthony Dimitrios. *The Poetics of the Machine Age: William Carlos Williams and Technological Modernism*. PhD diss., University of California, Berkeley, 1998.

Bart, Peter. "Advertising: Road Signs Will Stay." *New York Times*, February 23, 1963, 13.

Bean, Heidi R. and Mike Chasar, eds., *Poetry After Cultural Studies*. Iowa City: University of Iowa Press, 2011.

Belin, Alletta, Mercedes R. Bilotto, and Thaddeus Carhart. *A Legal Handbook for Billboard Control*. Palo Alto: Stanford Environmental Law Society, 1976.

Bell, Ed. "Do You Know." *Burma-Shavings,* November 1933, 2.

Berlant, Lauren. *The Queen of America Goes to Washington City: Essays on Sex and Citizenship*. Durham: Duke University Press, 1997.

Bers, Harold T. "Sing, O Sing of Billboards." *Holiday*, September 1947, 23.

Bishop, Elizabeth. *The Complete Poems, 1927–1979*. New York: Noonday Press, 1995.

——. *The Collected Prose*. New York: Farrar, Straus and Giroux, 1984.

Bourdieu, Pierre. *The Field of Cultural Production: Essays on Art and Literature*. Edited by Randall Johnson. New York: Columbia University Press, 1993.

Brennen, Bonnie. "Billboards of the Dream: Walker Evans on 1930s U.S. Advertising." In *In the Company of Media: Cultural Constructions of Communication, 1920s-1930s*, edited by Hanno Hardt. Boulder, Colo.: Westview Press, 2000.

Brinkman, Bartholomew. "Scrapping Modernism: Marianne Moore and the Making of the Modern Collage Poem." *Modernism/modernity* 18, no. 1 (January 2011): 43–66.

Brodhead, Richard. *Cultures of Letters: Scenes of Reading and Writing in Nineteenth-Century America*. Chicago: University of Chicago Press, 1993.

Brooks, Cleanth and Robert Penn Warren, eds. *Understanding Poetry: An Anthology for College Students*. New York: Holt, 1938.

Brown, Bob, ed. *Readies for Bob Brown's Machine*. Cagnes-sur-Mer: Roving Eye, 1931.

Brown, Carolyn. *The Mechanics of Sign Control*. Chicago: American Planning Association, 1980.

Bryant, Marsha. "Plath, Domesticity, and the Art of Advertising." *College Literature* 29, no. 3 (2002): 17–34.

Burma-Vita Company. *Advertising Copy Manual for "Burma-Shave" Road Signs*. Minneapolis: Burma-Vita, 1940.

——. *Burma-Shave Jingle Book*. No. 1. Minneapolis: Burma-Vita, 1931.

——. *Burma-Shave Jingle Book*. Minneapolis: Burma-Vita, 1936.

——. "Burma-Shave Signs Along the Pacific Highway." *Burma-Shavings*, November 1929, 1.

——. *The Burma-Shave Signs—A National Institution*. Minneapolis: Burma-Vita, 1938.

——. "City Extremists Plan Drive Against Roadside Property." *Burma-Shavings*, November 1944, 1.

——. "Forty-Three Legislatures to Convene Next Year." *Burma-Shavings*, November 1936, 1.

——. *Minutes of Directors' Meeting of the Board of Directors of Burma-Vita Company*, June 14, 1951, Burma-Vita, Minneapolis.

——. *Minutes of Directors' Meeting of the Board of Directors of Burma-Vita Company*, April 10, 1952, Burma-Vita, Minneapolis.

——. *Minutes of Directors' Meeting of the Board of Directors of Burma-Vita Company*, June 12, 1952, Burma-Vita, Minneapolis.

——. *Minutes of Directors' Meeting of the Board of Directors of Burma-Vita Company*, February 8, 1962, Burma-Vita, Minneapolis.

——. "New Jersey Taxes Road Signs." *Burma-Shavings*, March 1931, 1.

——. "1957 Burma-Shave Contest." Minneapolis: Burma-Vita, 1957.

——. "1930 Road Sign Copy." *Burma-Shavings*, June 1930, 2.

——. "No Rubbing." *Burma-Shavings*, November 1930, 2.

Burt, Stephen. "When Poets Ruled the School." *American Literary History* 20, no. 3 (Fall 2008): 508–20.

Canfield, Homer. "Ladies And Gentlemen—Ted Malone." *News-Press* (Glendale, Calif.). October 31, 1935, B-6.

Cannon, Lucius H. *Billboards and Aesthetic Legislation*. St. Louis: St. Louis Public Library, 1931.

Car Freshner Corporation. "About Car-Freshner." Accessed September 27, 2011. http://www.little-trees.com/us/about.php?section=aboutus.

Carson, Anne. *Nox*. New York: New Directions, 2010.

Cather, Willa. *My Antonia*. Boston: Houghton Mifflin, 1918.

Cavallo, Guglielmo and Roger Chartier. *A History of Reading in the West*. Translated by Lydia G. Cochrane. Amherst: University of Massachusetts Press, 2003.

Chasar, Mike. "Material Concerns: Incidental Poetry, Popular Culture, and Ordinary Readers in Modern America." In *The Oxford Handbook of Modern and Contemporary American Poetry*, edited by Cary Nelson, 301–30. Oxford: Oxford University Press, 2012.

——. *Poetry and Popular Culture* (blog). http://www.mikechasar.blogspot.com.

The Chuckle Corner. "Burmashave." C. Harris. Accessed October 10, 2003. http://www.lyfe.freeserve.co.uk/burmashave.htm.

Church, Arthur B. Papers, 1885–1980. Iowa State University Special Collections.

Churchill, Suzanne W. "William Carlos Williams and the Poetics of Ending Others." In Hatlen and Tryphonopoulos, *William Carlos Williams and the Language of Poetry*. Orono, Maine: National Poetry Foundation, 2002.

Cisneros, Sandra. *The House on Mango Street*. New York: Vintage, 1991.

Clemente, Vince. "Paul Engle's Long Reach: From Iowa City to Long Island." *South Carolina Review* 37, no. 2 (Spring 2005): 186–91.

Corbett, Scott. "Too Late I Read." *Atlantic*, September 1952, 82–84.

Corn, Wanda. *In the American Grain: The Billboard Poetics of Charles Demuth*. Poughkeepsie, N.Y.: Vassar College, 1991.

——. *The Great American Thing: Modern Art and National Identity, 1915–1935*. Berkeley: University of California Press, 2001.

Crane, Hart. Papers, 1917–1983. Kent State University Libraries Special Collections and Archives.

Crane, Maggie. "Air Freshener Responsible for Teen's Pricey Ticket." WHAS11.com, October 19, 2010. www.whas11.com/news/105263333.html.

Creeley, Robert. *For Love: Poems, 1950–1960*. New York: Scribner, 1962.

Damon, Maria and Ira Livingston, eds. *Poetry and Cultural Studies: A Reader*. Champaign: University of Illinois Press, 2009.

Dana, Robert, ed. *A Community of Writers: Paul Engle and the Iowa Writers' Workshop*. Iowa City: University of Iowa Press, 1999.

Darnton, Robert. *Poetry and the Police: Communications Networks in Eighteenth-Century Paris*. Cambridge, Mass.: Harvard University Press, 2010.

Davis, Russ. Introduction to *Jim and Bob's Victory Album of Poems as Performed on KMA*. [Shenandoah, Iowa?]: Spark-O-Lite Company, 1943.

Dawson, Nathaniel M. *The Scrap Book as an Educator*. Philadelphia: After School Club of America, [1925?].

de Certeau, Michel. *The Practice of Everyday Life*. Translated by Steven Rendall. Berkeley: University of California Press, 1988.

Deseret News. "Obituary: Afton Elaine Clegg Hicken." January 30, 2001. http://www.deseretnews.com/home/.

Douglas, Susan J. *Listening In: Radio and the American Imagination, from Amos 'n' Andy and Edward R. Murrow to Wolfman Jack and Howard Stern*. New York: Random House, 1999.

Drucker, Johanna. *Figuring the Word: Essays on Books, Writing, and Visual Poetics*. New York: Granary Books, 1998.

Drug Trade News. "Road Signs in Series, Presenting Jingles, Put Over Burma Shave." December 15, 1930.

Duerksen, Christopher J. and R. Matthew Goebel. *Aesthetics, Community Character, and the Law*. Washington, D.C.: American Planning Association, 1999.

Dugas, Gaille. "The Jingle Man of Burma Shave." *Saint Louis Post Dispatch Everyday Magazine*. October 5, 1947, 1.

Dunning, John. *On the Air: The Encyclopedia of Old-Time Radio*. New York: Oxford University Press, 1998.

Dunphy, Robert J. "A Lament for the Passing of the Highway Poets." *New York Times*, June 28, 1970, 344. http://www.proquest.com/en-US/.

Easthope, Antony. *Poetry as Discourse*. London: Methuen, 1983.

Eiseman, Alvord L. *Charles Demuth*. New York: Watson-Guptill, 1982.

Eliot, T. S. *Selected Essays*. 1960. New York: Harcourt, Brace, 1964.

Ellison, Ralph. *Invisible Man*. 1952. New York: Vintage Books, 1995.

Engle, Paul. "American Child: 3." *Ladies' Home Journal*, January, 1945.

——. "Country Ways." In *Country Ways: A Celebration of Rural Life*, 9–119. Pleasantville, N.Y.: Reader's Digest, 1988.

——. Curriculum Vitae. n.d., ca. 1962. Papers of Paul Engle, Box 4. University of Iowa Special Collections.

——. "Easter." *Better Homes and Gardens*, April 1960.

——, ed. *Midland: Twenty-five Years of Fiction and Poetry, Selected from the Writing Workshops of the State University of Iowa*. New York: Random House, 1961.

——. Papers of Paul Engle, 1959. University of Iowa Special Collections.

Favorite Poem Project. "About the Favorite Poem Project." http://www.favoritepoem. org/ project.html.

Fenza, David W. "About AWP: The Growth of Creative Writing Programs." Association of Writers and Writing Programs. http://www.awpwriter.org/aboutawp/ index.htm.

Fetterley, Judith and Marjorie Pryse. *Writing Out of Place: Regionalism, Women, and American Literary Culture*. Urbana: University of Illinois Press, 2005.

Filreis, Al. *Counter-Revolution of the Word: The Conservative Attack on Modern Poetry, 1945–1960*. Chapel Hill: University of North Carolina Press, 2007.

Fiske, John. "Popular Discrimination." In *Modernity and Mass Culture*, edited by James Naremore and Patrick Brantlinger, 103–16. Bloomington: University of Indiana Press, 1991.

——. *Understanding Popular Culture*. London: Routledge, 1989.

Fleming, Roscoe. "Perk Up, Jack / The Rhymes Are Back." *Pageant,* October 1946, 143–44.

Flint, Peter B. "Ted Malone, 81; Was Radio Pioneer with Talk Programs." *New York Times*, October 27, 1989.

Forbes. "We Still Pine for Those Rhyme Signs," January 22, 1996.

Fraser, James Howard. *The American Billboard: 100 Years*. New York: Abrams, 1991.

Frost, Robert. *Selected Letters of Robert Frost*. Edited by Lawrance Roger Thompson. New York: Holt, Rinehart and Winston, 1964.

Fumerton, Patricia. "Recollecting Samuel Pepys: His Life, His Library, and His Legacy." English Broadside Ballad Archive. University of California, Santa Barbara. Accessed June 20, 2011. http://ebba.english.ucsb.edu/page/pepys-collecting.

Furr, Derek. *Recorded Poetry and Poetic Reception from Edna St. Vincent Millay to the Circle of Robert Lowell*. Basingstoke, UK: Palgrave Macmillan, 2010.

Garvey, Ellen Gruber. *The Adman in the Parlor: Magazines and the Gendering of Consumer Culture, 1880s to 1910s*. New York: Oxford University Press, 1996.

——. "Scissoring and Scrapbooks: Nineteenth-Century Reading, Remaking, and Recirculating." In *New Media, 1740–1915*, edited by Lisa Gitelman and Geoffrey B. Pingree, 207–27. Cambridge, Mass.: MIT Press, 2003.

——. "Imitation Is the Sincerest Form of Appropriation: Scrapbooks and Extra-Illustration." *Common-Place* 7, no. 3 (April 2007). http://www.common-place.org/vol-07/no-03/garvey/ .

Gernes, Todd S. "Recasting the Culture of Ephemera." In *Popular Literacy: Studies in Cultural Practices and Poetics*, edited by John Trimbur, 107–27. Pittsburgh: University of Pittsburgh Press, 2001.

Gibran, Khalil. *The Prophet*. New York: Knopf, 1923.

Gibson, John Stanley Jr. "Notes on the Broadcast Interpretation of Ted Malone." PhD diss., University of Oklahoma, 1971.

Gioia, Dana. *Can Poetry Matter? Essays on Poetry and American Culture*. 10th anniversary edition. St. Paul, Minn.: Graywolf Press, 2002.

Glass, Loren. "Middle Man: Paul Engle and the Iowa Writers' Workshop." *Minnesota Review* 71–72 (Winter/Spring 2009): 256–68.

Golding, Alan. *From Outlaw to Classic: Canons in American Poetry*. Madison: University of Wisconsin Press, 1995.

Goldman, Emma. *Living My Life*. Vol. 1. New York: Knopf, 1931.

Goldsmith, Kenneth. *Uncreative Writing: Managing Language in the Digital Age*. New York: Columbia University Press, 2011.

Gramsci, Antonio. *Selections from the Prison Notebooks of Antonio Gramsci*. Edited and translated by Quintin Hoare and Geoffey Nowell Smith. New York: International Publishers, 1971.

Gudis, Catherine. *Buyways: Billboards, Automobiles, and the American Landscape*. New York: Routledge, 2004.

Halbfinger, David M. "'The Wake-Up Is a Victory.'" *New York Times*, March 4, 2011.

Hall, Joyce C. "Taste and Times." In *Poetry for Pleasure: The Hallmark Book of Poetry*, edited by Hallmark Cards. New York: Doubleday, 1960.

——. *When You Care Enough*. With Curtiss Anderson. 2nd edition. Kansas City: Hallmark Cards, 1992.

Hallmark Cards, ed. *Poetry for Pleasure: The Hallmark Book of Poetry*. New York: Doubleday, 1960.

Hall, Stuart. "Notes on Deconstructing 'the Popular.'" In *People's History and Socialist Theory*, edited by Raphael Samuel, 227–40. London: Routledge and Kegan Paul, 1981.

Harrington, Joseph. *Poetry and the Public: The Social Form of Modern U.S. Poetics*. Middletown, Conn.: Wesleyan University Press, 2002.

Hatlen, Burton and Demetres Tryphonopoulos, eds. *William Carlos Williams and the Language of Poetry*. Orono, Maine: National Poetry Foundation, 2002.

Hayles, N. Katherine. *How We Became Posthuman: Virtual Bodies in Cybernetics, Literature, and Informatics*. Chicago: University of Chicago Press, 1999.

Hejinian, Lyn. "The Rejection of Closure." In *Moving Borders: Three Decades of Innovative Writing by Women*, edited by Mary Margaret Sloan, 618–29. Jersey City, N.J.: Talisman, 1998.

Helfand, Jessica. *Scrapbooks: An American History*. New Haven: Yale University Press, 2008.

Hilmes, Michele. *Radio Voices: American Broadcasting, 1922–1952*. Minneapolis: University of Minnesota Press, 1997.

Howells, William Dean. *A Hazard of New Fortunes*. 1890. New York: Modern Library, 2002.

Hubbard, Elbert. *Elbert Hubbard's Scrap Book*. New York: Roycroft, 1923.

Huyssen, Andreas. *After the Great Divide: Modernism, Mass Culture, Postmodernism*. Bloomington: Indiana University Press, 1986.

Hyde, Lewis. *The Gift: Imagination and the Erotic Life of Property*. New York: Vintage, 1983.

Jack, Zachary Michael. "America's Forgotten Regionalist, Jay G. Sigmund." In *The Plowman Sings: The Essential Fiction, Poetry and Drama of America's Forgotten Regionalist J. G. Sigmund*, edited by Zachary Michael Jack, 1–17. Lanham, Md.: University Press of America, 2008.

Jackson, Leon. *The Business of Letters: Authorial Economies in Antebellum America*. Stanford: Stanford University Press, 2007.

Jackson, Virginia. *Dickinson's Misery: A Theory of Lyric Reading*. Princeton: Princeton University Press, 2005.

——. "Who Reads Poetry?" *PMLA* 123, no. 2 (January 2008): 181–87.

Jameson, Fredric. "Reification and Utopia in Mass Culture." *Social Text* 1 (Winter 1979): 130–48.

——. "The Vanishing Mediator; or, Max Weber as Storyteller." In *The Ideologies of Theory: Essays, 1971–1986*. Vol. 2, *Syntax of History*. Minneapolis: University of Minnesota Press, 1988.

Jarrell, Randall. "The Obscurity of the Poet." In *Poetry and the Age*, by Randall Jarrell, 3–25. New York: Vintage, 1959.

Jenkins, Henry. *Textual Poachers: Television Fans and Participatory Culture*. New York: Routledge, 1992.

——. *Confronting the Challenges of Participatory Culture: Media Education for the 21st Century*. White Paper, 2006.

Jensen, Emma P. Letter to the editor. *Burma-Shavings*, March 1935, 2.

Johnson, Steven. *Where Good Ideas Come From: The Natural History of Innovation*. New York: Riverhead, 2010.

Josephson, Matthew. "The Great American Billposter." *Broom: An International Magazine of the Arts* 3, no. 2 (Nov. 1922): 304–12.

Kaplan, Milton Allen. *Radio and Poetry*. New York: Columbia University Press, 1949.

Katriel, Tamar and Thomas Farrell. "Scrapbooks as Cultural Texts: An American Art of Memory." *Text and Performance Quarterly* 11, no. 1 (January 1991): 1–17.

Keillor, Garrison, ed. *Good Poems for Hard Times*. New York: Viking, 2005.

Kenner, Hugh. *The Mechanic Muse*. New York: Oxford University Press, 1987.

Kerouac, Jack. *The Dharma Bums*. 1958. New York: Penguin, 1976.

Kirsch, Adam. "The Old World of American Readers." Review of *Songs of Ourselves: The Uses of Poetry in America*, by Joan Shelley Rubin. *The Sun*, July 12, 2007. http://www.nysun.com/arts/old-world-of-american-readers/58323/.

Kizer, Carolyn, ed. *100 Great Poems by Women: A Golden Ecco Anthology*. Hopewell, N.J.: Ecco, 1995.

——. "Carolyn Kizer Interview." By Richard Zahler. University of Washington English Department, 1985. Accessed June 21, 2011. http://depts.washington.edu/engl/events/kizer.php.

——. *Cool, Calm and Collected: Poems, 1960–2000*. Port Townsend, Washington: Copper Canyon, 2001.

Kristol, William. "Thoroughly Unmodern McCain." *New York Times*, January 21, 2008.

Laird, Pamela Walker. *Advertising Progress: American Business and the Rise of Consumer Marketing*. Baltimore, Md.: Johns Hopkins University Press, 1998.

Lears, Jackson. *Fables of Abundance: A Cultural History of Advertising in America*. New York: Basic, 1994.

Lefebvre, Henri. *Everyday Life in the Modern World*. Translated by Sacha Rabinovitch. New Brunswick: Transaction, 1984.

Lentricchia, Frank. *Modernist Quartet*. Cambridge: Cambridge University Press, 1994.

Levine, Lawrence. *Highbrow/Lowbrow: The Emergence of Cultural Hierarchy in America*. Cambridge, Mass.: Harvard University Press, 1990.

Lewis, Sinclair. *Arrowsmith*. 1925. San Diego, Calif.: Harcourt, 1990.

——. *Babbitt*. 1922. New York: Signet, 1998.

Lowell, Robert. *Collected Poems*. Edited by Frank Bidart and David Gewanter. New York: Farrar, Straus and Giroux, 2003.

Mabie, Janet. "Robert Frost Interprets His Teaching Method." In *Interviews with Robert Frost*, edited by Robert Frost and Edward Connery Lathem, 67–71. New York: Holt, Rinehart and Winston, 1966.

Marchand, Roland. *Advertising the American Dream: Making Way for Modernity, 1920–1940*. Berkeley: University of California Press, 1985.

Marquis, Don. *The Annotated Archy and Mehitabel*. Edited by Michael Sims. New York: Penguin, 2006.

——. *Archy and Mehitabel*. Garden City, N.Y.: Doubleday, 1930.

——. *Archy Does His Part*. Garden City, N.Y.: Doubleday, 1935.

——. *Archy's Life of Mehitabel*. Garden City, N.Y.: Doubleday, 1933.

——. *The Lives and Times of Archy and Mehitabel*. Garden City, N.Y.: Doubleday, 1950.

Mariani, Paul. *William Carlos Williams: A New World Naked*. New York: McGraw-Hill, 1981.

Marotti, Arthur F. *Manuscript, Print, and the English Renaissance Lyric*. Ithaca: Cornell University Press, 1995.

Marsh, Alec. "Thaddeus Coleman Pound's 'Newspaper Scrapbook' as a Source for The Cantos." *Paideuma* 24 (Fall-Winter, 1995): 163–93.

Marshall, Paule. 1959. *Brown Girl, Brownstones*. New York: Feminist Press, 2006.

Mason, Nicholas. "Building Brand Byron: Early Nineteenth-Century Advertising and the Marketing of Childe Harold's Pilgrimage." *Modern Language Quarterly* 63, no. 4 (December 2002): 411–40.

——. "'The Quack Has Become God': Puffery, Print, and the 'Death' of Literature in Romantic-Era Britain." *Nineteenth-Century Literature* 60, no. 1 (June 2005): 1–31.

Mason, Walt. "A Kansas Poet's Income." *Literary Digest* 48 (1914): 341–42.

Mauss, Marcel. *The Gift: Forms and Functions of Exchange in Archaic Societies*. Translated by Ian Cunnison. New York: Norton, 1967.

McGann, Jerome. *Black Riders: The Visible Language of Modernism*. Princeton: Princeton University Press, 1993.

McGill, Meredith L. *American Literature and the Culture of Reprinting, 1834–1853*. Philadelphia: University of Pennsylvania Press, 2003.

McGurl, Mark. *The Program Era: Postwar Fiction and the Rise of Creative Writing*. Cambridge, Mass.: Harvard University Press, 2009.

McLuhan, Marshall. *Understanding Media: The Extensions of Man*. 2nd ed. New York: Signet, New American Library, 1964.

Milford, Nancy. *Savage Beauty: The Life of Edna St. Vincent Millay*. New York: Random House, 2002.

Mill, John Stuart. "Thoughts on Poetry and Its Varieties." In *Autobiography and Literary Essays*. Vol. 1, *The Collected Works of John Stuart Mill*. Toronto: University of Toronto Press, 1981.

Miller, Susan. *Assuming the Positions: Cultural Pedagogy and the Politics of Commonplace Writing*. Pittsburgh: University of Pittsburgh Press, 1998.

Minneapolis Star. "Signs of Spring / Make Poets Rave, / Writing Signs / — (For Burma Shave!)." February 18, 1949, 6.

Modern Highway. "St. Paul Picked Poet as Mayor," July 1919.

Monroe, Harriet. "The Radio and the Poets." *Poetry* 36, no. 1 (April 1930): 32–35.

Moody, Anthony David. *Ezra Pound: Poet*. Oxford: Oxford University Press, 2007.

Moretti, Franco. "Conjectures on World Literature." *New Left Review* 1 (2000): 54–68.

——. *Graphs, Maps, Trees: Abstract Models for Literary History*. New York: Verso, 2005.

——. *Signs Taken for Wonders: Essays on the Sociology of Literary Forms*. London: Verso, 1988.

Morris, Adalaide. *How to Live / What to Do: H. D.'s Cultural Poetics*. Urbana: University of Illinois Press, 2003.

Moss, Ann. "Commonplace Rhetoric and Thought-Patterns in Early Modern Culture." In *The Recovery of Rhetoric: Persuasive Discourse and Disciplinarity in the Human Sciences*, edited by R. H. Roberts and J. M. M. Good, 49–60. Charlottesville: University Press of Virginia, 1993.

——. *Printed Commonplace-Books and the Structuring of Renaissance Thought*. Oxford: Clarendon Press, 1996.

Munsey's Magazine. "The Advertising Poet," July 1900, 566.

Myers, D. G. *The Elephants Teach: Creative Writing Since 1880*. Chicago: University of Chicago Press, 1996.

Nelson, Cary. "Only Death Can Part Us: Messages on Wartime Cards." *Iowa Journal of Cultural Studies* 8/9 (Spring and Fall, 2006): 25–43.

——. *Repression and Recovery: Modern American Poetry and the Politics of Cultural Memory, 1910–1945*. Madison: University of Wisconsin Press, 1989.

——. *Revolutionary Memory: Recovering the Poetry of the American Left*. New York: Routledge, 2001.

Nelson, Cary and Mike Chasar. "American Advertising: A Poem for Every Product." In *U.S. Popular Print Culture, 1860–1920*. Vol. 6 of *The Oxford History of Popular Print Culture*, edited by Christine Bold, 133–167. Oxford: Oxford University Press, 2011.

Nelson, Ted. "Computer Lit / Dream Machines." In *The New Media Reader*, edited by Noah Wardrip-Fruin and Nick Montfort, 303–38. Cambridge, Mass.: MIT Press, 2003.

Newcomb, John Timberman. *Would Poetry Disappear? American Verse and the Crisis of Modernity*. Columbus: Ohio State University Press, 2004.

News. "Could It Be Verse?" July 11, 1955.

News-Week. "Poetry: A Tear-Jerking Cupid Seeks to Make Good in Big City," November 9, 1935.

New York Herald Tribune. "Doctor-Author Calls Writing Balance Wheel," January 18, 1932.

Niedecker, Lorine. *Collected Works.* Edited by Jenny Penberthy. Berkeley: University of California Press, 2002.

Ngai, Sianne. "Merely Interesting." *Critical Inquiry* 34 (Summer 2008): 777–817.

——. "Our Aesthetic Categories." *PMLA* 125, no. 4 (October 2010): 948–58.

——. "The Cuteness of the Avant-Garde." *Critical Inquiry* 31, no. 4 (Summer 2005): 811–47.

O'Brien, Robert Lincoln. "Machinery and English Style." *Atlantic Monthly,* October 1904, 464–72.

Odell, Allan G. *Burma-Vita Company President's Annual Message.* Minneapolis: Burma-Vita, 1953.

Odell, Clinton. "No Salesmen—No Reason-Why Copy—Sales Increase." *Printer's Ink,* May 3, 1932, 17.

——. "President's Corner." *Burma-Shavings,* April 1930.

——. "President's Corner." *Burma-Shavings,* November 1935.

Ong, Walter J. *Orality and Literacy: The Technologizing of the Word.* New York: Methuen, 1982.

Opdycke, John B. *The Language of Advertising.* New York: Isaac Pitman, 1925.

O'Rourke, Meghan. "The Unfolding." *New Yorker,* July 12, 2010. http://www.newyorker.com/arts/critics/books/2010/07/12/100712crbo_books_orourke.

Parker, David. "The Importance of the Commonplace Book: London, 1450–1550." *Manuscripta* 40, no. 1 (March 1996): 29–48.

Penberthy, Jenny. Introduction to *Lorine Niedecker: Collected Works.* Berkeley: University of California Press, 2002.

Perloff, Marjorie. *Radical Artifice: Writing Poetry in the Age of Media.* Chicago: University of Chicago Press, 1991.

Pinsky, Robert. Introduction to *William Carlos Williams: Selected Poems.* Edited by Robert Pinsky. New York: Library of America, 2005.

Plath, Sylvia. *The Bell Jar.* 1971. New York: Harper Perennial Modern Classics, 2005.

Pound, Ezra. "A Few Don'ts by an Imagiste." *Poetry* 1 no. 6 (1913): 200–206.

——. "A Retrospect." 1918. In *Literary Essays of Ezra Pound.* Edited by T. S. Eliot, 3–14. Norfolk, Conn.: New Directions, 1954.

——. *How to Read.* 1931. New York: Haskell House, 1971.

President's Research Committee on Social Trends. *Recent Social Trends in the United States, Report of the President's Research Committee on Social Trends.* Vol. 1. New York: McGraw-Hill, 1933.

Press release. "The Writer in a Mass Culture," 1959. Papers of Paul Engle, box 11. University of Iowa Special Collections.

Prins, Yopie. *Victorian Sappho*. Princeton: Princeton University Press, 1999.

Radway, Janice and Perry Frank. "Verse and Popular Poetry." In *Handbook of American Popular Culture*, edited by M. Thomas Inge, 299–322. New York: Greenwood, 1988.

Rainey, Lawrence. *Institutions of Modernism: Literary Elites and Public Culture*. New Haven: Yale University Press, 1998.

Ransom, John Crowe. *The New Criticism*. Norfolk, Conn.: New Directions, 1941.

——. *The World's Body*. New York: Scribner's, 1938.

Rasula, Jed. *The American Poetry Wax Museum: Reality Effects, 1940–1990*. Urbana, Ill.: National Council of Teachers of English, 1996.

——. "The Politics of, the Politics In." In *Poetics and Poetic Value*, edited by Robert von Hallberg, 315–22. Chicago: University of Chicago Press, 1987.

Reynolds, David. *Beneath the American Renaissance: The Subversive Imagination in the Age of Emerson and Melville*. Cambridge, Mass.: Harvard University Press, 1989.

Rittenhouse, Jessie, ed. *The Little Book of Modern Verse: A Selection from the Work of Contemporaneous American Poets*. Boston: Houghton Mifflin, 1913.

——, ed. *The Second Book of Modern Verse: A Selection from the Work of Contemporaneous American Poets*. Boston: Houghton Mifflin, 1919.

Rooney, Kathleen. "Freighted with Memory." *Contemporary Poetry Review*, 2008. Accessed June 15, 2011. www.cprw.com/Rooney/mcfarland.htm.

Rowsome, Frank, Jr. *The Verse by the Side of the Road: The Story of the Burma-Shave Signs and Jingles*. New York: Penguin-Plume, 1990.

Rubin, Joan Shelley. *The Making of Middlebrow Culture*. Chapel Hill: The University of North Carolina Press, 1992.

——. *Songs of Ourselves: The Uses of Poetry in America*. Cambridge, Mass.: Harvard University Press, 2007.

Ryan, Terry. *The Prize Winner of Defiance, Ohio: How My Mother Raised 10 Kids on 25 Words or Less*. New York: Simon and Schuster, 2001.

Scandura, Jani. *Down in the Dumps: Place, Modernity, American Depression*. Durham: Duke University Press, 2008.

Scherman, David E. "Speaking of Pictures . . ." *Life,* June 2, 1947, 14.

Schivelbusch, Wolfgang. *The Railway Journey: The Industrialization of Time and Space in the 19th Century*. Berkeley: University of California Press, 1986.

Schott, Webster. "Poetry, Yes." In *Poetry for Pleasure: The Hallmark Book of Poetry*, edited by Hallmark Cards, 23–37. New York: Doubleday, 1960.

Shortz, Will, ed. The New York Times Crossword. *New York Times,* April 30, 2003, E8.

Sleigh, Tom. "The Ordinary Reader." Review of *Songs of Ourselves: The Uses of Poetry in America*, by Joan Shelley Rubin. *New York Times*, June 24, 2007. http://www.nytimes.com/2007/06/24/books/review/Sleigh-t.html.

Smulyan, Susan. *Selling Radio: The Commercialization of American Broadcasting, 1920–1934*. Washington, D.C.: Smithsonian Institution Press, 1994.

Sorby, Angela. *Schoolroom Poets: Childhood, Performance, and the Place of American Poetry, 1865–1917*. Durham: University of New Hampshire Press, 2005.

Spahr, Juliana. *Everybody's Autonomy: Connective Reading and Collective Identity*. Tuscaloosa: University of Alabama Press, 2001.

Stabile, Susan. *Memory's Daughters: The Material Culture of Remembrance in Eighteenth-Century America*. Ithaca: Cornell University Press, 2004.

Stein, Gertrude. *Everybody's Autobiography*. 1937. New York: Cooper Square, 1971.

Steinbeck, John. *The Grapes of Wrath*. 1939. New York: Penguin, 2006.

Steinman, Lisa. *Made in America: Science, Technology, and American Modernist Poets*. New Haven: Yale University Press, 1987.

Stewart, Garrett. *Reading Voices: Literature and the Phonotext*. Berkeley: University of California Press, 1990.

Strachan, John. *Advertising and Satirical Culture in the Romantic Period*. Cambridge: Cambridge University Press, 2007.

Suckow, Ruth. "Iowa." *The American Mercury* 9, no. 33 (September 1926): 39–45.

Symposium transcript. "The Writer in a Mass Culture," 1959. Papers of Paul Engle. University of Iowa Special Collections.

Taussig, Michael. *The Devil and Commodity Fetishism in South America*. Chapel Hill: University of North Carolina Press, 1980.

Tichi, Cecelia. *Shifting Gears: Technology, Literature, Culture in Modernist America*. Chapel Hill: University of North Carolina Press, 1987.

Tiffany, Daniel. *Infidel Poetics: Riddles, Nightlife, Substance*. Chicago: University of Chicago Press, 2009.

Time. "Education: Trouble at Trinity." May 13, 1946. http://www.time.com/time/magazine/article/0,9171,776798,00.html.

Time. "Pilgrim." October 30, 1939.

Time. "Press: Scrapbookman." February 8, 1932. http://www.time.com/time/magazine/article/0,9171,743114,00.html.

Time. "Rhymes on the Road." April 21, 1947.

Time. "The Press: Eddie Guest's Rival." June 2, 1947. http://www.time.com/time/magazine/article/0,9171,934559,00.html.

Trachtenberg, Alan. Foreword to Schivelbusch, *The Railway Journey*, xiii–xvi. Berkeley: University of California, 1986.

Traubel, Horace. *With Walt Whitman in Camden*. Vol. 5. Edited by Gertrude Traubel. Carbondale: Southern Illinois University Press, 1964.

Tucker, Susan, Katherine Ott, and Patricia P. Buckler, eds. *The Scrapbook in American Life*. Philadelphia: Temple University Press, 2006.

Twain, Mark. *Mark Twain's Autobiography*. Vol. 1. New York: Harper, 1924.

Untermeyer, Louis, ed. *Modern American Poetry: An Introduction*. New York: Harcourt, Brace and Howe, 1919.

Van Wienen, Mark W. *Partisans and Poets: The Political Work of American Poetry in the Great War*. Cambridge: Cambridge University Press, 1997.

Ventura County Star. "Rhyme on the Highway." July 9, 1997.

Venturi, Robert, Denise Scott Brown, and Steven Izenour. *Learning from Las Vegas*. Cambridge: MIT Press, 1972.

Voils, Jessie Wiley. "Ted Malone Radio's Poetaster." *Everybody's Digest*, ca. 1944.

Volosinov, V. N. *Marxism and the Philosophy of Language*. Cambridge, Mass.: Harvard University Press, 1986.

Vossler, Bill. *Burma-Shave: The Rhymes, the Signs, the Times*. Saint Cloud, Minn.: North Star, 1997.

Warner, Michael. "Uncritical Reading." In *Polemic: Critical or Uncritical*, edited by Jane Gallop, 13–38. New York: Routledge, 2004.

Weber, Richard B. "Paul Engle: A Checklist." *Books at Iowa* 5 (1966): 11–37.

Wheeler, Lesley. *Voicing American Poetry: Sound and Performance from the 1920s to the Present*. Ithaca: Cornell University Press, 2008.

Wilbers, Stephen. *The Iowa Writers' Workshop: Origins, Emergence and Growth*. Iowa City: University of Iowa Press, 1980.

Williams, Raymond. *The Long Revolution*. London: Chatto and Windus, 1961.

Williams, William Carlos. *January: A Novelette and Other Prose (1921–1931)*. Toulon, France: TO Publishers, 1932.

——. *The Autobiography of William Carlos Williams*. New York: Random House, 1951.

——. *The Collected Poems of William Carlos Williams*. Edited by Christopher MacGowan. 2 vols. New York: New Directions, 1991.

——. *The Great American Novel*. 1923. Los Angeles: Green Integer, 2003.

——. *Interviews with William Carlos Williams*. Edited by Linda Wagner. New York: New Directions, 1976.

——. *In the American Grain*. Norfolk, Conn.: New Directions, 1925.

——. "Measure." *Spectrum* 3 (Fall 1959): 149.

——. *Paterson*. Edited by Christopher MacGowan. New York: New Directions, 1992.

——. *Selected Essays of William Carlos Williams*. New York: Random House, 1954.

——. *Selected Letters*. Edited by John C. Thurlwall. New York: McDowell, Obolensky, 1957.

Williams, William Eric. "Money." *William Carlos Williams Review* 9, no. 1–2 (Fall 1983): 42–43.

Wilson, Joseph. "Paul Engle." In *American Poets, 1880–1945: Second Series,* edited by Peter Quartermain. Detroit: Gale, 1985.

Wons, Anthony, ed. *Tony's Scrap Book* [Combined Radio Editions of 1927, 1928, and 1929]. Chicago: Reilly and Lee, 1930.

——, ed. *Tony's Scrap Book*. New York: Anthony Wons, 1930.

Woolf, Virginia. "Mr. Bennett and Mrs. Brown." In *The Virginia Woolf Reader*, edited by Mitchell A. Leaska, 192–212. San Diego: Harcourt Brace Jovanovich, 1984.

Yakima Herald-Republic. "For Ad Nostalgia / There Is No Lack; / Burma-Shave Signs / Are on Way Back." July 9, 1997, 5B.

Zaner, Ray. *My Poetry Scrap-Book*. York, Penn.: Dispatch Publishing, 1950.

Zinsser, William K. "Goodbye Burma-Shave." *Saturday Evening Post*, September 5, 1964.